W9-BWT-730

Folded Flowers

Fabric Origami With a Twist of Silk Ribbon

Kumiko Sudo

Breckling Press

Publisher's Cataloging-in-Publication
(Provided by Quality Books, Inc.)

Sudo, Kumiko
Folded flower : fabric origami with a twist of silk ribbon / Kumiko Sudo

p. cm.
ISBN: 0-9721-2180-3

1. Applique—Patterns. 2. Ribbon work. 3. Quilting—Patterns. 4. Flowers in art. 5. Origami.
I. Title.

TT779.S842 2002 746.44'5041
QBI02-200568

This book was set in Bembo and Scala by Bartko Design Inc.
Editorial direction by Anne Knudsen
Cover and interior design by Kim Bartko, Bartko Design Inc.
Cover and interior photographs by Sharon Hoogstraten
Calligraphy and water color paintings by Kumiko Sudo
Technical drawings by Kandy Petersen
Manufacturing direction by Patricia Martin

With special thanks to Hanah Silk, Offray, National Non Wovens, Yuwa Fabrics, and Quilters' Resource, Inc. for their support.

Published by
Breckling Press, a division of Knudsen, Inc.
124 North York Road, #266
Elmhurst, IL 60126
USA

Printed and bound in Singapore
International Standard Book Number: 0-9721-2180-3

Contents

A New Awakening

THE FLOWERS OF JAPAN speak a silent language that whispers to us through our arts and our traditions. They are a sweet and gentle reminder of our connection with the natural world. There is a story of an ancient cherry tree, once famed for its glorious blossoms. In time, the tree began to fade and its flowers sickened and died. A wise man stood beneath its withering branches. Murmuring words of hope and encouragement, he applied a purifying balm. To the amazement of all, the tree awoke and put forth beautiful, fragrant blossoms for all to see. I commune with the flowers that surround me in my garden. They reward me with fresh inspiration and I celebrate by folding fabric and ribbon into flowers anew.

A Calendar of Flowers

EACH MORNING, I STEP INTO MY GARDEN and discover anew the joy of nature as its secrets unfold before me. With dew drops glistening on its leaves, each flower curls back its petals and opens up to the morning sun. As I work with fabric and ribbon, I picture the delicate shapes and colors of the flowers that awaken each month in my garden. Layer after layer, my fingers fold the fabric and the shape of a new blossom emerges. A twist of silk ribbon adds a shimmer of sunlight and the flower comes to life in my hands.

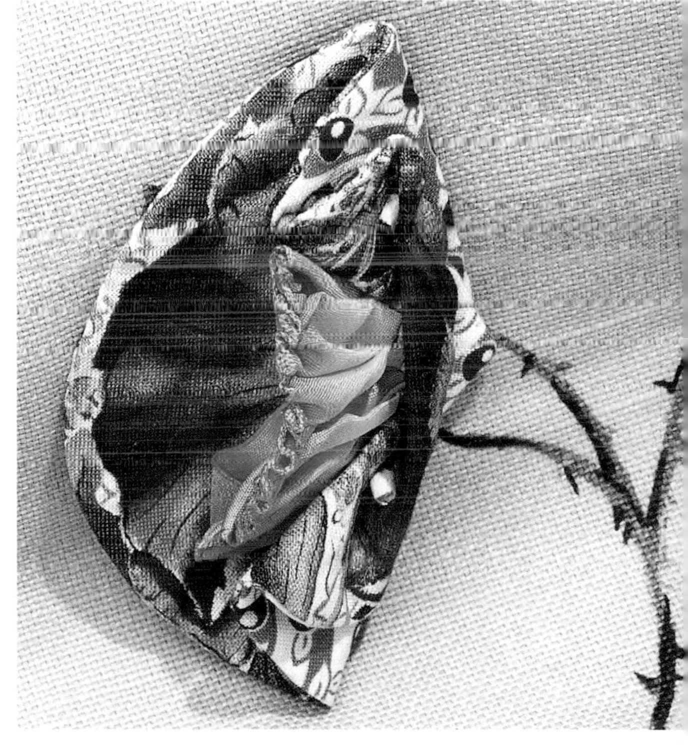

The Poetry of the Seasons

In Japan, the circle of the seasons is a theme that has always been close to our hearts. It is intertwined in our arts and crafts, our literature, and our culture and traditions. *Haiku,* a stylized form of poetry that is uniquely Japanese, requires that each poem make an allusion to the seasons. This *kigo* or season word might be as straightforward as a reference to cherry trees in bloom, reminiscent of spring, or it may be quite oblique—a withered petal suggesting the brevity of life. Deceptively simple in form, a *haiku* poem is usually made up of just seventeen syllables, written in three lines of five, seven, and five syllables. Yet the higher purpose of *haiku* is to capture a moment, a sensation, or an impression of life—a clear but fleeting glimpse of what the poet has thought or felt. This makes *haiku* a highly contemplative—it requires perception and meditation to create a true *haiku.*

Haiku matured in the Edo period in the late seventeenth century, but dates back to medieval times. The seasonal motifs threaded into these elegant verses also permeates other forms of Japanese art and literature. For the Japanese, all beauty derives from the natural world, for the purpose of art is to renew our connection with nature. Images or poetry that depict the moon, the sun, or, most especially, the fauna and flora of Japan are at the heart of the Japanese aesthetic.

Just as *haiku* poets through the ages have attempted to distill the essence of natural beauty into words, so I try to express my love of nature in the flowers I create from fabric and ribbon. I have spent my life among flowers. Every day, as I walk in my garden, I watch buds appear on the vine and break into glorious bloom. All too soon the winds shake new seeds to the ground, petals fall, and blossoms begin to wither. I often take a magnifying glass with me so that I can look closely at each flower, its foliage, and even the undersides of its leaves. Yet even the flowers that I have known and loved season after season, year after year, bring me surprises. Each day, I discover some new change, as layer upon layer the flower opens to the sun. Even as the outer petals die, I see new blossoms at its core. The delicate shades of color, the variations in shape and form, and the changing intensity of fragrances from day to day make each moment that I view a flower unique.

From Flowers into Fabric

The time I spend in my garden helps me appreciate the wonders of the flowers around me. In Spring, I watch as birds

busily gather twigs, grasses, and fallen petals for their nests, hidden deep in the bird houses I have set up just for them. I see a busy red woodpecker hammer away at the trunk of a shady cedar tree. A little green frog jumps across my path and disappears into the woods. On late summer afternoons, I lie in a hammock that is tied between two huge oak trees on a slight incline at the back of my house. Light blue patches of sky peek between the layers of deep green leaves. I listen as a summer breeze rustles the branches and as the crickets settle down to sing their evening song. The sounds, fragrances, and sensations of life around me all combine to give me the feeling of joy and thankfulness that I always associate with flowers.

When I work with fabric, I think not only of the flower I wish to recreate, but of the richness of the natural world. Sunlight, shadows, the fluttering of a bird's wings, the feeling of early morning mist in the air, and the call of the cricket to the autumn moon—all influence the impressions I have of the flowers in my garden. My fingers move, enjoying the textures of fabrics and ribbons, and a flower that had until now bloomed only in my imagination takes shape in my hands. Nothing gives me more joy.

An Ancient Calendar

In ancient Japan, each month was given a distinct name that related to the seasons. The meanings of these old names reflect the natural cycle of the year. In modern Japanese, the months are numbered sequentially. The Chinese character for "moon" makes up the last part of each name, demonstrating the influence of the lunar calendar.

		Ancient Japanese	***Modern Japanese***	***Meaning***
January	睦月	Mutsuki	Ichigatsu	Month of intimate gatherings
February	如月	Kisaragi	Nigatsu	Month for dressing in layers; buds begin to shoot out
March	弥生	Yayoi	Sangatsu	Month of the waning moon; signs of the end of spring
April	卯月	Uzuki	Shigatsu	Month of bloom for *uzuki* flowers in the mountains and fields
May	皐月	Satsuki	Gogatsu	Month for planting seedlings in the rice fields
June	水無月	Minazuki	Rokugatsu	Month for washing off and purifying—the blots of the last six months are washed away by streams and waterfalls

		Ancient Japanese	Modern Japanese	Meaning
July	文月	Fumuzuki	Shichigatsu	Month to enjoy learning, reading, and writing poems and letters
August	葉月	Hazuki	Hachigatsu	Month of the full moon, reflected in the colors of the leaves
September	長月	Nagatsuki	Kugatsu	Month of shadows bathed in moonlight on long autumn nights
October	神無月	Kannazuki	Jugatsu	Month to offer sake brewed for the new rice crop to the Gods
November	霜月	Shimotsuki	Juichigatsu	Month when winter begins and preparations for cold weather are made
December	師走	Shiwasu	Junigatsu	Month that is busiest for doctors, monks, and scholars

Notes on Technique

In this book you will find twenty-four designs that combine fabric and ribbon into flowers that celebrate the wonders of the seasons. Some of the flowers I have grown in my own garden and some I remember from my childhood. Still others are flowers of fantasy that I hope will inspire you to create a garden of your own on the quilts you sew. To show you how versatile fabric origami can be, I have included patterns for six purses, each decorated with three-dimensional flowers.

Selecting Fabrics

Before you begin to work with fabrics, look for inspiration in the world around you. Whether you find them on your own garden path, deep in the woods, or in exotic floral arrangements in a flower shop window, every blossom that you see can be recreated in fabric. Look carefully at the colors. A single flower offers an incredible range of hues. Look too at form of the petals, the buds, and the leaves. These are the shapes you will work with as you mold your fabric or twist your ribbons into place.

Most of the designs in *Folded Flowers* are made from contemporary American cottons. Many also use lengths of silk ribbon or wired silk ribbon. I love the texture of ribbon and the shimmer that it gives to the flowers I make. Wired silk ribbon comes in a wonderful variety of colors and is easy to mold into intricate shapes.

To make the projects here, you do not need to start with a large fabric collection. Most of the flowers can be made from quite small scraps and it is easy to combine several fabrics in the same design. For each project, I have suggested how much fabric you will need, but these quantities are always over generous. A ⅛ yd (15 cm) length, for example, will often allow enough fabric for two or even three flowers. Using the photographs as a guide to contrast (the use of light, medium, and dark tones), I suggest you choose colors and patterns that you enjoy. Lay them out on the background fabric you have selected. Make sure, too, the fabric you have chosen for the border complements the flowers and does not overwhelm them.

The more flowers you create, the more instinctive your color choices will become. Sometimes, I let the season affect my color selections. When I feel a gentle Spring breeze, for example, it may suggest pastel colors. At times, my mood determines the colors I want to use. If I'm in a calm and tranquil mood, I may want to use dramatic color combinations. To choose colors that are right for you, it is important to know your own heart and mind. Arrange the colors that you would most like to work with on a table. Then arrange them on your design. Remember that beautiful color schemes do not suggest themselves immediately. Take as much time as you need until you are satisfied with the ways your colors are working together.

BASIC TOOL KIT

A list of materials is supplied with every project. In addition, you will need the items listed here. Collect everything you need before you start and keep them in a box or basket within easy reach. A little preparation will save you time and frustration when you sit down to make a new project.

- Hand-sewing needles
- Pins and pincushion
- High-quality hand-sewing threads in variety of colors
- Thimble
- Thread snips
- Self-healing cutting mat
- Sharp fabric scissors
- Paper scissors
- Sharp pencils and eraser
- Compass
- Ruler
- Tracing paper

Using Templates

Full-size templates are provided for all pieces other than simple squares, rectangles, and circles. *The templates do not include seam allowances.* To all templates, unless otherwise indicated on the template or in the sewing directions, you will need to add a ⅛″ (0.4 cm) seam allowance. For squares, rectangles, and circles, the measurements in the sewing directions already include seam allowances. Most of the templates are curved, which means they are easier to cut with very sharp scissors than with rotary cutting equipment. Since the projects are small and multiples of the same pattern piece are rarely needed, hand-cutting is quick and easy. Remember to transfer any markings from the pattern onto the cut pieces of fabric.

Sewing

I sew everything—straight seams and curved seams, piecing and applique—by hand. I like the sense of intimacy that hand-sewing gives me. I feel that the hand is directed not only by the eye but by the heart. Since all the flower designs are small, you may want to sew them by hand, too. You'll find that some require only a few stitches. If you prefer to sew by machine, you will find it easy to do so. The circles, triangles, and hexagons of back-to-back fabric from which most of the flowers are formed are simple to sew by machine. Adding the backing and border is also easy on the machine.

Many of the designs involve sewing curved seams. For perfect curved seams, I use a form of applique or invisible stitching that is described below. My technique involves placing a fabric piece, with the seam allowance folded under, on top of a background piece; the piece is then blind-stitched by hand. In the instructions, this is what is meant by the term *applique*. The term *sew* indicates a more traditional method of sewing the pieces together, right sides facing, using a running stitch. Straight seams are sewn in this way, and you may use hand or machine stitching.

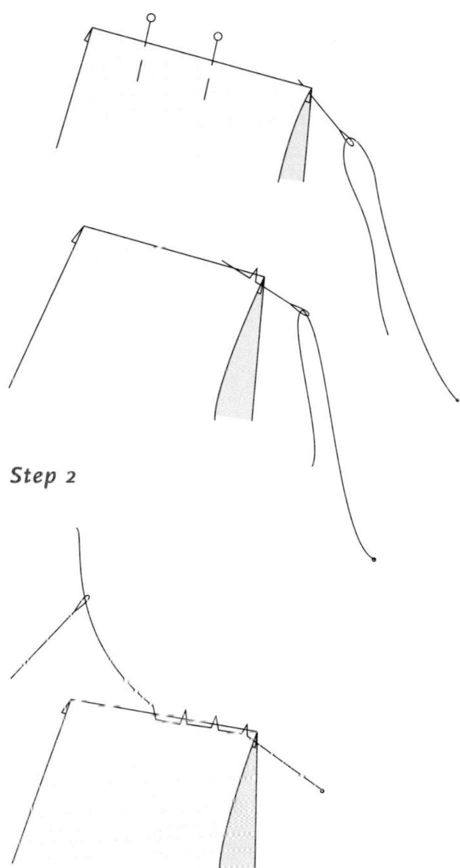

Step 2

Step 3

Invisible Stitches

The applique technique I use to attach flowers, leaves, and stems onto the background fabric results in tiny stitches that are not visible from the front of the quilt. The appliques lie flat, for a smooth, clean effect. This technique takes practice but you will soon be making perfect, invisible stitches.

1. Fold under the seam allowance of the applique and finger-press firmly in place. Pin in place through the seam allowance onto the background fabric. Knot the thread, then insert the needle through the fold line on the applique fabric at an angle, as shown. The knot will be hidden in the folded seam allowance.
2. Insert the needle through a single thread in the weave of the background fabric. As soon as it emerges, re-insert the needle into the applique fabric at the fold line. Exit at a point ¼″ (0.75) further down the fold line.
3. Repeat, pulling the thread firmly with each stitch. In effect, the thread is hidden in the "tunnel" inside the folded seam allowance of the applique fabric.

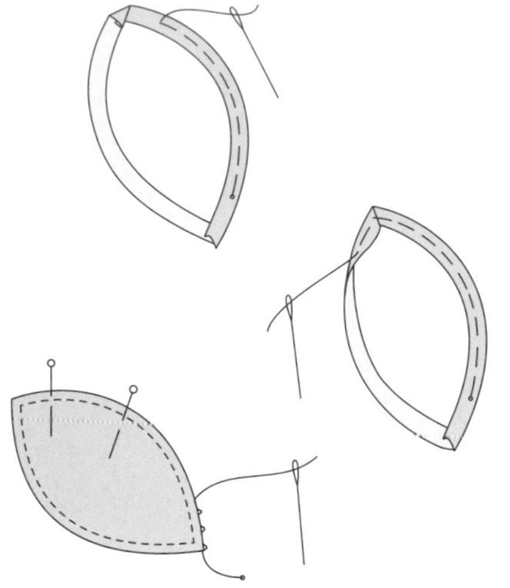

Basting before stitching

If you are working with slippery fabrics like silks or with small appliques, it is helpful to baste the seam allowance of the applique firmly in place before beginning the invisible stitch. This will prevent distortion of the fabric. Take care to fold over any tips or sharp corners precisely before basting. Remove basting stitches once the applique is in place.

Fabric Origami

All the flower designs in *Folded Flowers* are inspired by the Japanese art of origami, or paper folding. Like many Japanese children, I learned the basics of origami at my mother's knee. I loved the colors and patterns in decorative origami papers and would mold them into shapes of my own. Now, instead of paper, I fold fabrics. Even if you know nothing of origami, you will find that my fabric-folding techniques are easy to learn. These tips may help.

- Study each folding diagram carefully before you begin. Determine which is the right and wrong side of the fabric. Go through the step-by-step instructions mentally before you even pick up the fabric. You may find it helpful to practice each new shape on a sample so that you solve any difficulties before you begin on your final piece.
- Always fold accurately and neatly.
- Crease each fold firmly with the back of your thumbnail. Good creases make the folding easier, and they serve as guides to future steps.
- One difference between folding paper and folding fabric is that paper is available with different colors on the two

sides. To achieve the same effect when folding fabric, you must first sew the two colors of your choice together, then turn them right side out and press. Often, finger pressing will be adequate. Directions for this step are provided with each pattern.

You will find that the same procedures are used over and over again with every flower you make. You will soon become so proficient with them that you can carry them out almost without thinking.

Silk Ribbon

Ever since I was a little girl I have loved ribbons. My mother would arrange my long hair neatly every morning, tying it up with my favorite ribbons. Whenever our local craft store displayed it newest stock of ribbons, I would beg my mother to buy some for me. I still keep some of those ribbons from my childhood in a special box of childhood treasures. When I open it, the ribbons help me relive fond memories.

After graduating from high school, I worked as an assistant in a milliner's studio. The shelves were piled high with boxes filled with beautiful ribbons imported from Europe. They danced before my eyes in all the colors of the rainbow. While my hands were busy with the milliner's iron, my mind was filled with dreams of all those ribbons and the wonderful things I would do with them if they were mine.

As time passed, my fascination with ribbons grew and I began to incorporate them into my work. Just holding a new length of ribbon still sends my imagination reeling and,

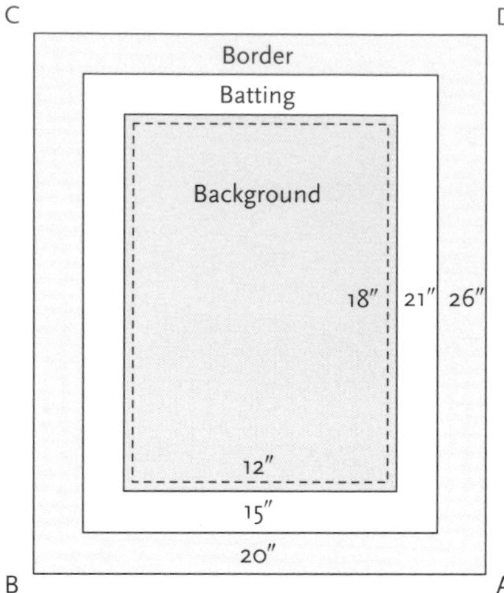

Step 2

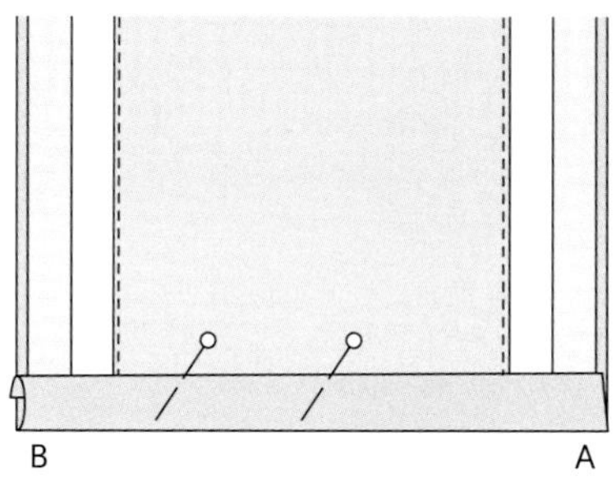

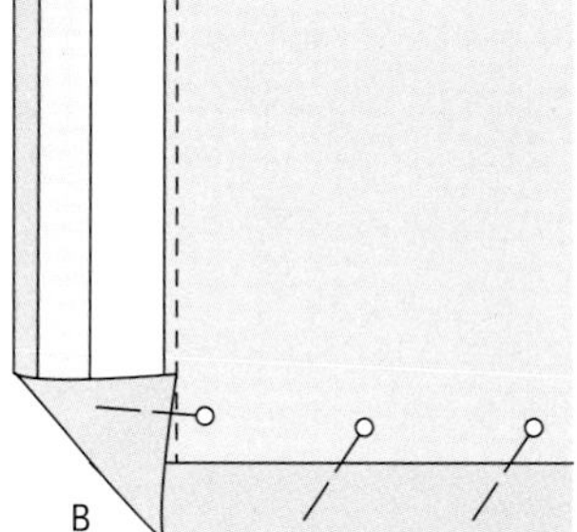

Step 3

almost without thinking, my hands shape it into beautiful flowers, petals, and leaves.

Many of the projects in *Folded Flowers* include silk ribbon. Quilt shops and craft shops now carry a very broad selection of ribbons in every width, pattern, and color imaginable. I especially enjoy working with wired silk ribbon. It is a pleasure to mold into different shapes and the wire holds those shapes perfectly. Once you have made one or two of the silk ribbon projects in this book, you will discover how easy it is to add ribbon to other projects you make.

Adding Backing and Borders

The first step in making each of the small quilts in *Folded Flowers* is to prepare the background base onto which you will applique the designs. Unlike traditional quiltmaking, I baste a layer of thin batting to the base before I begin the appliques. Once the design is complete, I add a combined backing/border made from a single piece of fabric.

Most of the blocks in this book are made on a base that is the same size for all designs. Most have a 2″ (5 cm) border, but for some the border is reduced to 1½″ (4 cm). Most of the borders are constructed in the same way out of a single piece of backing/border fabric. (There are some exceptions, for which the directions are provided with the pattern). Follow these steps to add the backing and border to the finished quilt top.

1. Pre-cut the background base, the batting, and the backing/border fabric as follows, or as directed in the pattern.

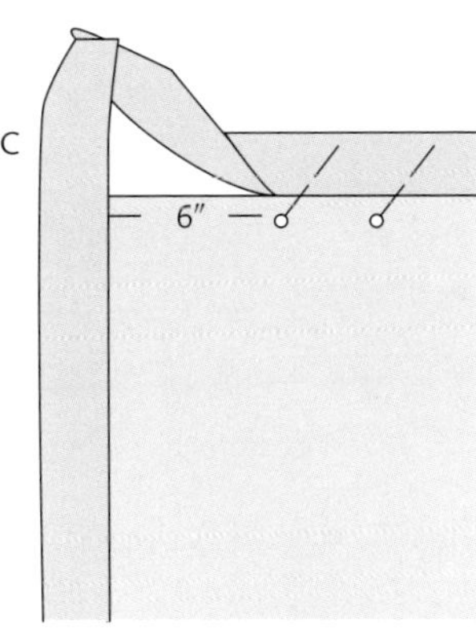

Background base	Batting	Backing/border
For 2″ (5 cm) border:		
12″ × 18″ (30 cm × 45 cm)	15″ × 21″ (37 cm × 52 cm)	20″ × 26″ (50 cm × 66 cm)
For 1½″ (4 cm) border:		
12″ × 18″ (30 cm × 45 cm)	14″ × 20″ (35 cm × 50 cm)	18″ × 24″ (45 cm × 60 cm)

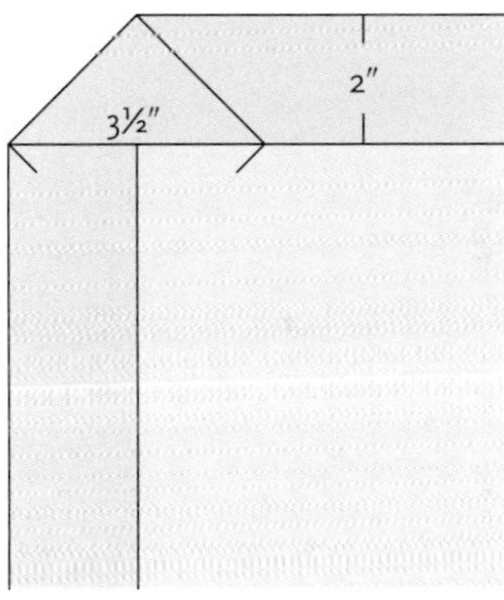

Step 6

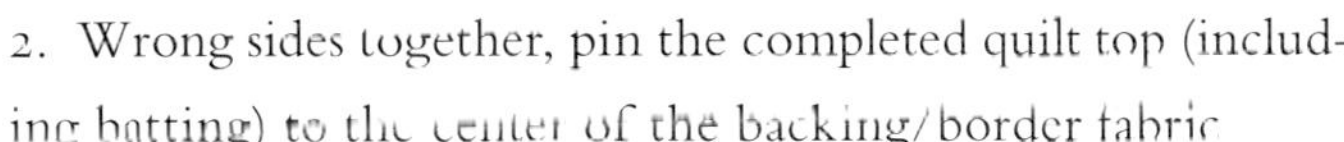

2. Wrong sides together, pin the completed quilt top (including batting) to the center of the backing/border fabric.
3. Fold inwards ½″ (1.5 cm) seam allowances around all sides of backing/border piece.
4. Fold bottom edge (A-B) inwards by 2″ (5 cm) to create bottom border. Folded-in seam allowance aligns with horizontal seam line previously marked on base, ½″ (1.5 cm) in from raw edge. Pin in place. Fold corner B diagonally to meet vertical seam line marked on base. Pin in place.
5. Repeat Step 4, folding top edge (C-D) and corner D.
6. Open out corner C completely (except turned-in seam allowance). Fold left edge (B-C) inwards by 2″ (5 cm) to create left border. Fold corner C diagonally to meet vertical seam line marked on base. Fold top edge (C-D) inwards by 2″ (5 cm) to create top border.
7. Repeat Steps 4 to 6, folding right edge D-A and opening out corner A to create right border.
8. Blind stitch around all seams, attaching front of border to front of base. There is no need to stitch across diagonals. They will lie flat if they are unstitched.

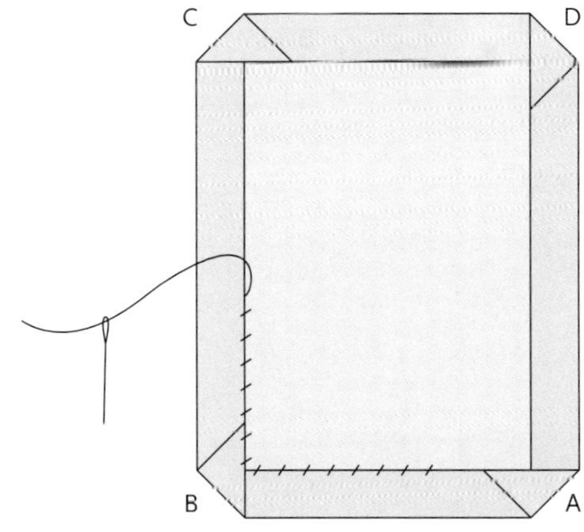

Step 8

Sashiko

Rather than use the traditional quilting stitch, I have adapted Japanese sashiko stitching to embellish the quilt blocks in *Folded Flowers.* This delicate yet distinctive form of stitching accents the folded flower designs beautifully. The stitching might suggest rays of sunshine, a sudden breeze, or the fluttering wings of a butterfly. Your choice of a contrasting thread color may highlight such effects.

The method of stitching I have used is a combination of the traditional sashiko stitch and the quilting stitch. It is done after the backing and border are completed.

1. Using the stencils provided, lightly mark the sashiko design on the quilt.
2. Without knotting the thread, insert the needle from the front of the quilt, at a point about ¼″ (0.75 cm) away from the first marked line of sashiko to be completed. Make a backstitch to secure the thread, then use simple stab stitches to complete the design. For each stitch, pull the thread though all layers of the quilt, exiting on the back. Reinsert the needle from the back to the front, taking care to stay on the marked design.

3. Follow the sequence shown with each sashiko pattern (see page 00, for example) to complete the design. To finish stitching, make another back stitch, then pull the needle about ¼″ (0.75 cm) from this point. Clip the thread as close to the quilt as possible, allowing the tail to slip within the layers of the quilt where it is hidden from view.

Once you have completed some of the sashiko designs included in *Folded Flowers* and understand the sequence of the stitching, you are ready to create designs of your own. Take your inspiration for the flowers you see around you and sketch new blossoms to translate into sashiko stitching.

Spring

As the last frosts of February give way to the new buds of March, the air fills with the intoxicating scents of Spring. This is a time of renewal, when we celebrate the re-awakening of nature. We flock to cherry or plum groves to admire the perfect formation of the flowers and to breathe in their glorious scents. Azaleas, Rhododendrums, Sweet Daphne, and Camellia—all are in bloom. *Haru ichiban*, the first wind of Spring, shakes their blossoms to the ground and their fragrances float in the breeze. We crush the fallen petals to make fresh teas. Children gaze into the windows of tea shops filled with seasonal sweets that are carefully molded by hand into the delicate shapes of the flowers of Spring. Ladies dressed in elegant *kimono* in pastel hues gather for the tea ceremony. The guests are greeted by beautiful flower arrangements in soft pinks, calming yellows, and peaceful greens that soothe the soul and renew the spirit.

On the first day of Spring, a friend brings me a bundle of *Kodemari* flowers, or Snowbells. They feel as soft as cotton candy in my hands. I arrange them in an intricately patterned vase. They tremble in the Spring breeze as their blossoms change from white to the lightest shade of green. It is as though they are bowing to me and so I invite them to stay in bloom for as long as they please.

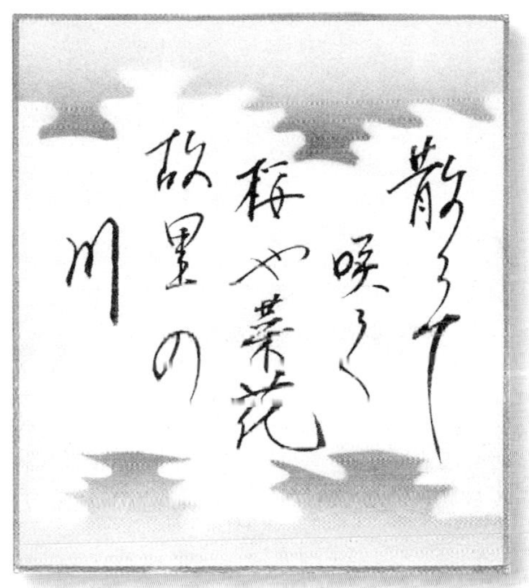

Chitte saku
Sakura ya Nanohana
Furusato no kawa

The haiku creates a picture of Spring blossoms floating on a river, blooming once more on the surface of the water. The scene imparts a feeling of peace to those who walk by.

MARCH

Malaleuca

In Japan, one of the many rites of Spring is the crushing of new leaves to make fresh tea. Malaleuca—or the tea tree—is native to Australia and its essential oils, with their sharp, spicy aroma, are considered medicinal. Captain Cook used the leaves of the tea tree to combat symptoms of scurvy.

Use ⅛" (0.4 cm) seam allowance, unless noted otherwise.

YOU WILL NEED

Base: ½ yd (45 cm)

Flower fabrics: ¼ yd (25 cm), each of two fabrics

Butterfly motif fabric: ¼ yd (25 cm) or scraps

For stems, 1½" (4 cm) wired silk ribbon: 2 yd (180 cm)

Backing/border: ¾ yd (70 cm)

Batting: ½ yd (45 cm)

Prepare block

1. Cut base rectangle of background fabric measuring 12" × 18" (30 cm × 45 cm). A floral print works well with this design. Mark a seam line ½" (1.5 cm) inwards from all raw edges, so that background base onto which you will applique measures 11" × 17" (27 cm × 42 cm). Cut batting to measure 15" × 21" (37 cm × 52 cm) and backing/border fabric to measure 20" × 26" (50 cm × 66 cm). Baste batting to wrong side of base.
2. From a fabric with a butterfly motif, cut three large butterflies, adding seam allowance. Turn under seam allowance and applique onto base. See page 5 for additional help.

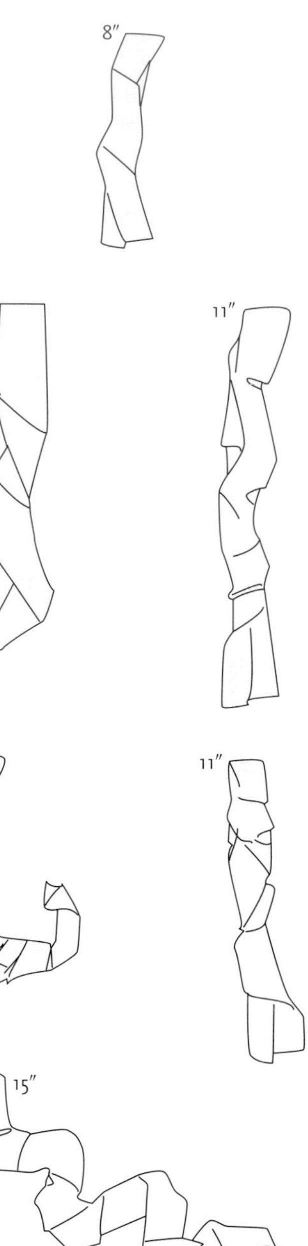

Step 3

Make six ribbon stems

3. Cut six lengths of wired silk ribbon, as follows: one length measuring 15″ (37 cm); four lengths of 11″ (27 cm); and one length of 8″ (20 cm). Fold as desired, pressing in place with fingers, into long stems. Pin then stitch in place on base, leaving open the ends at which flowers will be attached.

Make three flowers

4. Set compass to 3⅜″ (8.5 cm) radius to draw circle measuring 6¾″ (17 cm) in diameter. This includes ⅛″ (0.4 cm) seam allowance. Cut three from each of two fabrics. Match one of each color, right sides together, then sew them together around seam allowances, leaving a 1″ (2.5 cm) opening. Turn right side out. Blind stitch opening closed. Finger press seam.
5. Fold completed circle in half. Fold top layer back to center as shown and pin in place.

If you are new to applique, look for butterfly or other motifs that are not too intricately shaped. Use very sharp scissors to cut the motif out from the fabric, allowing ⅛" (0.4 cm) seam allowance all around. A wider seam allowance may be easier to sew, but it may be too bulky to lie flat as you sew. Fold under the seam allowance and finger press firmly in place. Pin the applique onto the background fabric. Read again the directions on page xv for achieving a clean, smooth line of invisible stitches around the entire applique.

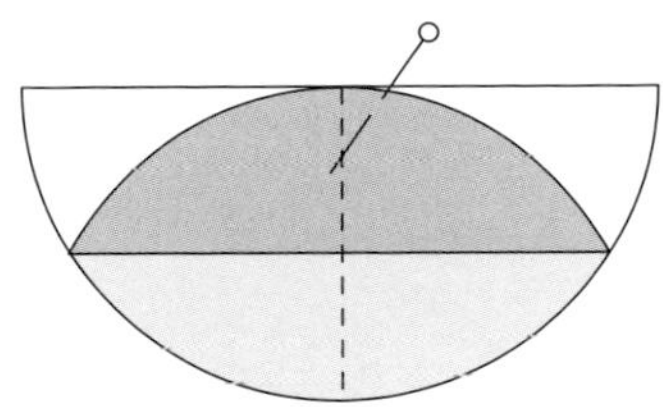

Step 5

6. Turn flower over, so that folded side lies against tabletop. Fold both sides in to center line, as shown. Pin to hold. Gather-stitch around top, 1" (2.5 cm) from tip, to create calyx of flower.

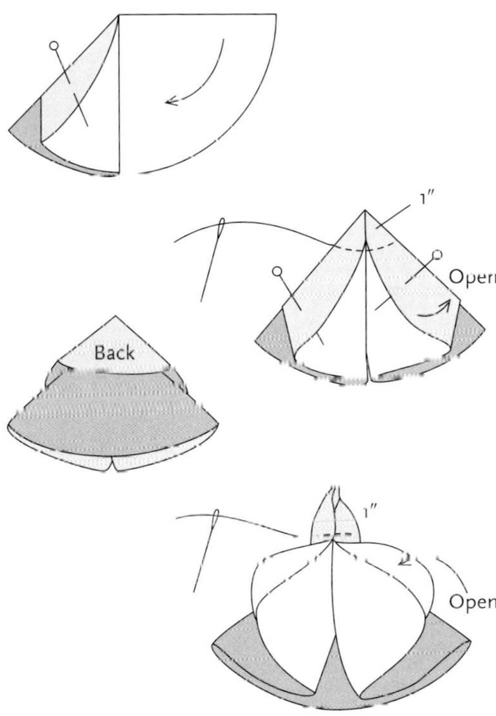

Step 6

Complete quilt

7. Insert the calyx of each flower into the top of its stem. Stitch ribbon in place around calyx. Use small stitches to secure underside of each flower in place on base.
8. To add backing and 2" (5 cm) border, see page xviii.

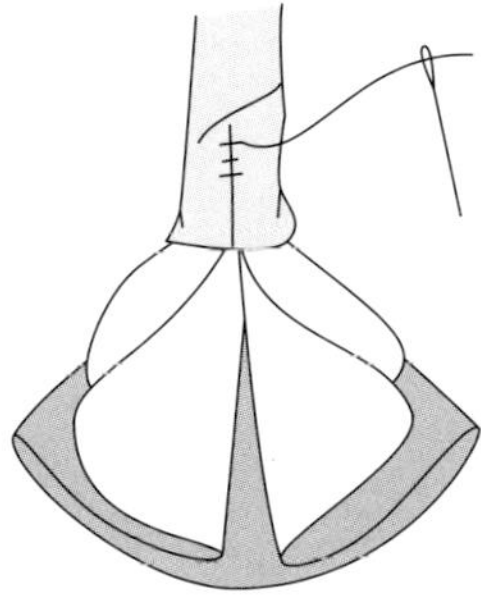

Step 7

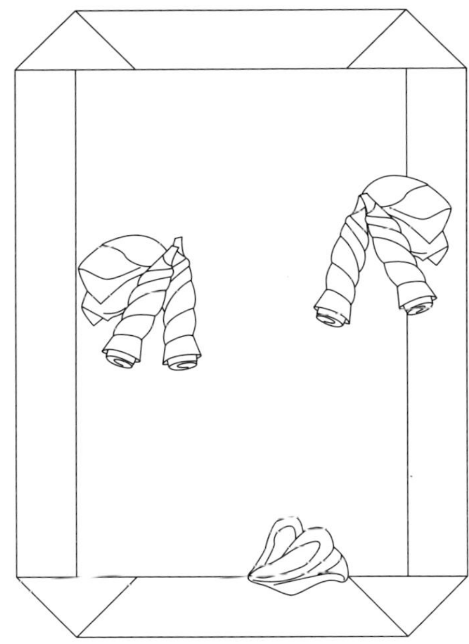

Magic Flower of the Incas

This fanciful flower from a fantasy landscape brings splashes of color into the budding Spring garden. Resplendent among the plant's arching branches, in dazzling hues of purple, pink, and gold, the flowers recapture the glory of a paradise lost.

Use ⅛" (0.4 cm) seam allowance, unless noted otherwise.

Prepare block

1. Cut base rectangle of background fabric measuring 12" × 18" (30 cm × 45 cm). Mark a seam line ½" (1.5 cm) inwards from all raw edges, so that background base onto which you will applique measures 11" × 17" (27 cm × 42 cm). Cut batting to measure 15" × 21" (37 cm × 52 cm) and backing/border fabric to measure 20" × 26" (50 cm × 66 cm). Baste batting onto wrong side of base.

Make four flowers

2. Set compass to 2⅜" (6 cm) radius to draw circle measuring 4¾" (12 cm) in diameter. This includes ⅛" (0.4 cm) seam allowance. Cut four from each of two fabrics (one light, one dark). Matching light to dark or matching two complemen-

YOU WILL NEED

Base: ½ yd (45 cm)

Flower fabrics: ¼ yd (25 cm), each of at least two fabrics

For leaves, 1½" (4 cm) wired silk ribbon: 2¼ yd (210 cm)

Backing/border: ¾ yd (70 cm)

Batting: ½ yd (45 cm)

If you choose a pictorial print for the base, depicting people, birds, animals, or scenery, you can use a simple applique technique to make that background even more rich. Here, I cut a half-circle from fabric with a bird motif and appliqued it to the top of the base. I added the green, blue, and teal leaves from other fabrics and appliqued those in the same way. To give the canopy and the table a little more emphasis, I appliqued colorful fabrics onto them, too. To give your applique motifs extra dimension, you can even stuff them with a little batting as you sew them down.

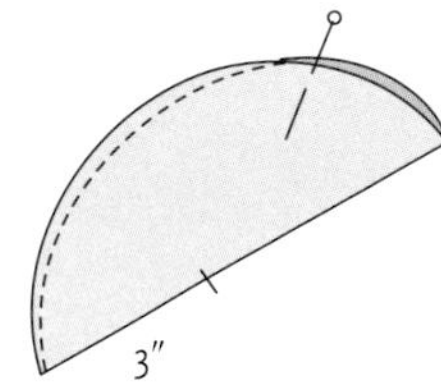

Step 3

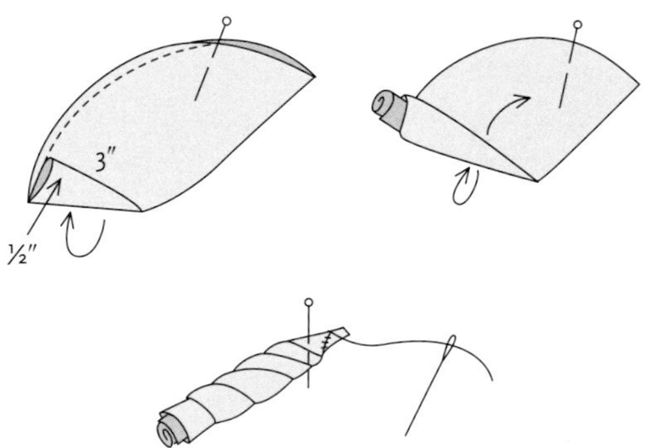

Step 4

tary fabrics, place them right sides together. Sew them together around seam allowances, leaving a 1″ (2.5 cm) opening. Turn right side out. Blind stitch opening closed. Finger-press seam.

3. Fold in half, then slide front half upwards by about ½″ (1.5 cm). Dotted line indicates position of back half. Pin to hold.

4. Make a ½″ (1.5 cm) fold along curve at one end, then continue rolling to opposite end. Pin in place while rolling. Make three stitches to hold, as shown.

Make three leaves

5. Cut three lengths of wired silk ribbon, each measuring 25″ (64 cm). At one end, make a ½″ (1.5 cm) fold, holding ribbon

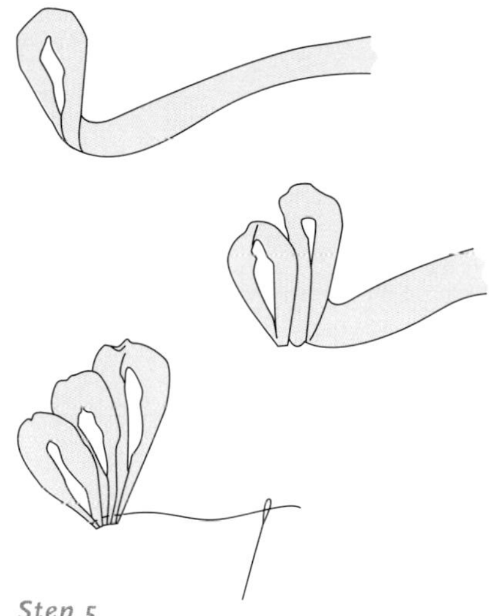
Step 5

firmly between your finger and thumb. Make a 2½″ (6.5 cm) fold, then a 3″ (8 cm) fold. Continue, increasing size of fold by ½″ (1.5 cm) across length of ribbon. Gather-stitch across folds to hold them in place. Pull thread lightly to gather. Backstitch twice to hold.

Complete

6. Arrange flowers and leaves on base. Use small stitches to secure at underside. If you would like your leaves or flowers to overlap the borders, as in the photograph, make final stitches once the border is in place.
7. To add backing and 2″ (5 cm) border, see page xviii.

APRIL

Sweet Pea

The sweet-scented flowers on their climbing vine fill the air with the intoxicating aromas of Spring. Delicate petals in pinks, lilacs, and lavenders remind us that the joys of the season are to be cherished. Like beauty itself, they will all too soon wilt on the vine.

Use ⅛" (0.4 cm) seam allowance, unless noted otherwise.

YOU WILL NEED

Base: ½ yd (45 cm)

Flower fabrics: Scraps, up to eight different prints

For leaves, 1½" (4 cm) wired silk ribbon: 1¾ yds (160 cm)

Backing/border: ¾ yd (70 cm)

Batting: ½ yd (45 cm)

Prepare block

1. Cut base rectangle of background fabric measuring 12" × 18" (30 cm × 45 cm). Mark a seam line ½" (1.5 cm) inwards from all raw edges, so that background base onto which you will applique measures 11" × 17" (27 cm × 42 cm). Cut batting to measure 15" × 21" (37 cm × 52 cm) and backing/border fabric to measure 20" × 26" (50 cm × 66 cm). Baste batting onto wrong side of base.

Make eight flowers

2. Set compass to 2" (5 cm) radius to draw circle measuring 4" (10 cm) in diameter. This includes ⅛" (0.4 cm) seam allowance. Cut eight from each of two fabrics. Match one of each color together, right sides together, then sew them

Try adding some decorative touches to the background base before you begin. Here, I cut the base from a wide piece of border fabric that featured parallel blue stripes enclosing a rambling vine. I cut out extra strips of the striped portion of the fabric (with added seam allowance) and applique them on the base to give the appearance of a lattice. Notice, too, that some of my vines extend beyond the lattice. To achieve this effect, simply cut out some extra stems from the vine fabric, adding seam allowance. Applique them in place.

together around seam allowances, leaving a 1″ (2.5 cm) opening. Turn right side out. Blind stitch opening closed. Finger press seam.

3. Fold right side of completed circle inwards, leaving ½″ (1.5 cm) gap between curves. Pin to hold. Make a diagonal fold 1½″ (4 cm) from base, as shown. Pin to hold then gather-stitch along fold. Pull thread lightly to gather. Backstitch twice to hold.

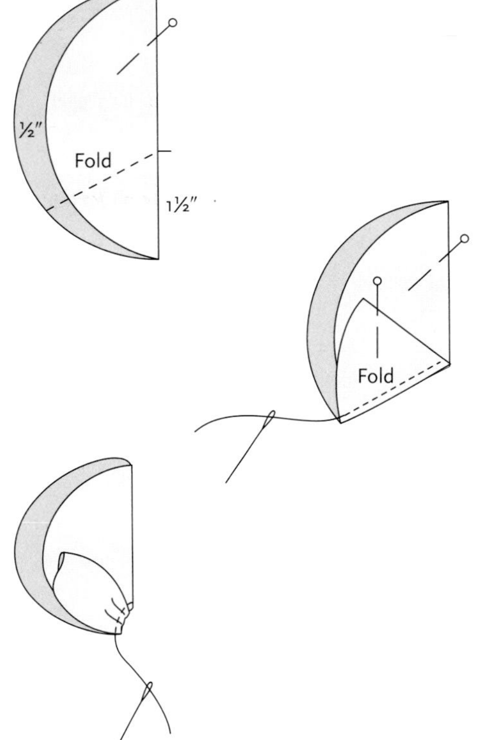

Step 3

Make five leaves

4. Cut five lengths of wired silk ribbon, each measuring 12″ (20 cm). Leaving ½″ (1.5 cm) at center unfolded, loosely fold

both sides of ribbon in toward center, then out, then back in, as shown. Fold under one raw edge, then tuck other raw edge behind it. Pin in place.

5. Gather-stitch in a slight arc across bottom, as shown. Pull thread lightly to gather. Backstitch twice to hold. Turn under bottom ¼″ (0.75 cm) of stem, then sew onto base. Add extra stitches as needed to undersides of leaves to hold.

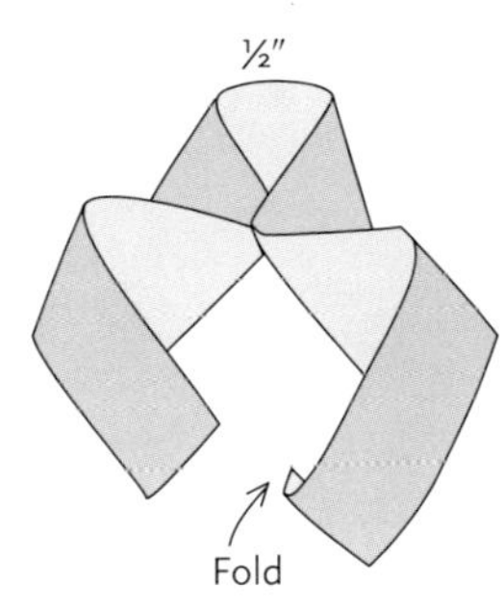

Step 4

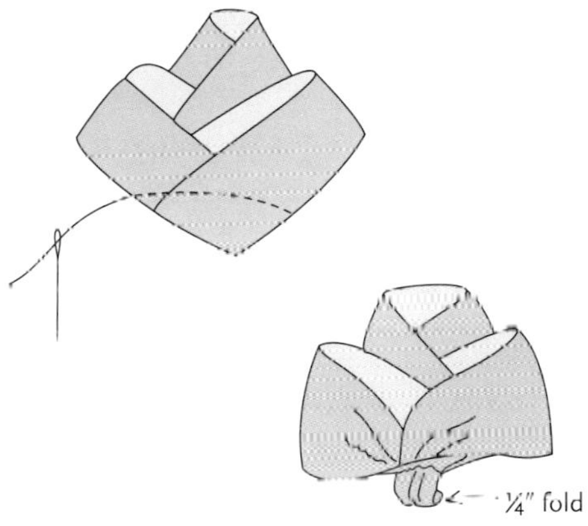

Step 5

Complete

6. Arrange flowers on base as desired. Use small stitches to secure underside of each flower in place.

7. To add backing and 2″ (5 cm) border, see page xviii.

Cockscomb

The shining, silky texture of the blossoms of the Cockscomb charm the imagination. Brilliant pink and crimson buds dance in the Spring breeze.

See templates on page 129. Use ⅛" (0.4 cm) seam allowance, unless noted otherwise.

Prepare block

1. Cut base rectangle of background fabric measuring 12" × 17" (30 cm × 42 cm). Mark a seam line ½" (1.5 cm) inwards from all edges, so that background base onto which you will applique measures 11" × 16" (27 cm × 40 cm).

2. Using Templates A and B and adding ½" (1.5 cm) seam allowance, cut left and right house pieces from complementary fabrics. Right sides together, sew house pieces together down center seam. Applique onto base rectangle, positioning so that bottom of house extends a full 5" (13 cm) below bottom raw edge of base rectangle. Background base now measures 12" × 22" (30 cm × 55 cm).

3. To create roof line, cut two strips: ⅝" × 8" (1.8 cm × 20 cm) for left roof and ⅝" × 10" (1.8 cm × 25 cm) for right roof. Turn under by ⅛" (0.4 cm) along each edge and baste to hold. Strips now measure ⅜" (1 cm) wide. Applique roof lines

YOU WILL NEED

Base: ½ yd (45 cm)

House: 9 " × 12" (23 cm × 30 cm)

Roof line: ⅛ yd (15 cm) or scraps

Flower fabrics: ¼ yd (25 cm), each of two fabrics

For leaves, 2½" (6.5 cm) wired silk ribbon, two or more colors: total of 1¼ yds (120 cm)

For stems and bow, 2½" (6.5 cm) plain silk ribbon: 1 yd (90 cm)

Side borders: ⅓ yard (30 cm)

Top border: ⅛ (15 cm) yard or scrap

Backing: ¾ yd (70 cm)

Batting: ½ yd (45 cm)

If, like mine, the fabric you choose for the base has a bird print, give the wings and tail feathers more emphasis by appliquéing tiny scraps of fabric over them. Create a template by tracing the area of the design you wish to cover. Add ⅛" (0.4 cm) seam allowances. Cut the fabric and applique in place. You can even stuff a little batting inside the appliques as you stitch to make them three dimensional.

over stitches that attach house to background fabric. Fold once at each roof peak.

4. Cut batting to measure 15" × 21" (37 cm × 52 cm) and backing fabric to measure 12" × 18" (13 cm × 45 cm). Baste batting onto wrong side of completed base.

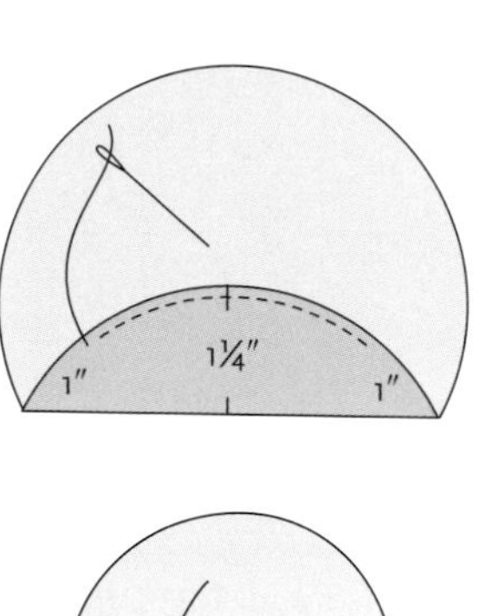

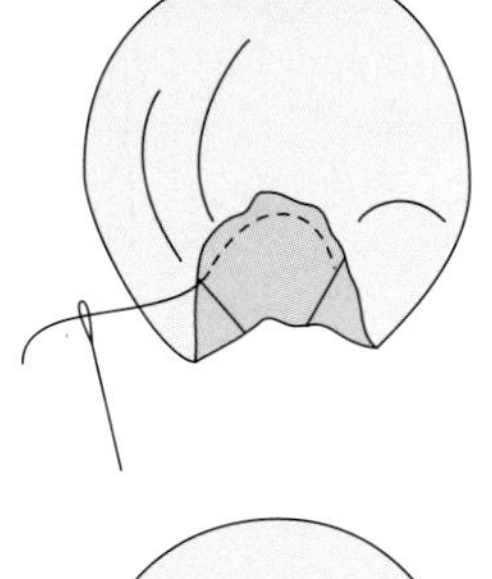

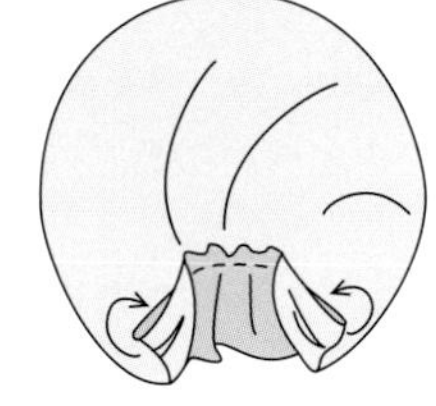

Step 6

Make three flowers

5. Set compass to 2⅜" (6 cm) radius to draw circle measuring 4¾" (12 cm) in diameter. This includes ⅛" (0.4 cm) seam allowance. Cut three from each of two fabrics (one light, one dark). Matching light to dark and right sides together, sew them together around seam allowances, leaving a 1" (2.5 cm) opening. Turn right side out. Blind stitch opening closed. Finger-press seam.

6. Fold upwards from bottom by 1¼" (3.2 cm) as shown. Gather-stitch through all layers along curve, leaving 1" (2.5 cm) free at either side. Lightly pull thread to gather. Backstitch twice to hold. Fold back top layer that remains unstitched at each side.

7. Arrange flowers on base as desired. Use small stitches to secure at underside.

Make three leaves, two stems, one bow

8. Cut three lengths of wired silk ribbon, each measuring 18" (45 cm). Fold in one end by 2" (5 cm). Continue folding, zig

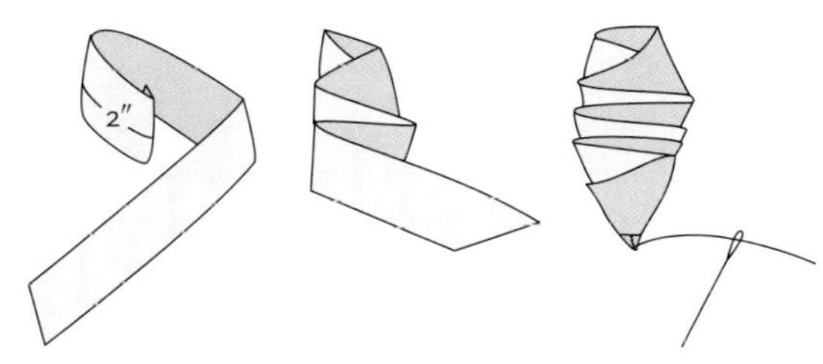

Step 8

zag fashion, along entire length of ribbon. Stitch twice at end to hold. Sew onto base.

9. Cut two lengths of plain silk ribbon measuring 12″ (30 cm) Twist each from top to bottom as shown, making small stitches to secure twists in place. Sew onto base.

10. Make a simple bow from remaining length of ribbon. Sew onto base.

Step 9

Complete

11. Wrong sides together, pin completed base in place onto backing fabric. Turn under ½″ (1.5 cm) seam allowance along bottom edge of base. Press or pin to hold in place. Fold bottom of base toward back by 2″ (5 cm). Blind stitch in place to complete bottom border.

12. Cut two strips of fabric measuring 5″ × 22″ (13 cm × 55 cm) for side borders and one strip measuring 5″ × 13″ (13 cm × 32.5 cm) for top border. Fold under raw edges on all sides by ½″ (1.5 cm) and press in place. Fold each border piece in half lengthwise and press.

13. Position and pin top border in place, aligning folded edge at front with line marked on base in Step 1. Blind stitch in place at front and back.

14. Repeat Step 11 to stitch vertical borders in place. Blind stitch front border to back border at top and bottom.

MAY

Passion Flower

The brilliant pink or purple corona of the Passion Flower atop its pretty twining vines bedeck shady woodland spots in late Spring. The fruit has a sweet, lemon-like scent. If you chance to step on it, you'll hear a loud popping sound that gives that passion flower its nickname—the Maypop. The Passion Flower is thought to have medicinal qualities—tea brewed from its woody vines brings calm and tranquility.

See templates on pages 130–131. Use ⅛" (0.4 cm) seam allowance, unless noted otherwise.

Prepare block

1. Cut base rectangle of background fabric measuring 12" × 18" (30 cm × 45 cm). Mark a seam line ½" (1.5 cm) inwards from all raw edges, so that background base onto which you will applique measures 11" × 17" (27 cm × 42 cm). Cut batting to measure 14" × 20" (35 cm × 50 cm) and backing/border fabric to measure 18" × 24" (45 cm × 60 cm). Baste batting onto wrong side of base.
2. Using template A, cut four leaves (reverse template for one). Pin in place onto base.

YOU WILL NEED

Base: ½ yd (45 cm)
Flower fabrics: variety, for total of ¼ yd (25 cm)
Leaves: Scraps, variety
For center vine, decorative cord or Poly String
For other vines, #25 embroidery floss
For border, 2⅜" (6 cm) plain silk ribbon: 6" (15 cm)
Backing/border: ¾ yd (70 cm)
Batting: ½ yd (45 cm)
Quilting thread

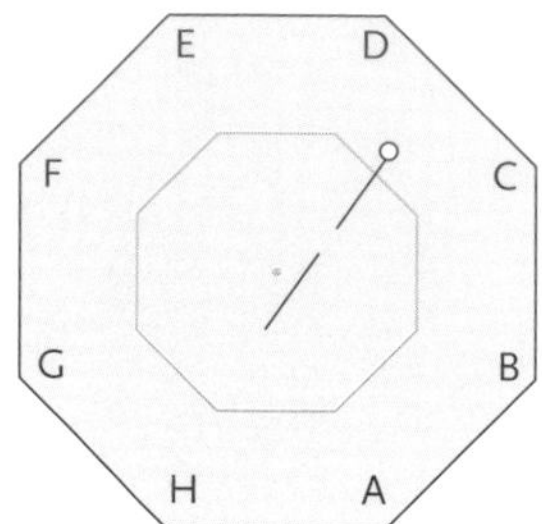

Step 5

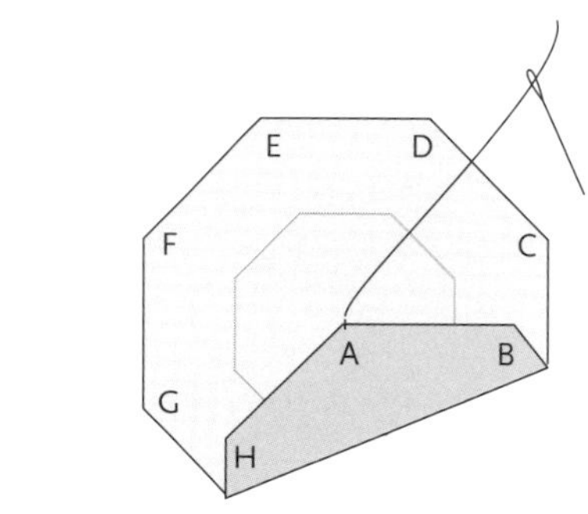

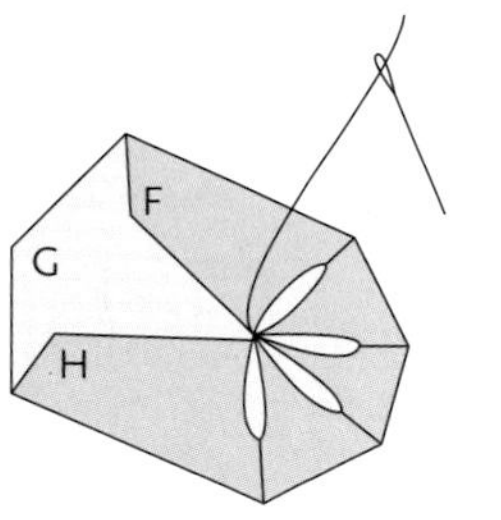

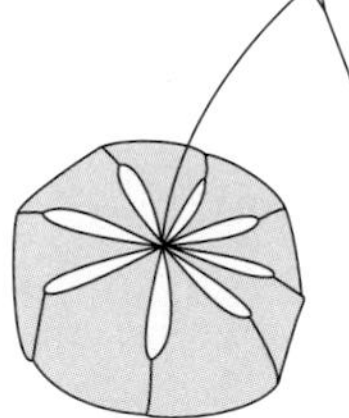

Step 6

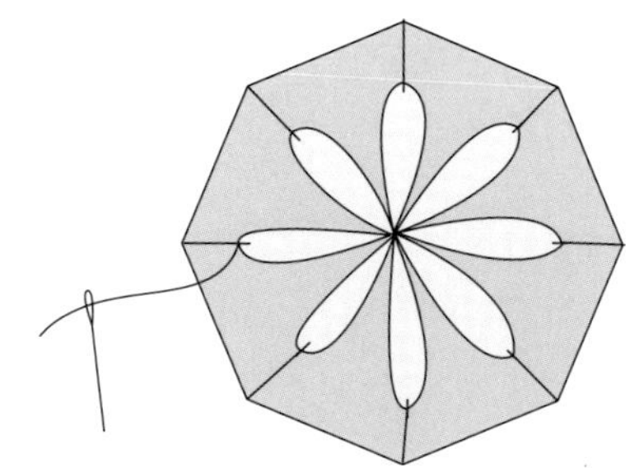

Step 7

3. To make central strand of vine, cut a 25″ (65 cm) strand of decorative cord. Arrange cord on base, tucking underneath pinned leaves as needed. Make small stitches at underside of cord to sew in place. Use layout diagram as a guide. Applique leaves onto base. Where leaves jut into border, leave those portions unstitched. Use embroidery floss and embroidery stitching to add the remaining strands of vine.

Make three flowers

4. Using template B, cut six flower pieces from a variety of light and dark fabrics. Matching light to dark and with right sides together, sew them together around seam allowances, leaving a 1″ (2.5 cm) opening. Turn right side out. Blind stitch opening closed. Finger press seam.
5. Using template C, cut three small octagons from batting. Do not add seam allowance. Pin and baste one at center of each flower piece.
6. Fold point A to center as shown and stitch to hold. Repeat until points B to H are stitched in place.
7. Gently open out the petals that form at the center so that more of the fabric shows. Make a single stitch at the tip of each petal to hold in place.

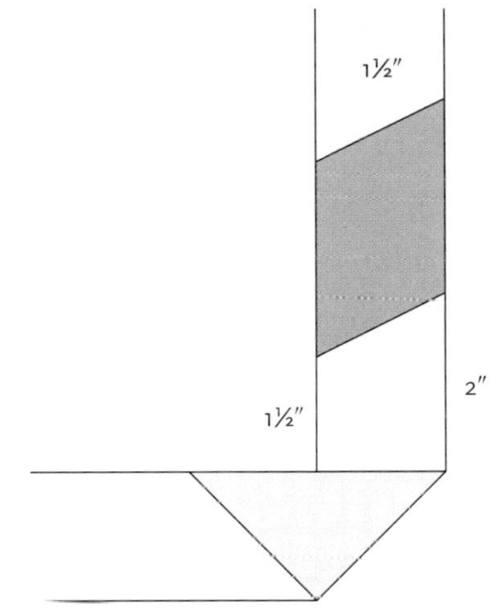

Step 10

Complete

8. Attach flowers to base. Use small stitches to secure underside of each in place.

9. Cut ribbon in two to make two 3″ (7.5 cm) lengths. Fold and press all four sides under by ¼″ (0.75 cm).

10. To add backing and 2″ (5 cm) border, see page xviii. Before blindstitching vertical borders in place, tuck ribbon into border as shown. Wrap ribbon to reverse of quilt. Blindstitch in place around entire ribbon.

11. Using stencil below, trace sashiko design onto base as desired. Stitch in sequence shown.

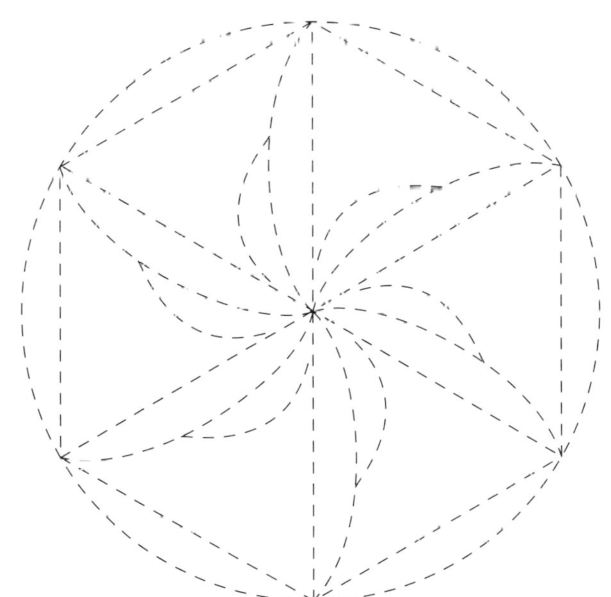

Sashiko stencil

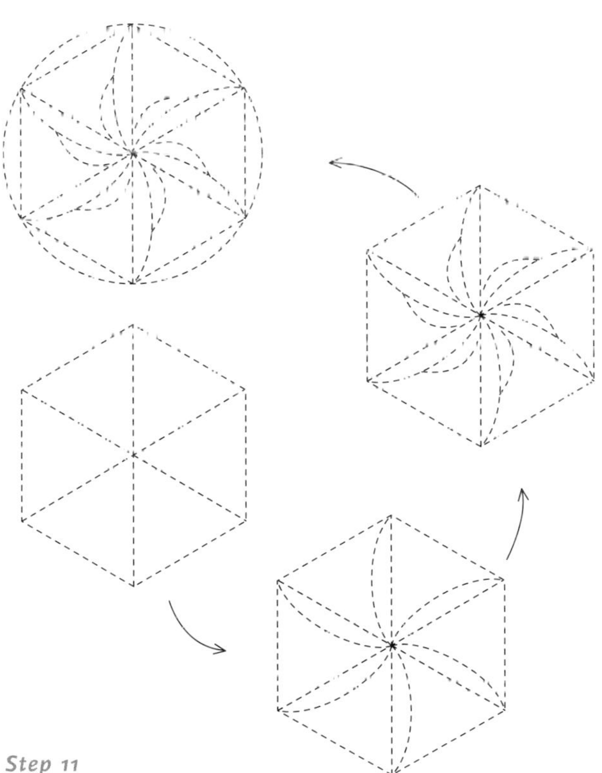

Step 11

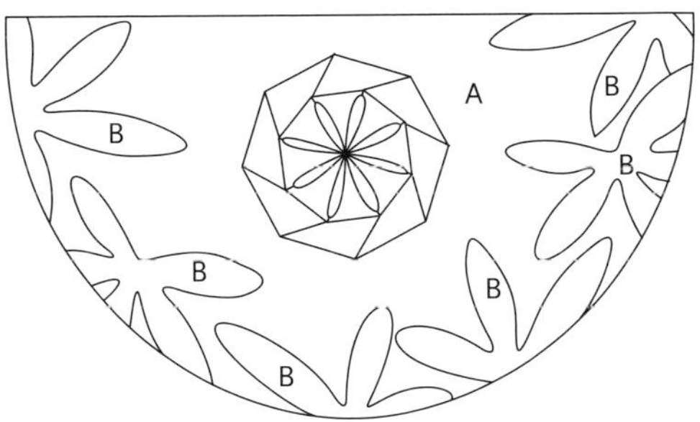

Front

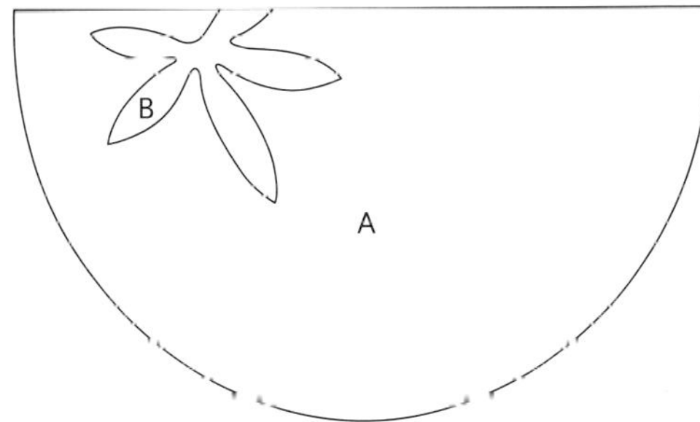

Back

Maypop Sachet

Bright and sunny, this pretty purse bursts with the joys and surprises of Spring. Drop inside a sachet of pot pourri that is made in part from lemon rind to give the purse the fresh lemon scent associated with the Passion Flower.

See templates on pages 131–133. Use ⅛" (0.4 cm) seam allowance, unless noted otherwise.

1. Join two template A pieces to create full template. Adding ½" (1.5 cm) seam allowance to curved edge only, cut two each from fabric, lining, and batting. Baste batting to wrong side of fabric for front and back of purse. Trim batting to scant ⅛" (0.4 cm).

2. Using template A from *Passion Flower* (page 131), cut seven leaf pieces from two shades of green felt. Do not add seam allowance. Position leaves on front of purse. Turn the leaves a little to give each one a slightly different look. Trim off any excess felt that overlaps the edges of the purse. Pin in place. Use a running stitch and matching thread to sew each leaf in place. Sew one leaf onto the back of purse as desired. Add decorative beads. (See diagrams on page 24.)

YOU WILL NEED

Purse fabric: ½ yd (45 cm) or less

Lining fabric: ½ yd (45 cm) or less

Flower fabric: Light and dark scraps

Leaf fabric: Scraps of felt

For handle, ½" (1.5 cm) plain silk ribbon: 10" (25 cm)

Thin batting: ½ yd (45 cm) or less

Beads for embellishment

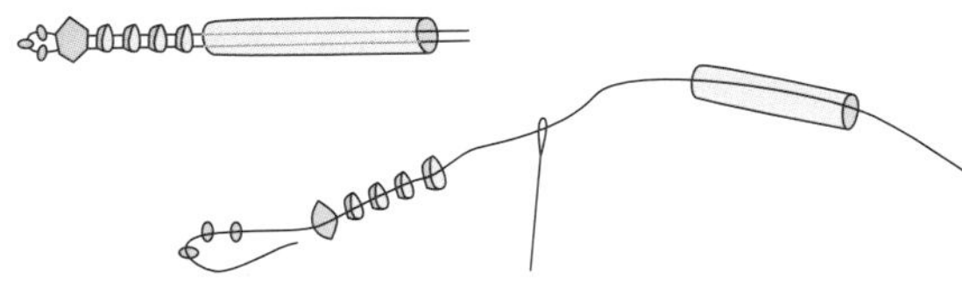

Step 2

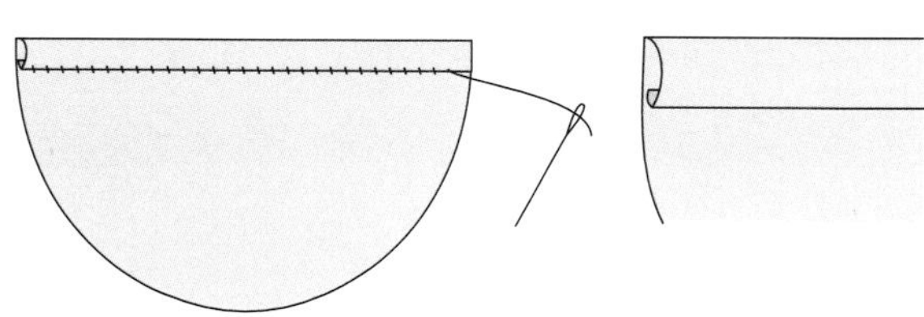

Step 5

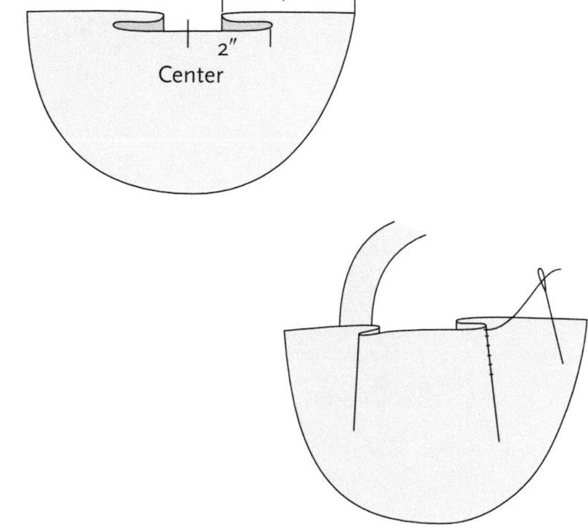

Step 6

3. Using Template B, cut one from each of two fabrics (one light, one dark). Follow Step 4 then Steps 6 to 7 of *Passion Flower* to complete flower. Stitch to purse, using small stitches to secure underside. Add a bead to center of flower.

4. Right sides together and using a ½″ (1.5 cm) seam allowance, sew front and back of purse together around bottom curve. Do not turn right side out. Repeat with lining pieces.

5. Wrong sides together, position lining on top of purse and pin in place, aligning center bottom of lining with center bottom of purse. Make two or three small stitches through all layers at center bottom to secure lining to purse. Repeat at about 2″ (5 cm) at either side of first set of stitches. Remove pins. Turn purse right side out, with lining falling in place inside. Fold under top edge of purse by a ¾″ (2 cm). Press to hold. Fold top to inside along edge of batting. Blind stitch in place onto lining.

6. Make tucks at center front and center back of purse as shown. Blindstitch to hold along folds at front and back for about ½″ (1.5 cm).

7. To make two handles, cut two strips of fabric to match purse, each measuring 1¼″ × 10″ (3.2 cm × 25 cm). This includes ¼″ (0.75 cm) seam allowances. Press seam allowances

Back view

to wrong side. Using template C, cut two from batting and two from felt. Do not add seam allowance. Right sides facing up, sew a fabric strip on top of a felt piece. Turn over and stitch short raw edges in place.

8. Baste batting to wrong side of felt piece. Fold in half lengthwise. Stitch around all edges to completely hide batting. Blindstitch silk ribbon to handle to disguise previous seam.

9. Position first completed handle with felt facing inside at tucks in purse front. About 1″ (2.5 cm) of each end of handle will be on inside of purse. Blindstitch in place. Repeat to attach second handle to back of purse.

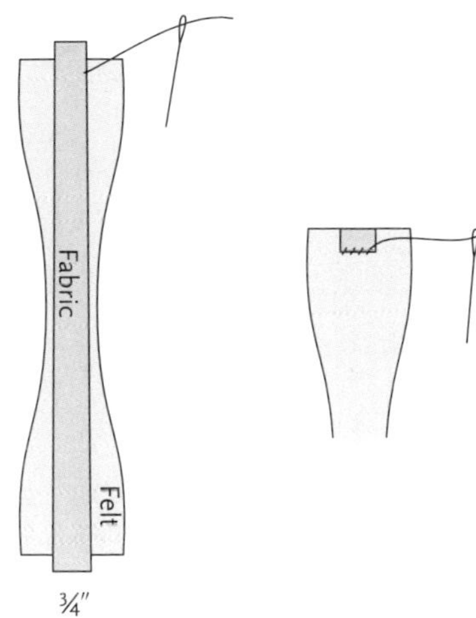

Step 7

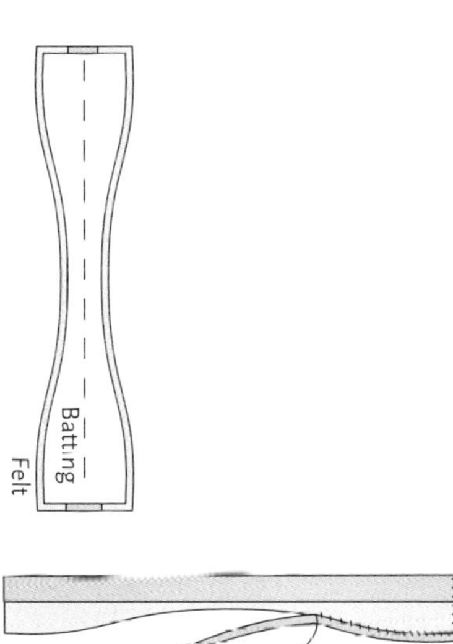

Step 8

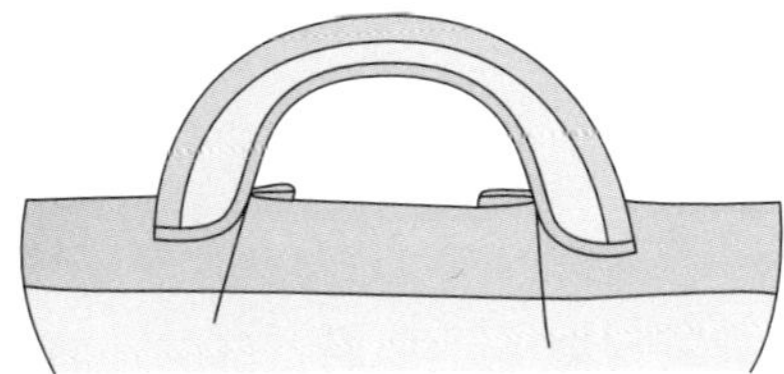

Step 9

Phlox

Its amazing range of bright colors make Phlox a favorite in the Spring or Summer garden. The name derives from Greek and means flame—Phlox glimmers and glows in lovely shades of pink, primrose, amber, scarlet, crimson, rose and lavender.

See templates on pages 134–135. Use ⅛" (0.4 cm) seam allowance, unless noted otherwise.

Prepare block

1. Cut base rectangle of background fabric measuring 12" × 18" (30 cm × 45 cm). Mark a seam line ½" (1.5 cm) inwards from all raw edges, so that background base onto which you will applique measures 11" × 17" (27 cm × 42 cm). Cut batting to measure 14" × 20" (35 cm × 50 cm) and backing/border fabric to measure 18" × 24" (45 cm × 60 cm). Baste batting onto wrong side of base.
2. Transfer markings of stencil on page 29 onto base. You may complete the sashiko stitching now or once the appliques are in place.
3. Using templates A to I, cut three leaves and six stem pieces. Applique leaves A and B onto base. Next applique stems D and E, then leaf C, fitting the leaf neatly between the two

YOU WILL NEED

Base: ½ yd (45 cm)

Flower fabrics: ⅛ yd (15 cm), each of two fabrics. Use more than two fabrics if desired.

For bud, leaves, and stems: Scraps, variety

Backing/border: ¾ yd (70 cm)

Batting: ½ yd (45 cm)

Quilting thread

If you wish to highlight sections of the sashiko design, as in the photograph, use the stencil as a template to cut out small pieces of fabric, adding ⅛″ (0.4 cm) seam allowances. Applique in place between the marked sashiko lines. Follow the sashiko sequence diagrams on page 29 to complete sashiko.

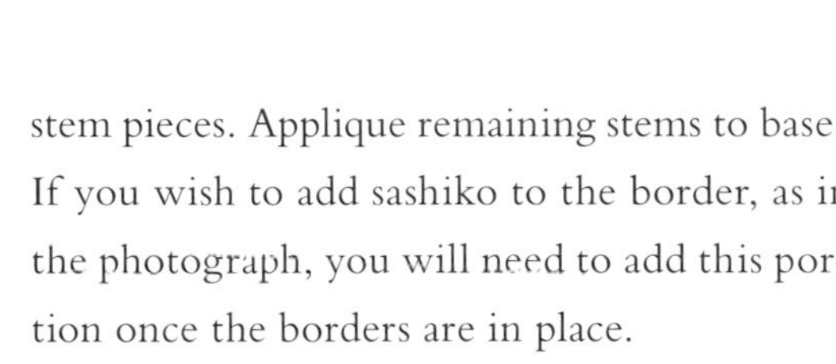

stem pieces. Applique remaining stems to base. If you wish to add sashiko to the border, as in the photograph, you will need to add this portion once the borders are in place.

Make five flowers

4. Using template J, cut five flower pieces from each of two fabrics. Match one of each color together, right sides together, then sew them together around seam allowances, leaving a 1″ (2.5 cm) opening. Turn right side out. Blind stitch opening closed. Finger press seam.

5. Fold points A to E to center as shown, stitching each tip in place. Then stitch each to its neighbors, about ¼″ (0.75 cm) from the tip.

6. Gently open out the petals so that more of the fabric shows. Fold back each outer tip over itself by about ¼″ (0.75 cm) to form final flower.

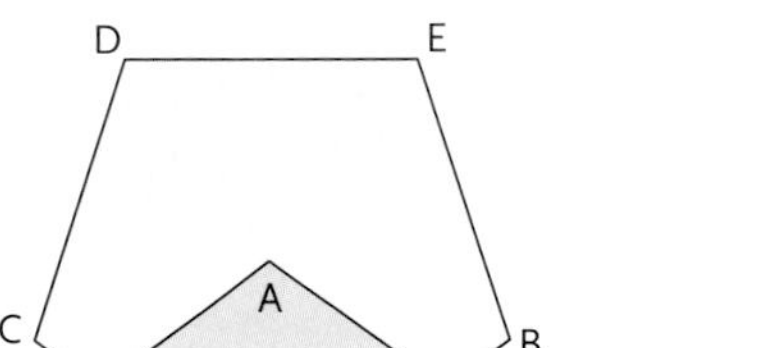

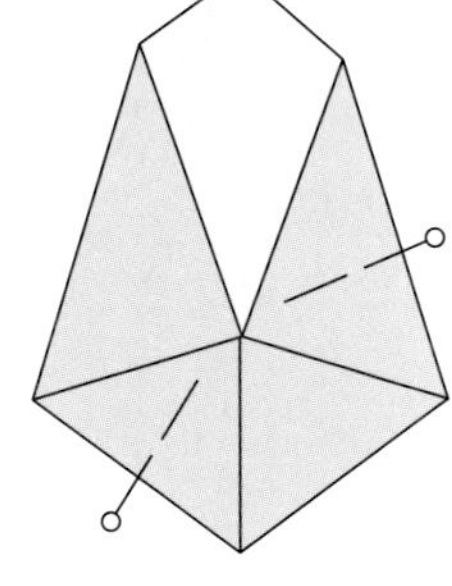

Step 5

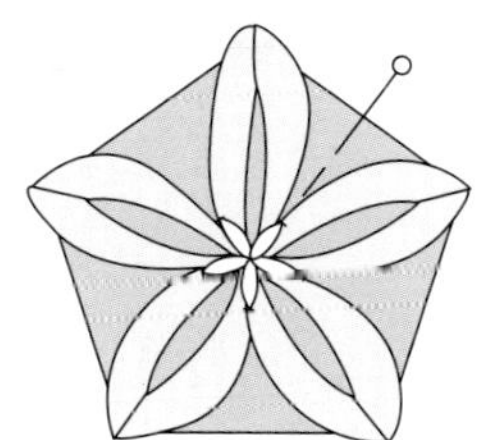

Step 6

Complete

7. Attach flowers to base at ends of stems. Use small stitches to secure underside of each in place. Complete as much as you can of the sashiko stitching before adding border.
8. To add backing and 1½″ (4 cm) border, see page xviii.
9. Complete any sashiko stitching that overlaps into border.

Sashiko sequence

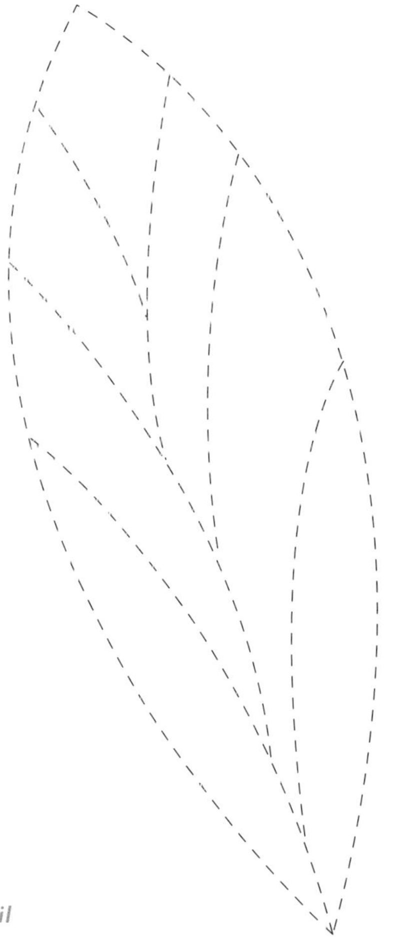

Sashiko stencil

Summer

The Morning Glory has been highly prized since the Edo period in the seventeenth century, when people competed to produce exceptional varieties for trade. Few sights are as memorable to me as its budding vines twisting and twining their way through bamboo fences in the neighborhood of my childhood days. When I was little, I would gather these fragrant summer blossoms in as many colors as I could find. I would soak them in water then set up a row of colorful glass jars outside our garden gate. I would make believe this was a store and that I was selling magical potions in all the colors of the rainbow. As street merchants sauntered by, their carts filled with flowers, fruits, and handicrafts, I would imagine that I was one of them.

Another favorite is the delicate purple flower of the *Kiri* tree. These lovely tubular blossoms have a mild aroma that I always associate with Summer. The tree's immense heart-shaped leaves give shade on the hottest days. The wood of the *Kiri* tree has been used for centuries to build fine furniture, particularly *tansu* chests, which are used to store *kimono*. There is an ancient custom of planting a *Kiri* tree to celebrate the birth of a daughter. When the girl marries, a chest is made from the tree to carry her *kimono*—along with her hopes, dreams, and memories—to her new home.

Asagao ni
Tsurube torarete
Morai mizu

This ancient haiku tells of a lady drawing water from a well. She sees that a vine of Morning Glory in bloom has twined around the bucket. Thankful for this singular glimpse of beauty, she leaves the well undisturbed and asks her neighbor for water instead.

Calypso

The Calypso flower—or fairy slipper—with its delicate pink, purple, and yellow blossoms, dances through the Summer woodlands. Catching a glimpse of Calypso petals will bring good fortune!

See templates on pages 136–138. Use ⅛" (0.4 cm) seam allowance, unless noted otherwise.

Prepare block

1. Cut base rectangle of background fabric measuring 12" × 18" (30 cm × 45 cm). Mark a seam line ½" (1.5 cm) inwards from all raw edges, so that background base onto which you will applique measures 11" × 17" (27 cm × 42 cm). Cut batting to measure 15" × 21" (37 cm × 52 cm) and backing/border fabric to measure 20" × 26" (50 cm × 66 cm). Baste batting onto wrong side of base.
2. Using templates A to D, cut two leaves and two stems. Applique onto base in following order: stem A, stem B, leaf C, leaf D.
3. Using templates E to I, cut three stones and seven cloud pieces. Applique onto base in following order: clouds E and F; then stones G, H, and I. For additional clouds, cut four small rectangles measuring 3½" × 1" (9 cm × 2.5 cm) and one

YOU WILL NEED

Base: ½ yd (45 cm)

Flower fabrics, variety of light/dark: ¼ yd (25 cm) or less

For leaves, stems, and clouds: Scraps, variety

Backing and border: ¾ yd (70 cm)

Batting: ½ yd (45 cm)

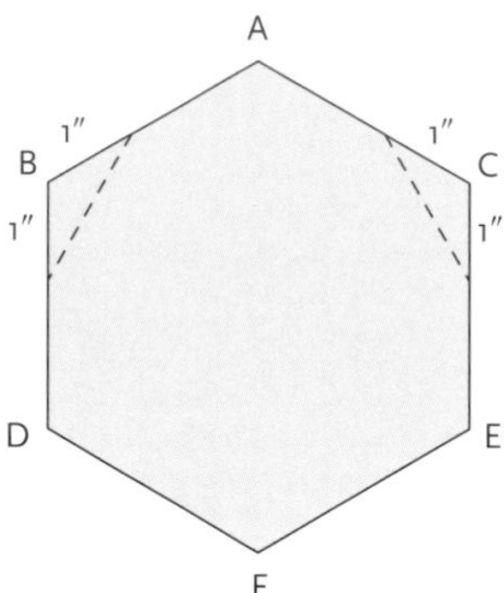

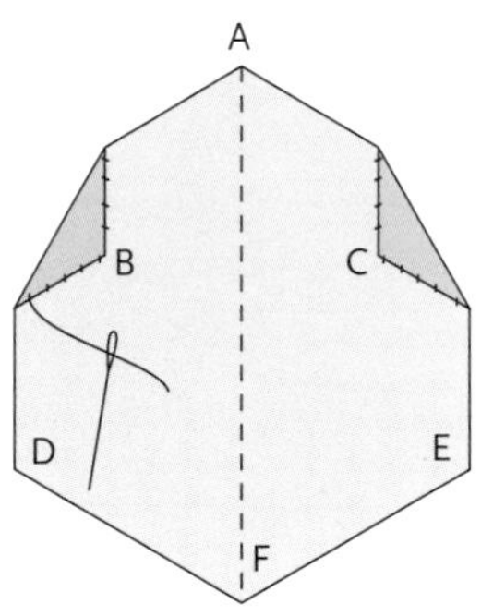

Step 5

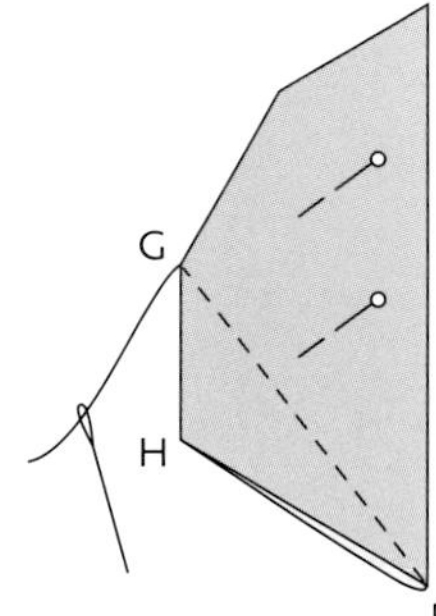

Step 6

large rectangle measuring 3½″ × 1¾″ (9 cm × 4.5 cm). All pieces include seam allowances.

Make five flowers

4. Using template J, cut five flower pieces from light fabrics and five from dark fabrics. Matching light to dark and with right sides together, sew them together around seam allowances, leaving a 1″ (2.5 cm) opening. Turn right side out. Blind stitch opening closed. Finger press seam.

5. Lightly mark at 1″ (2.5 cm) from either side of points B and C as shown. Fold and pin to hold. Stitch in place. Fold in half down center line A-F. Pin to hold

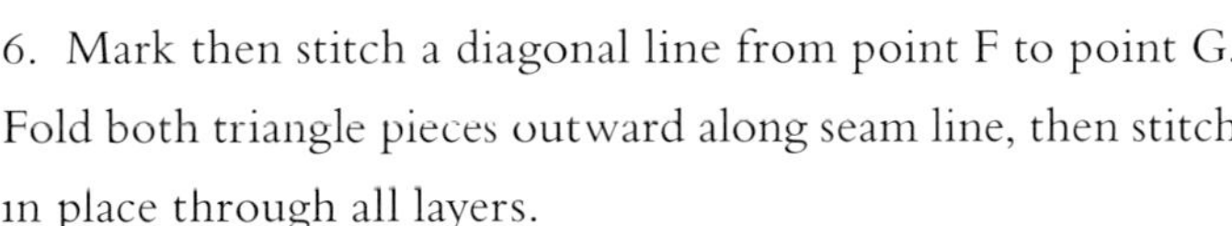

6. Mark then stitch a diagonal line from point F to point G. Fold both triangle pieces outward along seam line, then stitch in place through all layers.

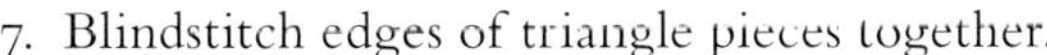

7. Blindstitch edges of triangle pieces together.

8. Gather stitch as shown, at about the midpoint of F-G. Pull point A over the center of the flower, toward point F as shown.

Complete

9. Attach flowers to base as desired. Use small stitches to secure underside of each in place.

10. To add backing and 2″ (5 cm) border, see page xviii.

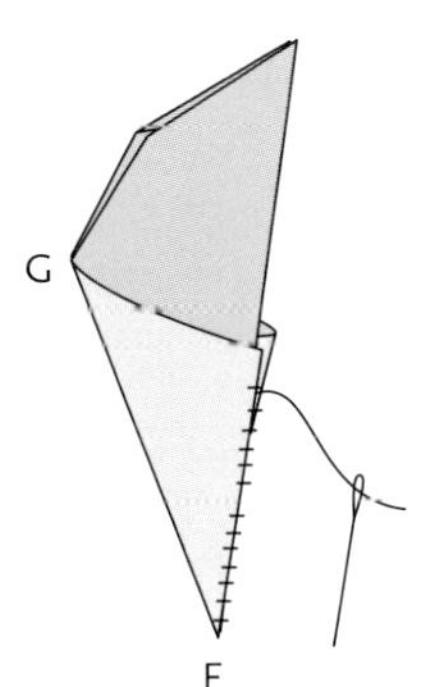

Step 7

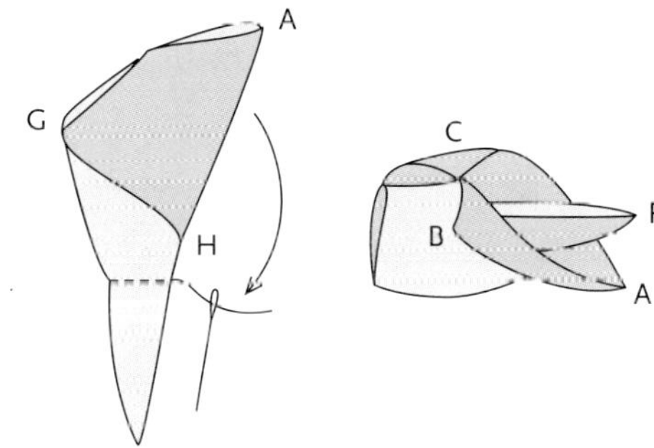

Step 8

Framboise

Glowing with color as they put forth their fruits, raspberry vines are a sign that Spring has gone. Sweet and succulent, the scent of Framboise fills the air, coaxing hatchlings from their nests to discover the tastes of Summer.

Use ⅛" (0.4 cm) seam allowance, unless noted otherwise.

Prepare block

1. Cut base rectangle of background fabric measuring 12" × 18" (30 cm × 45 cm). Mark a seam line ½" (1.5 cm) inwards from all raw edges, so that background base onto which you will applique measures 11" × 17" (27 cm × 42 cm). Cut batting to measure 15" × 21" (37 cm × 52 cm) and backing/border fabric to measure 20" × 26" (50 cm × 66 cm). Baste batting onto wrong side of base.

Make three flowers

2. Set compass to 2⅜" (6 cm) radius to draw circle measuring 4¾" (12 cm) in diameter. This includes ⅛" (0.4 cm) seam allowance. Cut three flower pieces from each of two fabrics (one light, one dark). Matching light to dark and with right

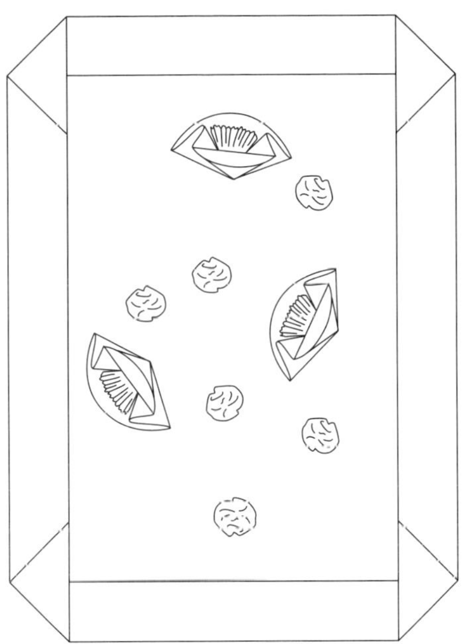

YOU WILL NEED

Base: ½ yd (45 cm)

Flower fabrics: ¼ yd (25 cm), each of two fabrics.

For flower centers, 1½" (4 cm) wired silk ribbon: ¾ yd (70 cm)

For buds, 1" (2.5 cm) plain silk ribbon: 1 yd (90 cm)

Backing/border: ¾ yd (70 cm)

Batting: ½ yd (45 cm)

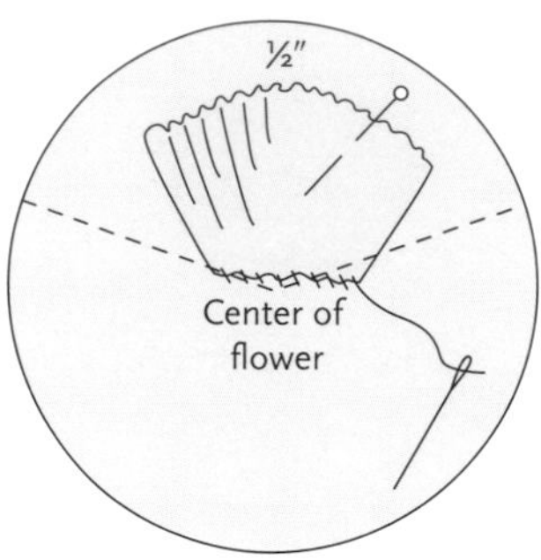

Step 4

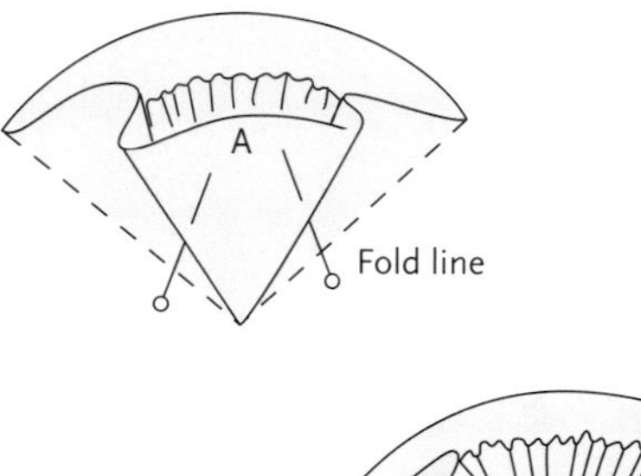

Step 5

sides together, sew them together around seam allowances, leaving a 1″ (2.5 cm) opening. Turn right side out. Blind stitch opening closed. Finger press seam.

3. For flower centers, cut three lengths of wired silk ribbon, each measuring 8″ (20 cm). Fold in each end by ½″ (1.5 cm). Gather ribbon with your fingers, reducing length to 2½″ (6.5 cm). Gather stitch across tucks. Pull thread lightly, reducing length to 1¼″ (3.2 cm). Backstitch to hold.

4. Position tucked edge of ribbon at center of flower piece, leaving a space of 1½″ (4 cm) at top center. Pin then stitch in place.

5. Fold flower inwards at fold lines, then out again, as shown. Fold front curve A outward by ½″ (1.5 cm). Stitch in place through all layers.

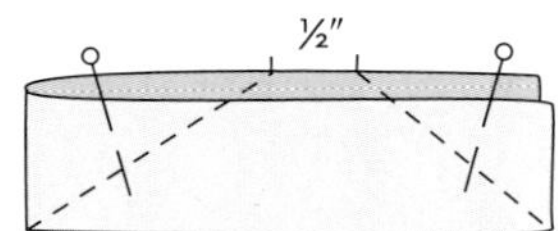

Step 6

Make six buds

6. Cut six lengths of plain silk ribbon, each measuring 6″ (15 cm). Fold in half and pin to hold. Leaving ½″ (1.5 cm) at center unfolded, fold diagonally as shown. Pin to hold.

7. Using small running stitches, stitch up first diagonal, across top, and down opposite diagonal. Turn right side out, then gather-stitch along same stitched line, leaving ¼″ (0.75 cm) unstitched at each end. Pull lightly to gather, manipulating with your fingers to create a "wrinkled" effect. Backstitch twice to hold.

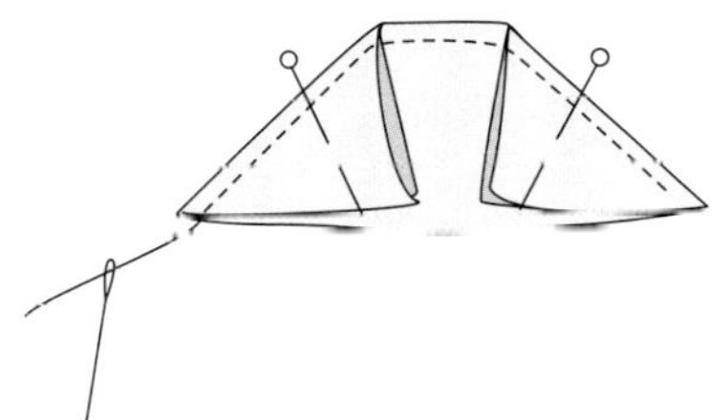

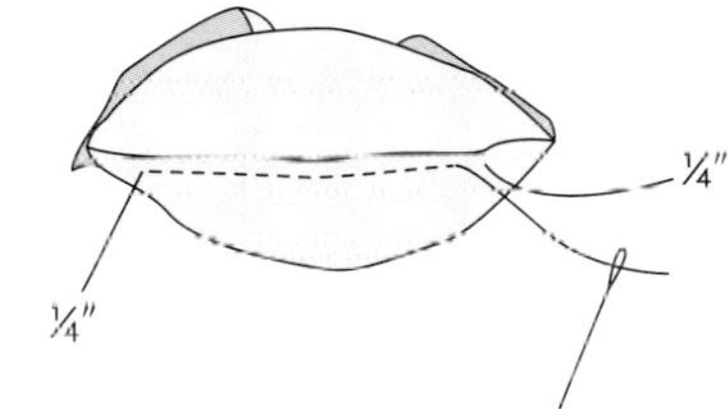

Step 7

Complete

8. Attach flowers and buds to base as desired. Use small stitches to secure underside of each in place.

9. To add backing and 2″ (5 cm) border, see page xviii.

Summer Surprise

As you walk through gardens or woodlands, collect the fallen blossoms of Spring and Summer in this pretty pouch. Dried sprigs of cherry and plum blossoms or petals of Azaleas, Hydrangea, or Magnolia will make a wonderfully scented summer sachet.

See templates on pages 139–142. Use ⅛" (0.4 cm) seam allowance, unless noted otherwise.

1. Join four template A pieces to create full template. Adding ½" (1.5 cm) seam allowance, cut two each from fabric, lining, and batting. Baste batting to wrong side of fabric for front and back of purse. Trim batting to scant ⅛" (0.4 cm).
2. Cut seven strips of felt measuring ¼" × 12" (0.75 cm × 30 cm). Use a single line of running stitch to sew stems onto front and back of purse, as shown in photographs. Stitch out to the raw edges of the purse fabric so that ends of felt will later be enclosed in seam allowance. Stitch decorative beads in place along each edge of stems.
3. Cut two flower pieces from each of two fabrics (one light, one dark). Follow Steps 2 to 5 of *Framboise* to complete two flowers. Stitch flowers in place on front of purse. Use small stitches to secure underside of each.

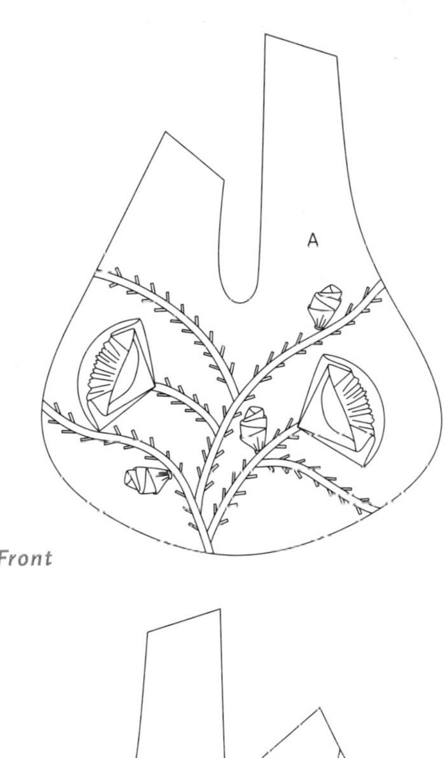

Front

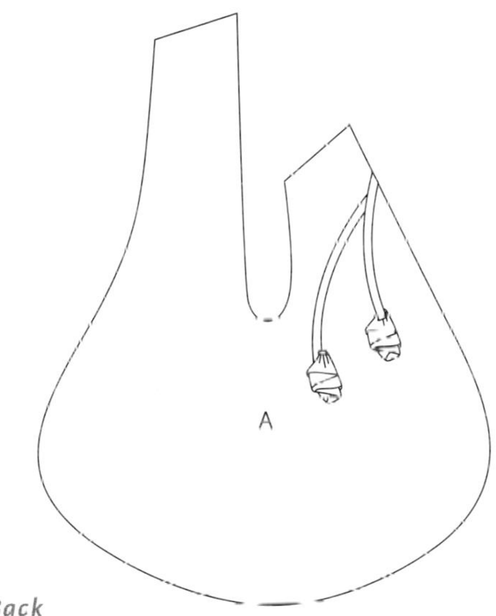

Back

YOU WILL NEED

Purse fabric: ½ yd (45 cm) or less

Lining fabric: ½ yd (45 cm) or less

Flower fabric: ¼ yd (25 cm) or scraps

For stems: Felt scraps

For flowers, 1½" (4 cm) wired silk ribbon: ½ yd (70 cm)

For buds, 1½" (4 cm) wired silk ribbon: 1¼ yds (115 cm)

Thin batting: ½ yd (45 cm) or less

Decorative beads; purse photographed uses ¼" (0.75 cm) cylindrical beads

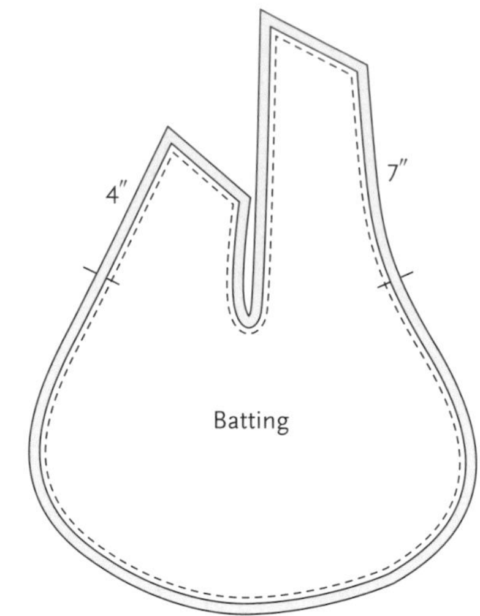

Step 1

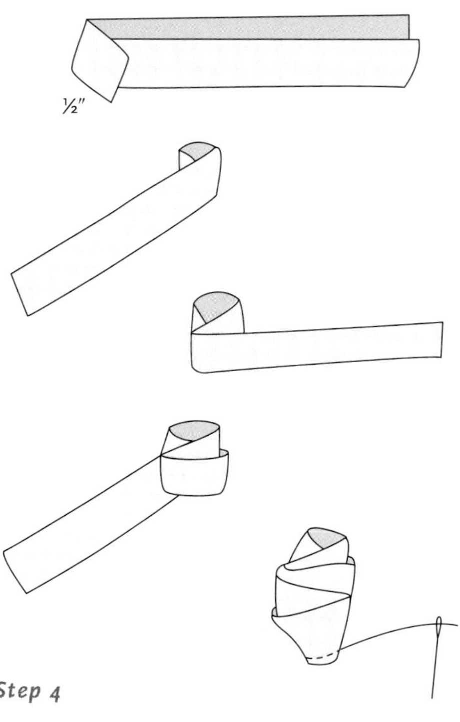

Step 4

4. For buds, cut five lengths of 1½" (4 cm) wired ribbon, each measuring 8" (20 cm). Fold in by ½" (1.5 cm) at one end. Starting here, fold alternately from left to right as shown. Gather stitch across bottom. Pull thread to gather and backstitch twice to hold. Attach three buds to the front and two to back of purse.

5. Right sides together, sew front to back, using ½" (1.5 cm) seam allowance. Leave top and handles open, as marked on Template A. Clip curves and press seams open. Repeat with lining front and lining back. Turn under seam allowance around handles and purse top and baste in place. Repeat with lining.

6. Wrong sides together, position lining on top of purse and pin in place, aligning center bottom of lining with center bottom of purse. Make two or three small stitches through all layers at center bottom to secure lining to purse. Repeat at about 2" (5 cm) at either side of first set of stitches. Remove pins. Turn purse right side out, with lining falling in place inside. Blindstitch lining to purse around handles and top. You may need to adjust the seam allowances so that purse fab-

Back view

ric overlaps the lining fabric a little. Remove all basting stitches. Arrange handles so that longer handle slips easily inside shorter handle. Press lightly in place.

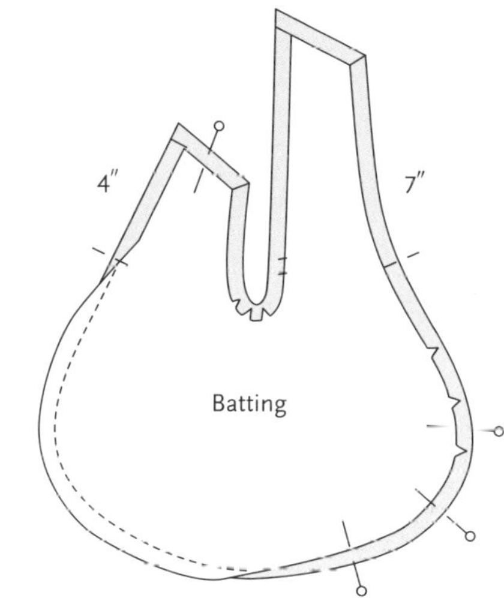

Step 5

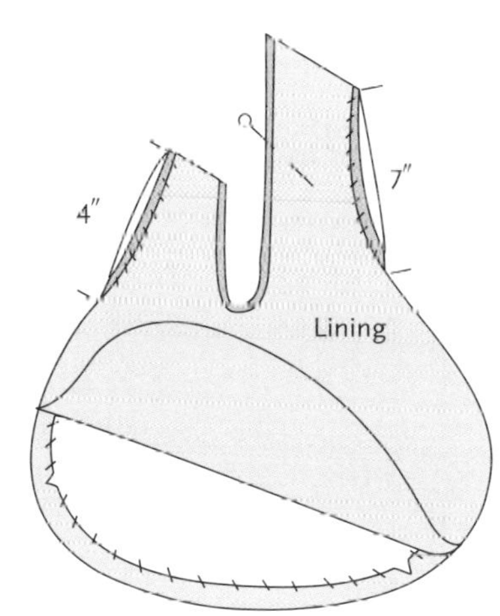

Step 6

JULY

Campanula

The Campanula—or Bellflower—sways gracefully in the soft woodland shade. Caught in the Summer sunlight, pretty rosettes bud at the top of the bell, bursting into flower to celebrate the season.

Use ⅛" (0.4 cm) seam allowance, unless noted otherwise.

YOU WILL NEED

Base: ½ yd (45 cm)

Flower fabrics: ¼ yd (25 cm), each of two fabrics. Use more than two fabrics if desired.

For leaves, 1½" (4 cm) wired silk ribbon: ¾ yd (70 cm)

Backing/border: ¾ yd (70 cm)

Batting: ½ yd (45 cm)

Prepare block

1. Cut base rectangle of background fabric measuring 12" × 18" (30 cm × 45 cm). Mark a seam line ½" (1.5 cm) inwards from all raw edges, so that background base onto which you will applique measures 11" × 17" (27 cm × 42 cm). Cut batting to measure 15" × 21" (37 cm × 52 cm) and backing/border fabric to measure 20" × 26" (50 cm × 66 cm). Baste batting onto wrong side of base.

2. Choose strong motifs from a pictorial fabric—moons, stars, birds, or a favorite motif—and applique them onto the base as desired.

Make five flowers

3. Using template J from *Calypso* (see page 138), cut five flower pieces from each of two fabrics. Match one of each

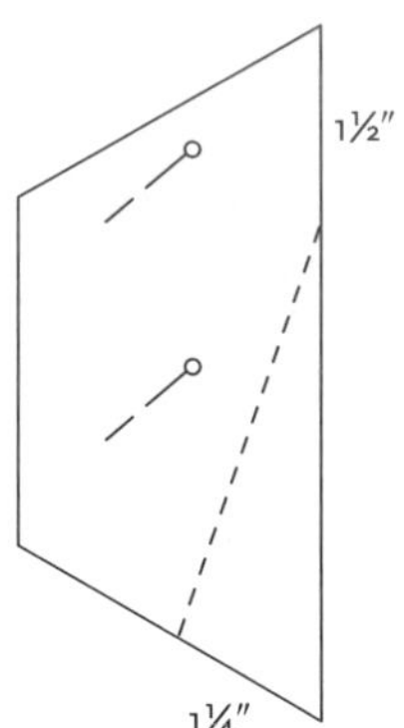

Step 4

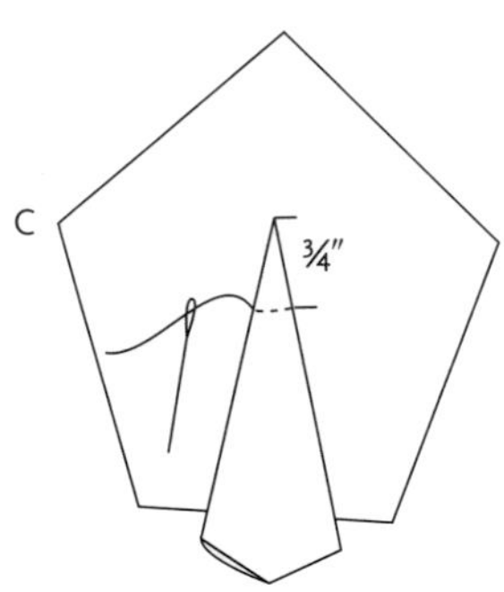

Step 5

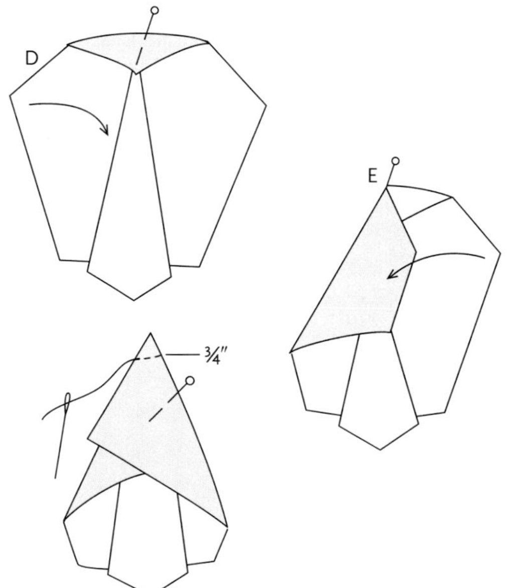

Step 6

color together, right sides together, then sew them together around seam allowances, leaving a 1″ (2.5 cm) opening. Turn right side out. Blind stitch opening closed. Finger press seam.

4. Fold hexagonal flower piece in half. Pin to hold. Mark then sew dart as shown, starting 1½″ (4 cm) from top center and ending 1¼″ (3.2 cm) from bottom center.

5. Open out hexagon so that it lies flat, with sewn seam on top. Open out dart. Sew across dart, ¾″ (2 cm) from top of stitched seam.

6. Fold top of hexagon downwards to meet top of dart. Pin to hold. Fold left side of hexagon inward as shown. Fold right side of hexagon over left. Pin to hold. Gather stitch across top, ¾″ (1.5 cm) from tip. Pull thread to gather. Backstitch twice to hold. Stitch pearl or bead to bottom tip of completed flower.

Make three leaves

7. Cut three lengths of wired ribbon, each measuring 9" (23 cm). Make tucks along the entire length of each ribbon, starting at raw edges and working inwards toward center. Gather stitch along tucked edge. Pull thread to gather. Backstitch to hold.

8. Fold in half as shown, and stitch raw edges of ribbon together. Turn leaf over and arrange tucks with your fingers for final shape.

Complete quilt

9. Arrange flowers and leaves on base as desired. Use small stitches to secure underside of each flower or leaf in place.

10. To add backing and 2" (5 cm) border, see page xviii.

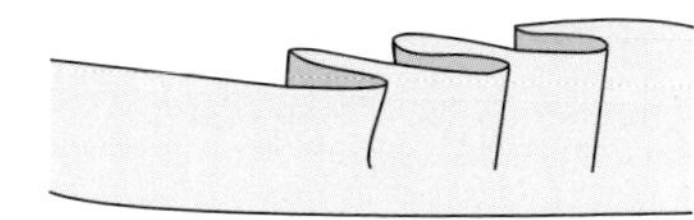

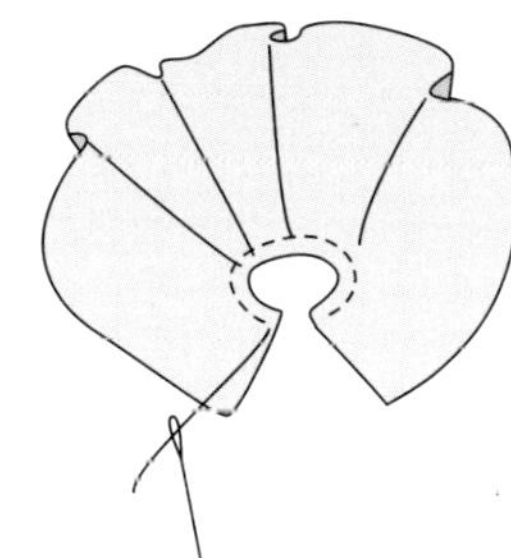

Step 7

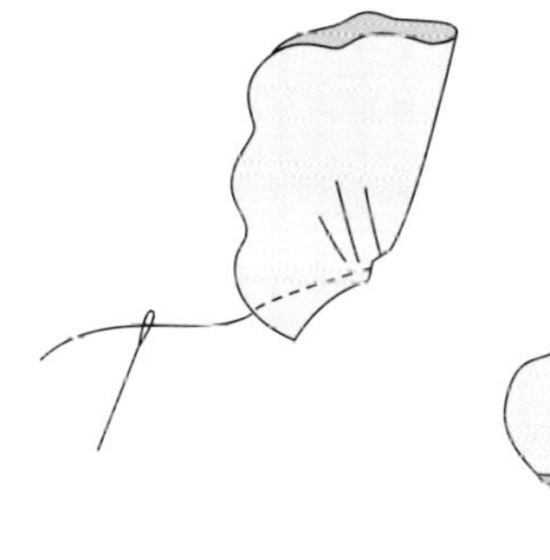

Step 8

Protea

Protea is one of the world's most ancient plants, native to South Africa. Its exotic flowers come in various shapes and an incredible range of colors. The plant takes its name from the Greek sea god, Proteus, who could transform his shape at will to elude capture. Protea are very long lasting, making them a wonderful choice for season-long ikebana arrangements.

See templates on pages 143–146. *Use ⅛" (0.4 cm) seam allowance, unless noted otherwise.*

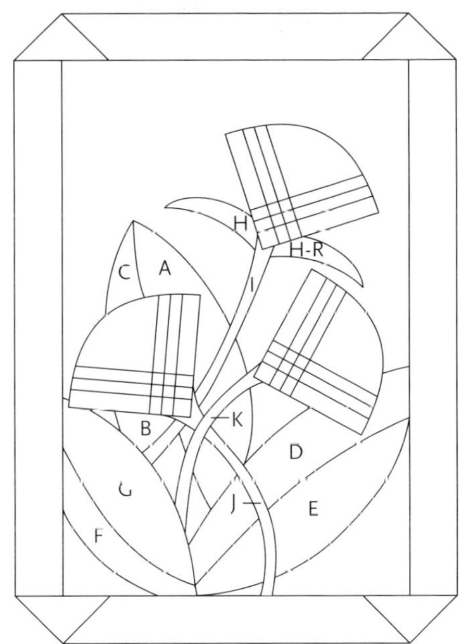

YOU WILL NEED

Base: ½ yd (50 cm)

Flower fabric: ¼ yd (25 cm)

For leaves and stems: Scraps, variety

For flowers, ½" (1.5 cm) plain silk ribbon: 1 yd (90 cm)

Backing/border: ¾ yd (70 cm)

Batting: ½ yd (45 cm)

7 decorative beads or covered buttons

Prepare block

1. Cut base rectangle of background fabric measuring 12" × 18" (30 cm × 45 cm). Mark a seam line ½" (1.5 cm) inwards from all raw edges, so that background base onto which you will applique measures 11" × 17" (27 cm × 42 cm). Cut batting to measure 14" × 20" (35 cm × 50 cm) and backing/border fabric to measure 18" × 24" (45 cm × 60 cm). Baste batting onto wrong side of base.

2. Using templates A to K, cut out leaf and stem pieces. Applique onto base in following order: leaves A to E, stems I, J, K, leaves F, G, H, and H-R.

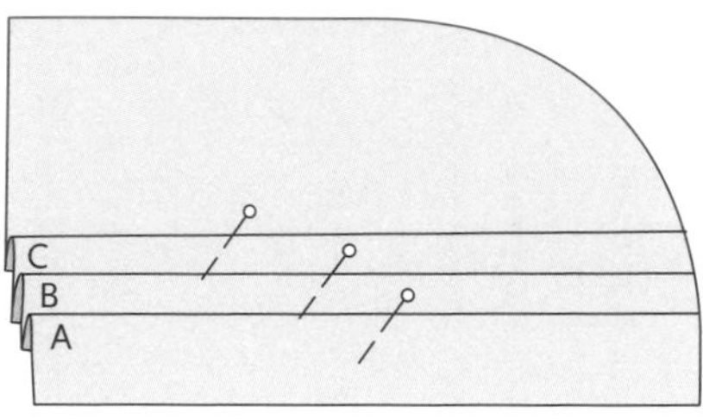

Step 3

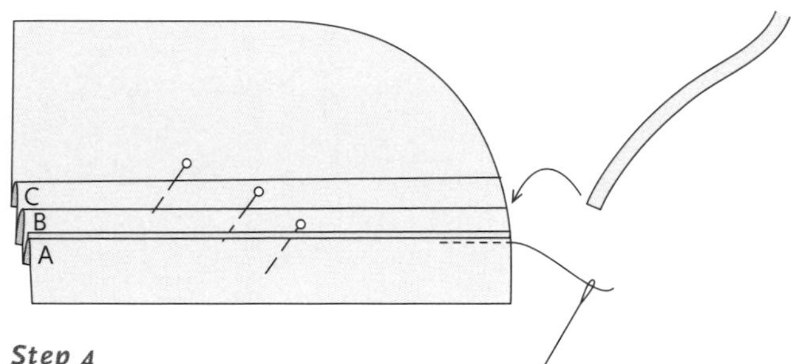

Step 4

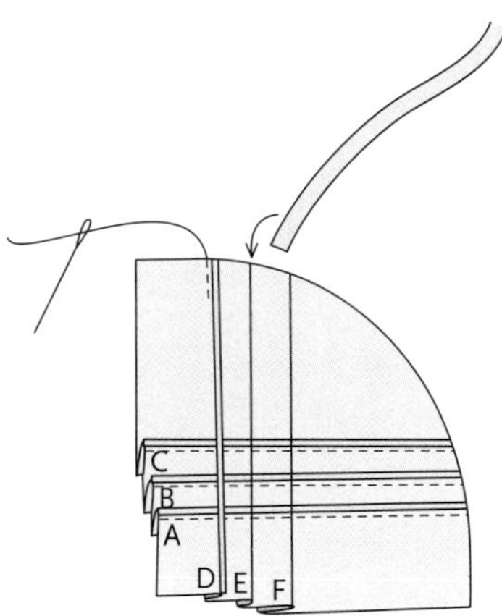

Step 5

Make three flowers

3. Using template L, cut three. Transfer markings. Using markings as a guide, fold lines A, B, and C as shown. Pin to hold.

4. Cut six lengths of plain silk ribbon, each measuring 6¾" (17 cm). Place first length of ribbon behind folded line A. Pin then stitch in place, allowing ¼" (0.75 cm) of ribbon to show. Repeat, adding ribbon behind folds B and C.

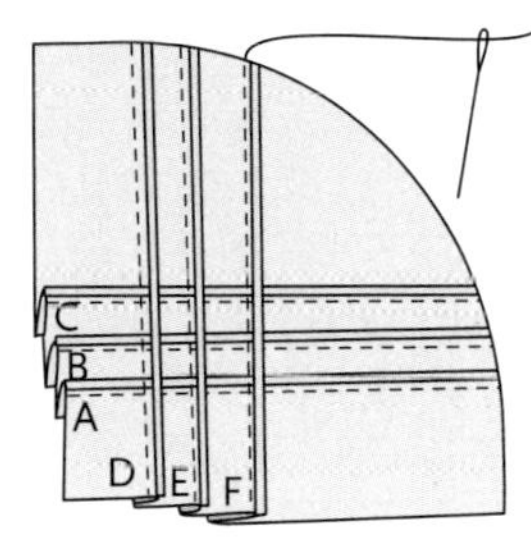

Step 5

5. In same way, make folds D, E, and F. Attach ribbon behind folds.

Complete

6. Fold in seam allowances around each flower, hiding raw edges of ribbon. Applique onto base, over tops of stems.
7. Stitch buttons covered with fabric or decorative beads onto leaves as in photograph.
8. To add backing and 1½″ (4 cm) border, see page xviii.

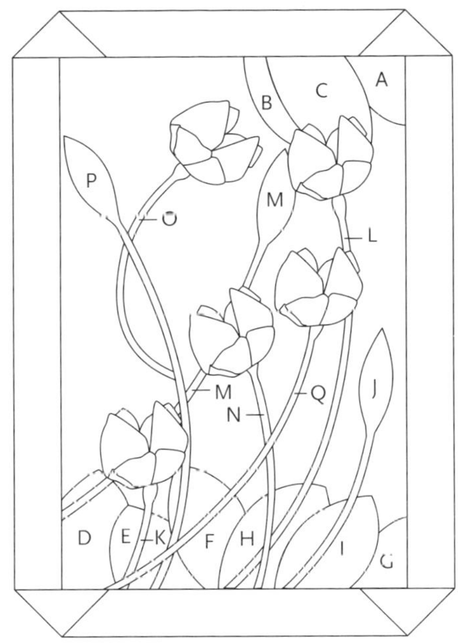

Lantern Flower

Hozuki, the Chinese lantern plant, is known for its fragile, papery blooms formed by bright orange sepals around a rich red fruit. In the long hot summer, Japanese children make hozuki squeakers—the fruit, emptied of its pulp, makes a sharp squeaking sound when pressed between the tongue and the roof of the mouth.

See templates on pages 147–150. Use ⅛" (0.4 cm) seam allowance, unless noted otherwise.

YOU WILL NEED

Base: ½ yd (45 cm)

Flower fabrics, variety of light/dark: ½ yd (45 cm)

For leaves: ⅙ yd (15 cm) or scraps of various fabrics

For stems: Scraps, variety

Backing/border: ¾ yd (70 cm)

Batting: ½ yd (45 cm)

Prepare block

1. Cut base rectangle of background fabric measuring 12" × 18" (30 cm × 45 cm). Mark a seam line ½" (1.5 cm) inwards from all raw edges, so that background base onto which you will applique measures 11" × 17" (27 cm × 42 cm). Cut batting to measure 14" × 20" (35 cm × 50 cm) and backing/border fabric to measure 18" × 24" (45 cm × 60 cm). Baste batting onto wrong side of base.
2. Using templates A to I, cut nine leaf pieces. Applique in alphabetical order onto base. Using templates J to Q, cut eight stem pieces. Make sure you join the two-piece templates L, M, and P before cutting fabrics. Applique onto base in alphabetical order.

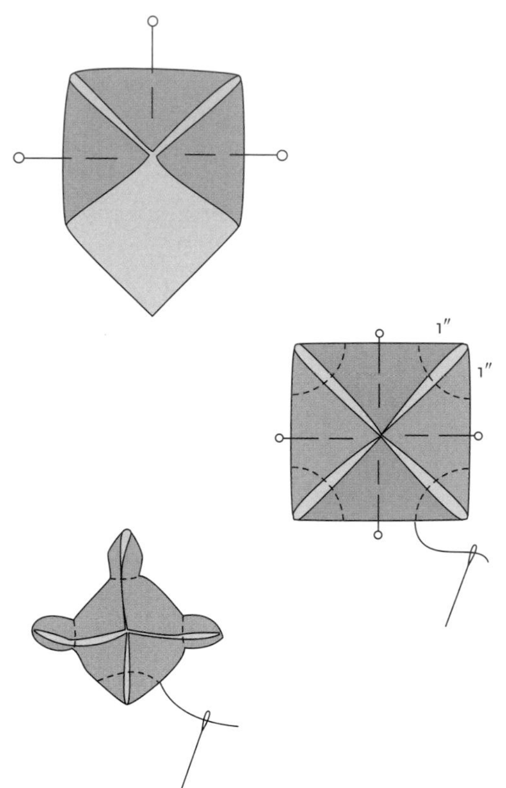

Step 4

Make five flowers

3. Cut five squares of dark fabric measuring 6½″ × 6½″ (16.5 cm × 16.5 cm), which includes a ¼″ (0.75 cm) seam allowance. Cut five squares from light fabric. Matching light to dark and with right sides together, sew two squares together around seam allowances, leaving a 1″ (2.5 cm) opening. Turn right side out. Blind stitch opening closed. Finger press seams.

4. Fold all four corners to center and pin in place. Lightly mark each side of resulting square 1″ (2.5 cm) from each corner. Draw a curve connecting marks at each corner as shown.

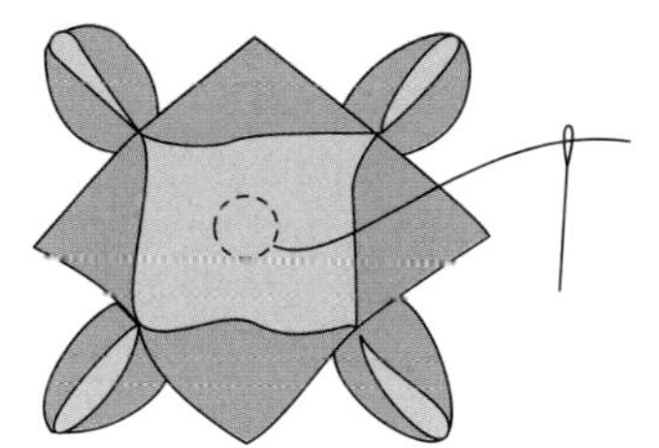

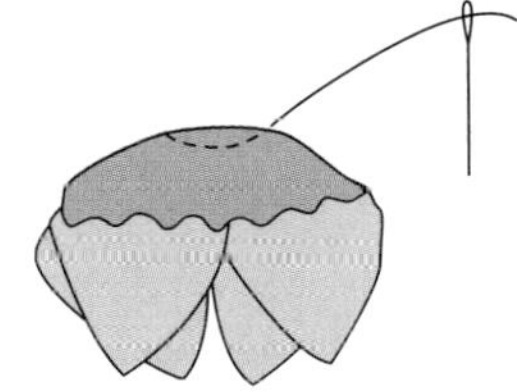

Gather-stitch each curve. Pull thread lightly to gather. Backstitch twice to hold.

5. Open out points at center of flower. Mark then gather stitch a ½″ (1.5 cm) diameter circle at center. Pull thread to gather. Backstitch twice to hold. You can let the flowers hang down or you can face them upwards, as shown.

Complete

6. Attach flowers to base at ends of stems. Use small stitches to secure underside of each in place.

7. To add backing and 2″ (5 cm) border, see page xviii.

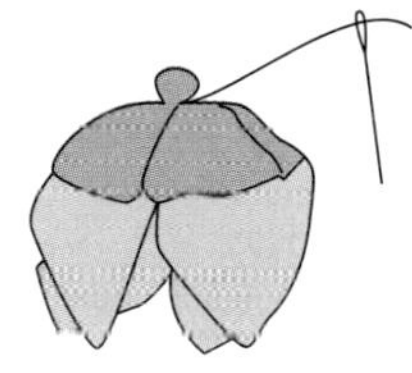

Step 5

Hozuki

This exquisite purse, with its brightly colored blossoms and intricate embellishments, makes a perfect accessory. Take it with you on hot Summer nights, since the Hozuki flower is believed to deflect the glare of the sun and drive away Summer heat.

See templates on pages 151–153. Use ⅛" (0.4 cm) seam allowance, unless noted otherwise.

1. Join two template A pieces to create full template. Adding ½" (1.5 cm) seam allowance, cut two each from fabric, lining, and batting. Baste batting to wrong side of lining pieces. Trim batting to scant ⅛" (0.4 cm).
2. Cut stem pieces B to H from two shades of green felt. Do not add seam allowance. You will have five leaves and five stems. Use a small, even running stitch to sew the felt stems in place on front and back of purse, as shown in the photograph. Sew in following order: B, C, D, E-1, C-R, B R, E-2, F, G, and H. String then sew decorative beads to the leaves and the stems on the handle.
3. From each of two fabrics (one light, one dark) cut five squares, each measuring 5" × 5" (13 cm × 13 cm). Follow Steps 3 to 5 of *Lantern Flower* to complete five flowers. Arrange and sew on front of purse.

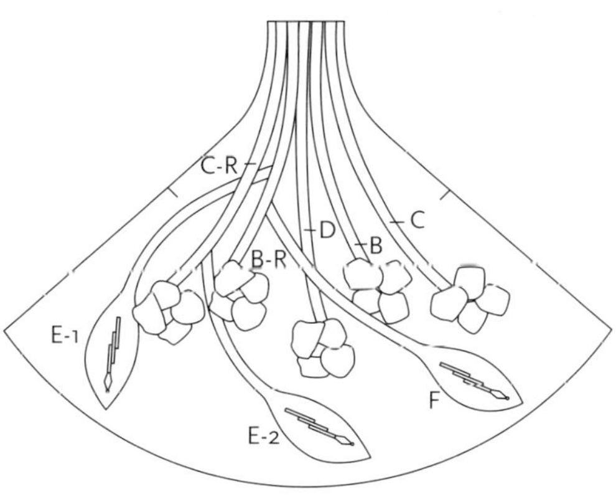

Front

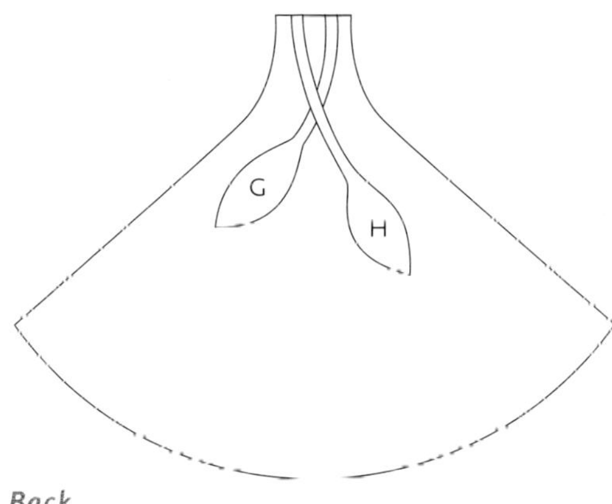

Back

YOU WILL NEED

Purse fabric: ½ yd (45 cm) or less

Lining fabric: ½ yd (45 cm) or less

Flower fabric, variety of light/dark: ½ yd (45 cm) or scraps

For leaves and stems: Scraps of felt, two shades of green

Thin batting: ½ yd (45 cm) or less

Decorative beads, ¾" (2 cm)

Decorative button

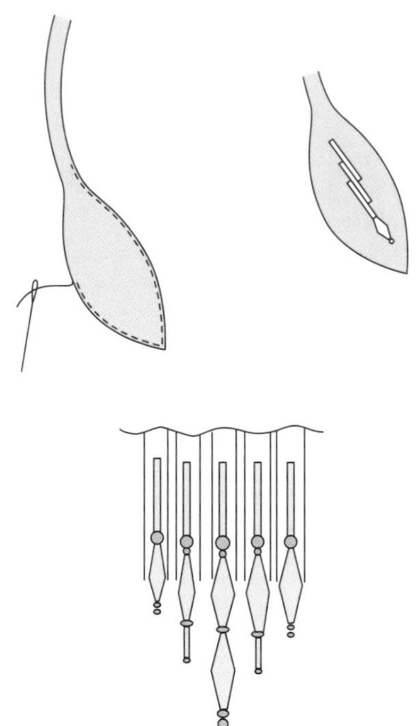

Step 2

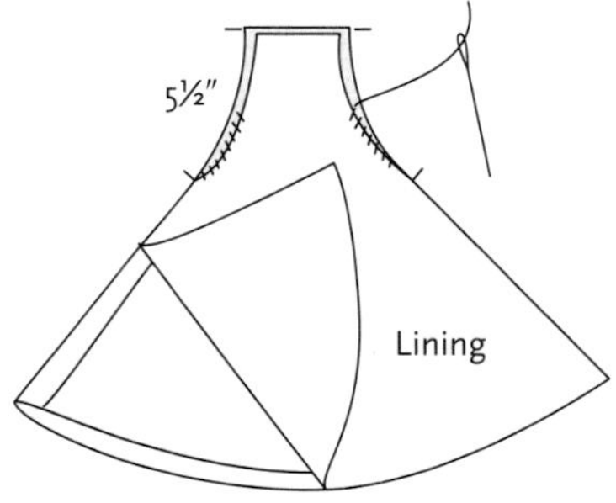

Step 4

4. Right sides together, sew front to back, using ½″ (1.5 cm) seam allowance. Leave top open as shown on template A for about 5½″ (14 cm) at each side. Clip curves, if necessary, and press seams open. Repeat with lining front and lining back. Turn under seam allowance around handles and purse top and baste in place. Repeat with lining.

5. Wrong sides together, sew across top of handle pieces. Repeat for lining.

6. Wrong sides together, position lining on top of purse and pin in place, aligning center bottom of lining with center bottom of purse and aligning handles pieces. Make two or three small stitches through all layers at center bottom to secure lining to purse. Repeat at about 2″ (5 cm) at either side

Back view

of first set of stitches. Remove pins. Turn purse right side out, with lining falling in place inside. Blindstitch lining to purse around handles and top. You may need to adjust the seam allowances so that purse fabric overlaps the lining fabric a little. Remove all basting stitches.

7. Add a button to the handle at the top of the purse.

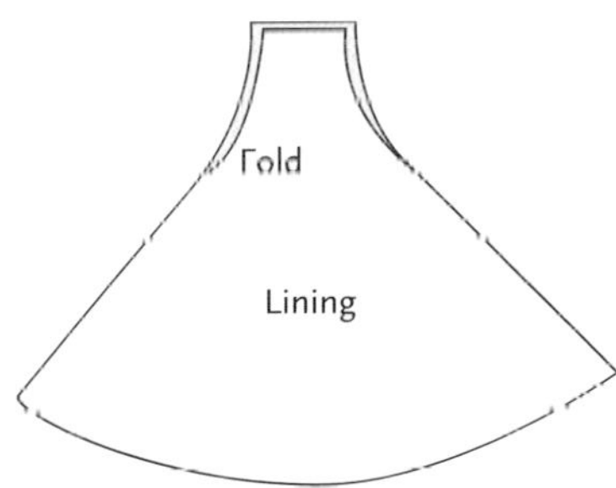

Step 6

Rose Hortensia

Tiny fairies peek from the blossoms of this sweetly scented flower. Originating in Japan, Rose Hortensia's ball-shaped flowers and rich green foliage make it a perfect hiding place for Summer sprites.

Use ⅛" (0.4 cm) seam allowance, unless noted otherwise.

Prepare block

1. Cut base rectangle of background fabric measuring 12" × 18" (30 cm × 45 cm). Mark a seam line ½" (1.5 cm) inwards from all raw edges, so that background base onto which you will applique measures 11" × 17" (27 cm × 42 cm). Cut batting to measure 15" × 21" (37 cm × 52 cm) and backing/border fabric to measure 20" × 26" (50 cm × 66 cm). Baste batting onto wrong side of base.
2. Set compass to 2" (5 cm) radius to draw circle measuring 4" (10 cm) in diameter. This includes ⅛" (0.4 cm) seam allowance. Cut two large handballs from floral fabric. Set compass to 1¾" (4.5 cm) radius to draw circle measuring 3½" (9 cm) in diameter. Cut one small handball. Turn under seam allowance and applique to base. Leave the portion of the bottom left handball that juts into the border unstitched.

YOU WILL NEED

Base: ½ yd (45 cm)

Handball fabrics: Scraps, decorative prints

Flower fabrics: ¼ yd (25 cm), each of two fabrics

White cotton: Scraps

For leaves, 3" (8 cm) wired silk ribbon: ¾ yd (70 cm)

For fairy's frill, 1" (2.5 cm) wired silk ribbon (dark): ¾ yd (70 cm)

For inner bow, 1½" (4 cm) wired silk ribbon (light): ¾ yd (70 cm)

For outer bow, 1½" (4 cm) wired silk ribbon (dark): 1¼ yd (120 cm)

Backing and border: ¾ yd (70 cm)

Batting: ½ yd (45 cm)

Fine-tip marker or embroidery floss

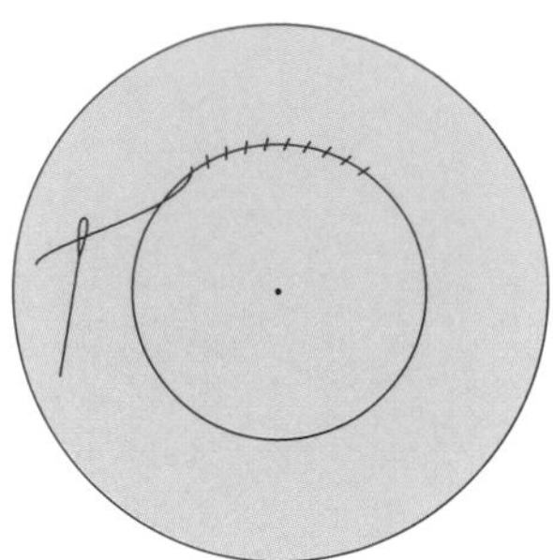

Step 3

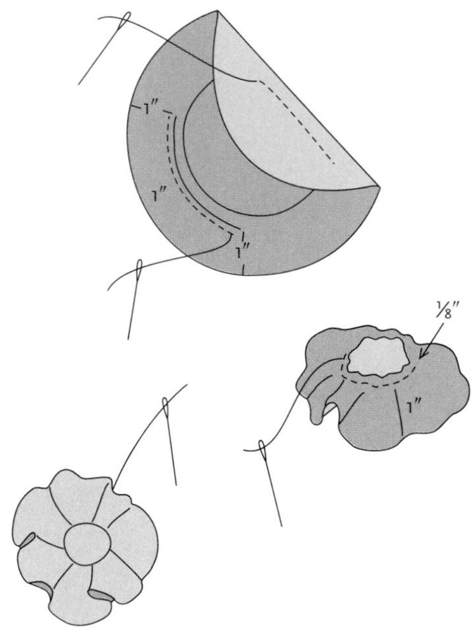

Step 4

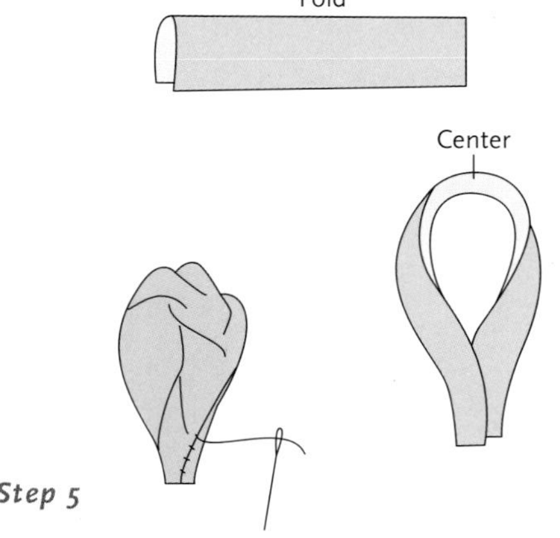

Step 5

Make three flowers

3. Set compass to 2½″ (6.5 cm) radius to draw circle measuring 5″ (13 cm) in diameter. This includes ⅛″ (0.4 cm) seam allowance. Cut three from each of two fabrics (one light, one dark). Set compass to 1½″ (4 cm) radius to draw circle measuring 3″ (8 cm) in diameter. This includes ⅛″ (0.4 cm) seam allowance. Cut three. Applique a small circle to center of each of three large circles. Matching light to dark and with right sides together, sew a circle with applique to a circle without. Stitch around seam allowances, leaving a 1″ (2.5 cm) opening. Turn right side out. Blind stitch opening closed. Finger press seam.

4. By folding the outer circle inwards over the inner circle by 1″ (2.5 cm), gather-stitch around outside of inner circle, about ⅛″ (0.4 cm) away from its perimeter. Pull thread lightly to gather, letting petal pop out to front. Backstitch twice to hold.

Make three leaves

5. Cut three lengths of 3″ (8 cm) wired ribbon, each measuring 8″ (20 cm). Fold in half lengthwise by ½″ (1.5 cm). Fold to make curve and stitch loose edges together as shown. Manipulate wire with your fingers to create desired shape.

Make two fairies

6. Set compass to 1″ (2.5 cm) radius to draw circle measuring 2″ (5 cm) in diameter. This includes ⅛″ (0.4 cm) seam

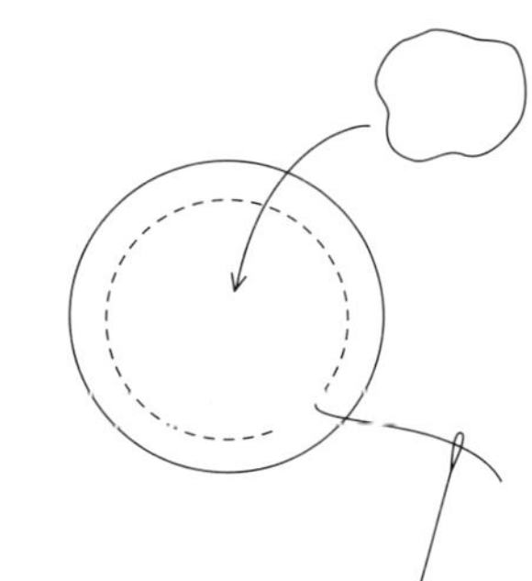

Step 6

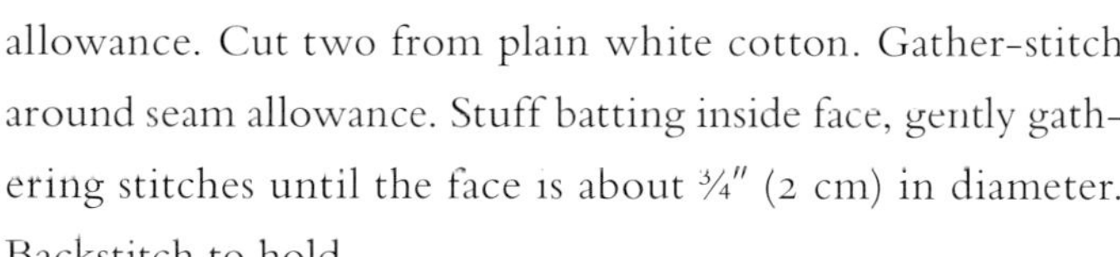
allowance. Cut two from plain white cotton. Gather-stitch around seam allowance. Stuff batting inside face, gently gathering stitches until the face is about ¾″ (2 cm) in diameter. Backstitch to hold.

7. With fine-tip marker, lightly draw hair, eyes, nose, and, and mouth. If you prefer, embroider features onto face.

8. Create ribbon frills by bunching a 12″ (30 cm) length of 1″ (2.5 cm) wired ribbon around the face line. Make small stitches to hold in place at back of face.

9. To make two fairy bows, cut four lengths of wired silk ribbon (light shade) measuring 4″ (10 cm). Fold each in half lengthwise, then fold from end to end. Manipulate with fingers to create petal shape. Stitch across bottom as shown, about ¼″ (0.75 cm) from raw edge. Stitch two back of each fairy face to create bow.

10. Wrap a 22″ (55 cm) length of wired ribbon (darker shade) loosely around each fairy, behind bow. Stitch in place.

Complete

11. Arrange leaves, flowers, and fairies on base as desired. Using small stitches at underside, stitch leaves in place first, then overlap edges with flowers. Stitch flowers and fairies to base.

12. To add backing and 2″ (5 cm) border, see page xviii. Once border is in place, applique rest of final handball in place.

Step 7

Step 8

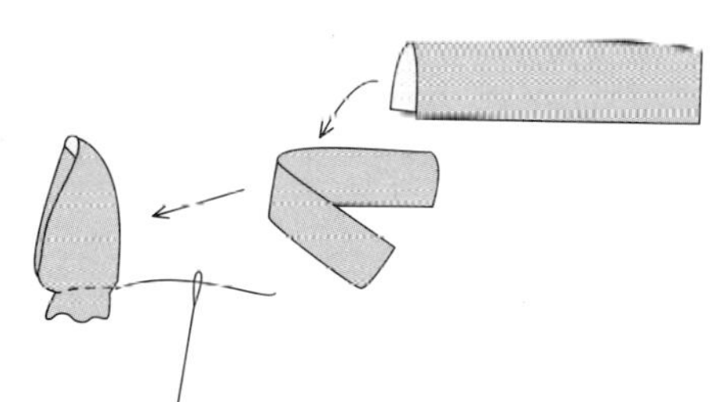

Step 9

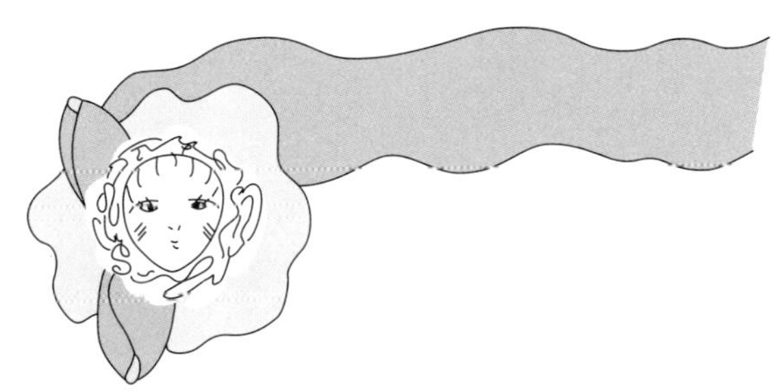

Step 10

Autumn

When I was a child, Japanese street merchants would call from door to door, selling cleverly crafted bamboo baskets filled with several varieties of crickets. We would hang our basket in the eaves of the house or in the garden and listen to this curious Autumn chorus deep into the evening hours. My brother and I would even try to catch our own crickets, running with our little white nets along the riverside near our home. Even today, the nostalgia of the music made by the wings of crickets carries me back to those Fall nights. I can still see the pink and white blooms of the bush clover in my mother's garden and the graceful pampas grasses waving in the cool breeze.

Another memory of Autumn comes to me. I am running to catch up with my mother as she sets off down a footpath alongside a rice paddy. I look up and see thunder clouds begin to spread over the blue sky as though they wish to conquer the world. Amid the waves of golden rice stalks, ready for harvest, stands a lone scarecrow. As sparrows flutter cheerfully about his head, he seems to glance over at me. I look onwards down the path and see that it is covered with floating ribbons of *Higanbana* or liquorice plant in bloom. I feel as though I am stepping into a dream world.

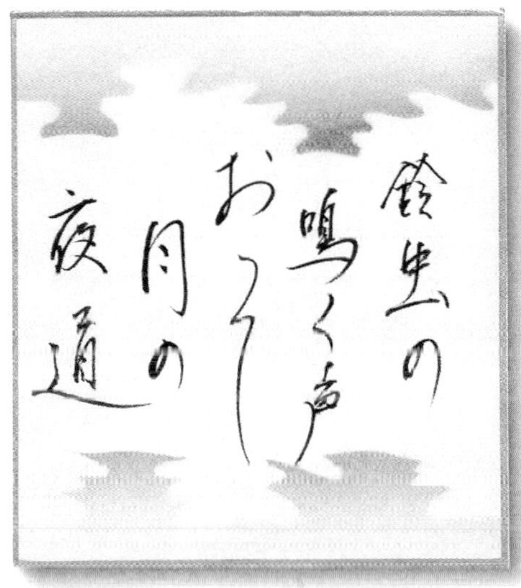

Suzumushi no
Naku koe otte
Tsuki no yomichi

The haiku describes the harmonious music of the crickets, whose song rings out on a still Autumn night when the moon is full. No matter how closely you listen, it's hard to tell where the echo comes from.

SEPTEMBER

Calceolaria

The golden yellow blooms of the Calceolaria—or slipper flower— are the jewels of the Fall garden. Their dusty blue-green leaves show off the flowers to perfection.

Use ⅛" (0.4 cm) seam allowance, unless noted otherwise.

Prepare block

1. Cut base rectangle of background fabric measuring 12" × 18" (30 cm × 45 cm). Mark a seam line ½" (1.5 cm) inwards from all raw edges, so that background base onto which you will applique measures 11" × 17" (27 cm × 42 cm). Cut batting to measure 15" × 21" (37 cm × 52 cm) and backing/border fabric to measure 20" × 26" (50 cm × 66 cm). Baste batting onto wrong side of base.

Make four flowers

2. Set compass to 3½" (9 cm) radius to draw circle measuring 7" (18 cm) in diameter. This includes ⅛" (0.4 cm) seam allowance. Cut four from each of two fabrics. Match one of each color, right sides together, then sew them together around seam allowances, leaving a 1" (2.5 cm) opening. Turn right side out. Blind stitch opening closed. Finger press seam.

YOU WILL NEED

Base: ½ yd (45 cm)

Flower fabrics: ¼ yd (25 cm), each of two fabrics

For leaves, 1½" (4 cm) wired silk ribbon: 2 yds (180 cm)

Border/backing: ¾ yd (70 cm)

Batting: ½ yd (45 cm)

Decorative beads

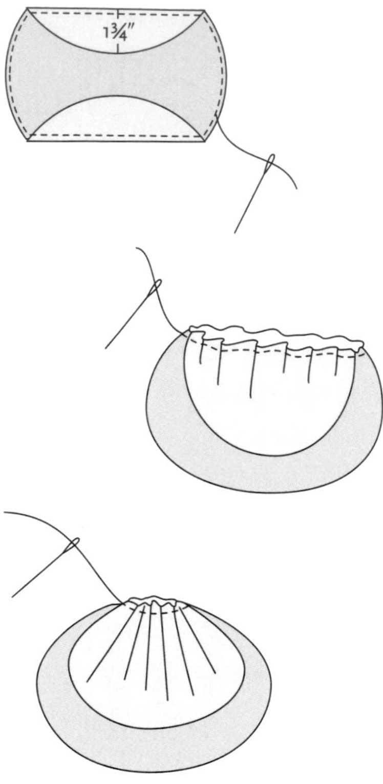

Step 3

3. Fold top and bottom curves in by 1¾″ (4.5 cm). Pin in place. Gather stitch around perimeter, ⅛″ (0.4 cm) from edge, as shown. Fold in half, with curved flaps to outside. Pull thread to gather. Backstitch to hold.

Make four leaves

4. Cut four lengths of wired silk ribbon, each measuring 17″ (43 cm). Starting at center, fold as shown. Wrap one raw edge

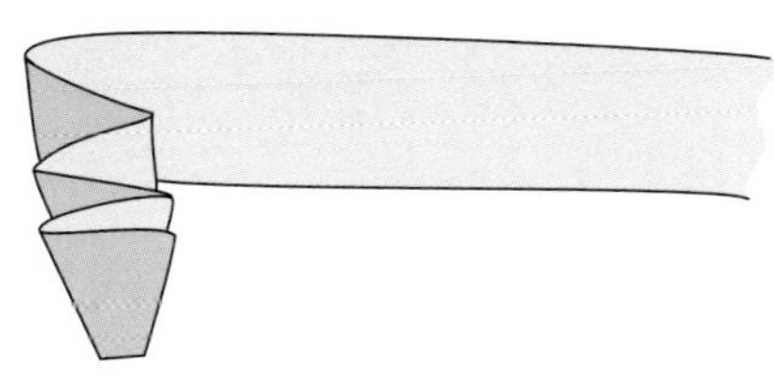

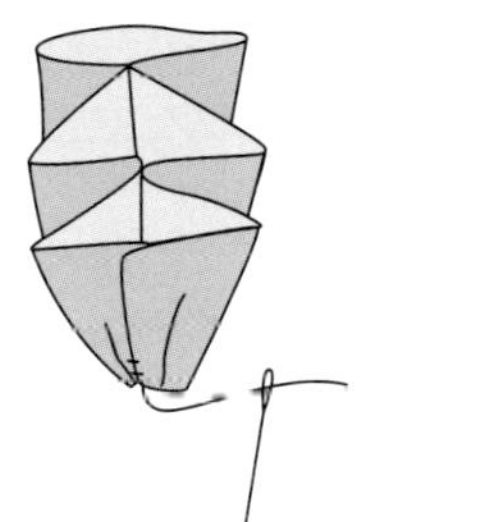

Step 4

over the other, turn hem under and stitch as shown. Manipulate leaves with fingers into pleasing, natural shapes.

Complete

5. Arrange flowers and leaves on base as desired. Use small stitches to secure underside of each flower or leaf in place. Stitch decorative beads onto base as desired.
6. To add backing and 2″ (5 cm) border, see page xviii.

Mandarin

Bearing the sweetest of the fruits of Autumn, the Mandarin plant erupts into flower just as the heat of Summer fades. Richly aromatic, its essential oils are thought to be medicinal, having a calming, uplifting quality.

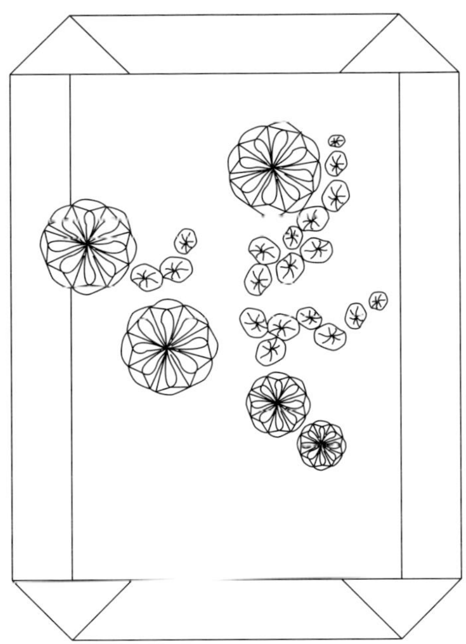

See templates on page 154. Use ⅛″ (0.4 cm) seam allowance, unless noted otherwise.

YOU WILL NEED

Base: ½ yd (45 cm)

Flower fabrics: ¼ yd (25 cm), each of at least four fabrics

For buds, 1″ (2.5 cm) plain silk ribbon: 1¾ yds (150 cm)

Backing/border: ¾ yd (70 cm)

Batting: ½ yd (45 cm)

Prepare block

1. Cut base rectangle of background fabric measuring 12″ × 18″ (30 cm × 45 cm). Mark a seam line ½″ (1.5 cm) inwards from all raw edges, so that background base onto which you will applique measures 11″ × 17″ (27 cm × 42 cm). Cut batting to measure 15″ × 21″ (37 cm × 52 cm) and backing/border fabric to measure 20″ × 26″ (50 cm × 66 cm). Baste batting onto wrong side of base.

Make three large, one medium, and one small flower

2. Using template A, cut six large flower pieces from a variety of light and dark fabrics; using template B, cut three from batting. Baste a batting octagon to wrong side at center of

Highlight portions of the background print you select by appliqueing contrasting fabrics of portions of the print. Here, I've added extra color to some of the leaves. I've also enhanced the butterfly motif by adding fabric stuffed with batting to the body and embellishing the wings with beads. As an added touch, I embroidered antennae in place. If you cannot find a fabric with a butterfly motif that pleases you, use the technique described on page 5 to cut and applique butterflies from an alternative fabric.

each of three flower octagons. Matching light to dark and matching an octagon with batting to one without, right sides together, sew around seam allowances, leaving a 1″ (2.5 cm) opening. Turn right side out. Blind stitch opening closed. Finger press seam.

3. Repeat Step 2, this time using template C to cut two from fabric and template D to cut one from batting. Repeat again, using template B to cut two from fabric and template E to cut one from batting.

4. Fold point A to center as shown and stitch to hold. Repeat until points B to H are stitched in place.

5. Gently open out the petals that form at the center so that more of the fabric shows. Make a single stitch at the tip of each petal to hold in place.

6. Gather-stitch around perimeter of octagon, ⅛″ (0.4 cm) from outer edge. Pull thread to gather. Stuff with scraps of batting, then pull thread tight. Backstitch twice to hold. To

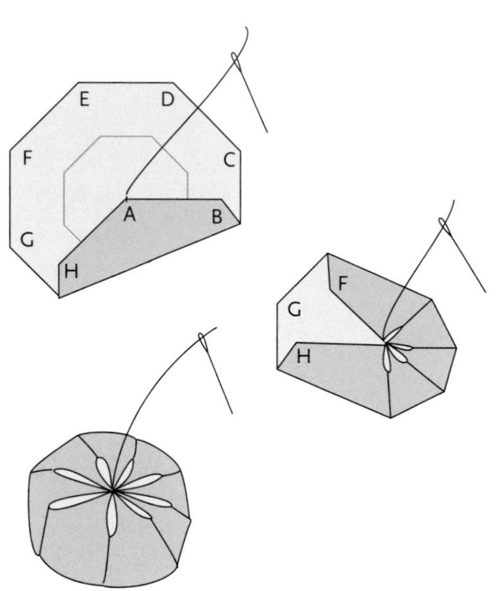

Step 4

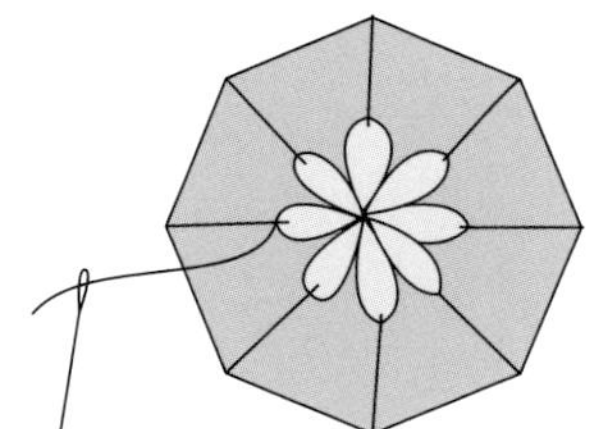

Step 5

give each flower a unique look, stuff some lightly and others more tightly.

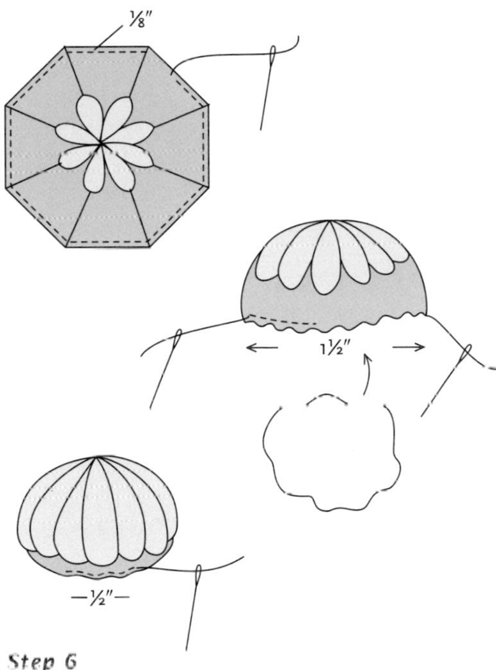

Step 6

Make nineteen buds

7. Cut ribbon into nineteen 3″ (8 cm) lengths. Fold end-to-end, then stitch ends together to make loop.

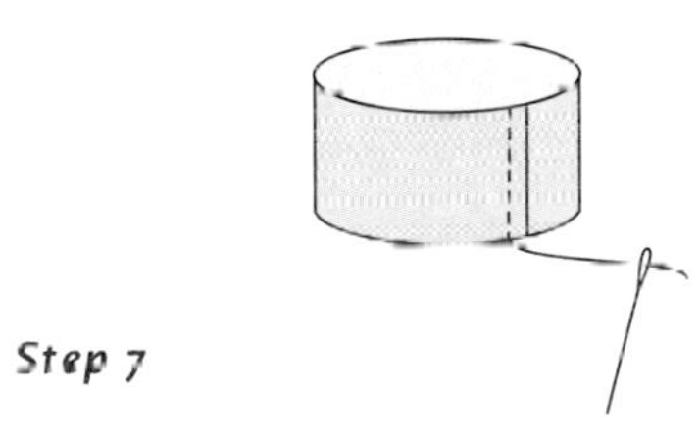
Step 7

8. Fold loop in half horizontally, right sides out, so that edges are together. Gather-stitch along unfolded edges. Pull thread to gather bud into desired shape. Backstitch twice to hold.

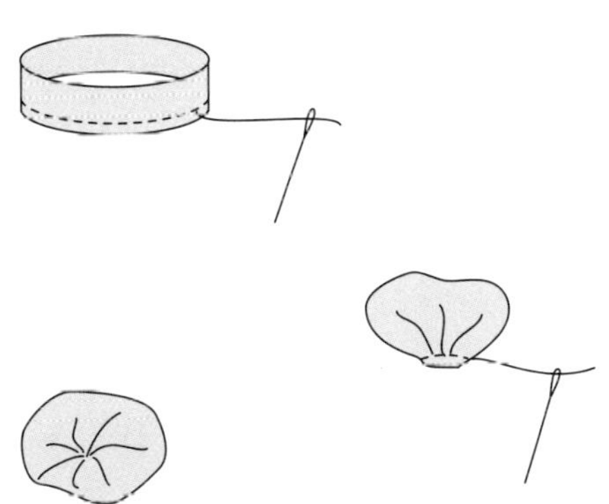
Step 8

Complete

9. Arrange flowers and buds on base as desired. Use small stitches to secure underside of each in place. If you decide to allow one of the flowers to overlap the border, make sure you do not stitch that portion of the flower to the base until you have completed the border.

10. To add backing and 2″ (5 cm) border, see page xviii.

Sweet September

Let the Mandarin flowers on this colorful purse remind you of the beauty of Autumn. Although the seasons of flowers are soon to end, the bright blossoms and sweet scent of the Mandarin enrich the Autumn landscape.

See templates on pages 155–156. Use ⅛" (0.4 cm) seam allowance, unless noted otherwise.

1. Using templates A and B and adding ½" (1.5 cm) seam allowance, cut two each from fabric, lining, and batting. Baste battings to wrong side of lining pieces. Trim seam allowance of batting to scant ⅛" (0.4 cm). Using a ½" (1.5 cm) seam allowance, sew front purse top to front purse bottom along curved seam. Repeat for back pieces and linings.
2. Using template C, cut 16 leaves from fabric and 8 from felt. Do not add seam allowance to felt leaves. Stitch beads to felt leaves for embellishment. Applique all fabric leaves and stitch all felt leaves in place on purse front and back, using photographs as a guide. Stitch button and more beads to the top front as in photograph.
3. Using template A from *Mandarin*, cut three octagons from each of two fabrics (one light, one dark). Follow Steps 2 to 7 of *Mandarin* to complete three flowers, but do not insert bat-

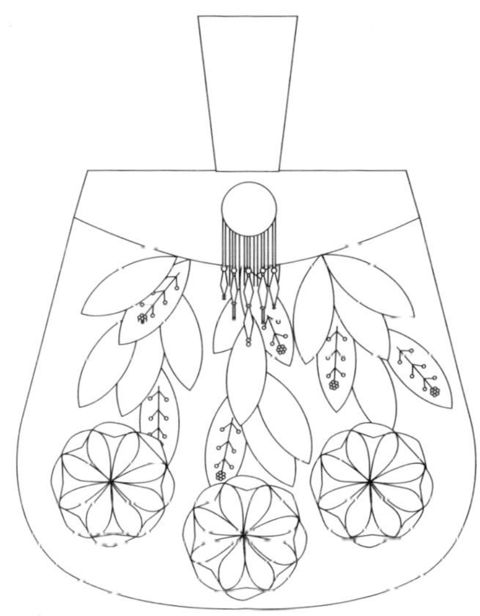

Front

Back

YOU WILL NEED

Purse fabric: ½ yd (45 cm) or less

Lining fabric: ½ yd (45 cm) or less

Flower fabric: ¼ yd (25 cm) each light and dark

For leaves: Scraps of fabric and felt

Batting: ½ yd (45 cm)

Beads for embellishment

Button

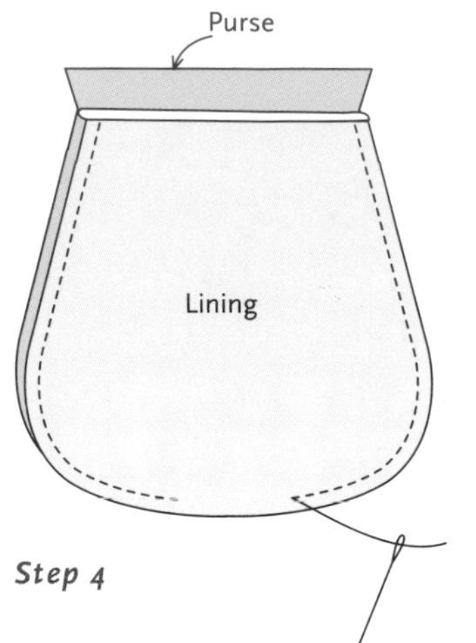

Step 4

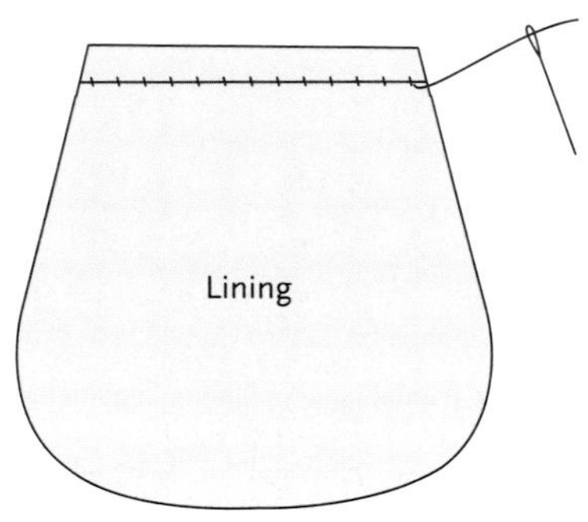

Step 5

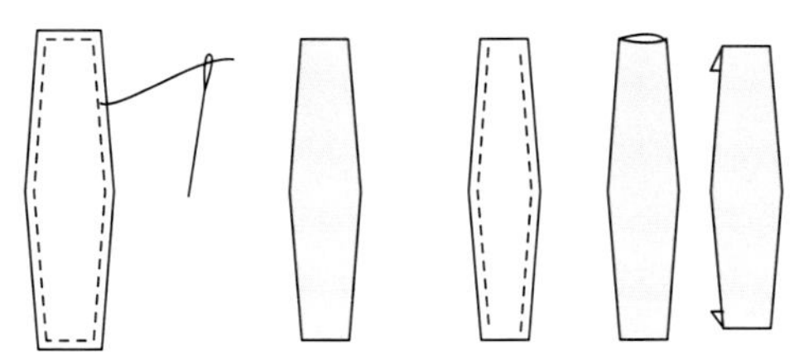

Step 6

ting. Stitch flowers to front of purse. Use small stitches to secure underside of each. Add a bead to the center of each flower.

4. Right sides together and using a ½″ (1.5 cm) seam allowance, sew front and back of purse together, leaving top open. Do not turn right side out. Repeat for lining.

5. Wrong sides together, position lining on top of purse and pin in place, aligning center bottom of lining with center bottom of purse. Make two or three small stitches through all layers at center bottom to secure lining to purse. Repeat at about 2″ (5 cm) at either side of first set of stitches. Remove pins. Turn purse right side out, with lining falling in place inside. Fold under top edge of purse by a ¾″ (2 cm). Press to hold. Turn under seam allowance and blindstitch folded seam to lining.

6. Using template E and adding ½″ (1.5 cm) seam allowances, cut two handle pieces from fabric and one from batting. Baste batting to one of fabric pieces. Trim batting to scant ⅛″ (0.4 cm). Right sides together, sew handle pieces together along long sides. Turn right side out. Turn under seam allowances

Back view

at each end of handle and press to hold. Position handle inside purse along line marked on template. Pin in place at point where the purse fabric and lining meet. Blindstitch around all sides.

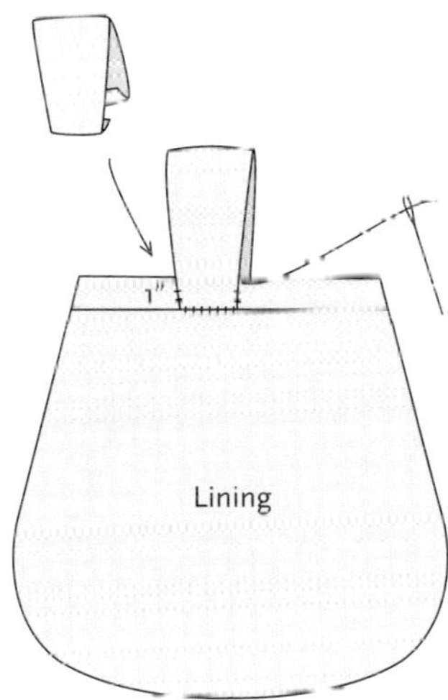

Step 6

Pompon Dahlia

In bloom from midsummer until frost, the Pompon Dahlia lends the brilliance of sunny days to the fading light of Autumn. The charming ball-shaped flowers grow in shades of deep purple, rosy red, and rich lavender.

See templates on pages 156–157. *Use ⅛″ (0.4 cm) seam allowance, unless noted otherwise.*

Prepare block

1. Cut base rectangle of background fabric measuring 12″ × 18″ (30 cm × 45 cm). Mark a seam line ½″ (1.5 cm) inwards from all raw edges, so that background base onto which you will applique measures 11″ × 17″ (27 cm × 42 cm). Cut batting to measure 14″ × 20″ (35 cm × 50 cm) and backing/border fabric to measure 18″ × 26″ (45 cm × 66 cm). Baste batting onto wrong side of base.
2. Using templates A and B, cut two full leaves and one shortened leaf. Applique A-1, B, then A-2 onto base.
3. Using templates C to F, cut stems. If you wish, piece the stems from different fabrics, using the dotted lines on the templates as a guide. Remember to add extra seam allowance. Applique stems to base. Note that some stems loop behind others. To achieve the same effect, begin with stem C and

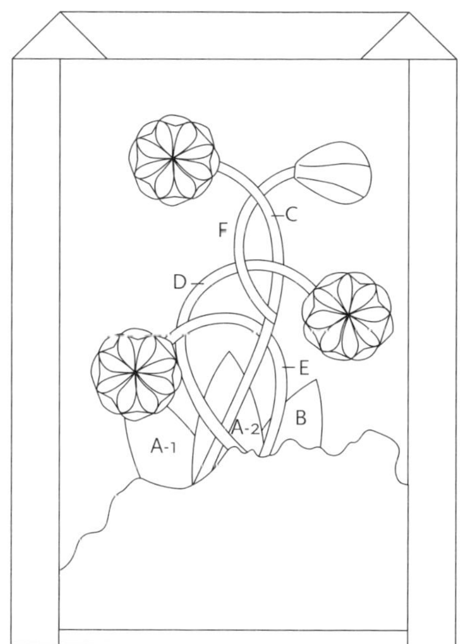

YOU WILL NEED

Base: ⅙ yd (15 cm)

Flower fabrics: ¼ yd (25 cm), each of two fabrics

For leaves and stems: Scraps, variety

Backing/border: ¾ yd (70 cm)

Batting: ½ yd (45 cm)

If you wish to create a scene like mine in the foreground, search out a fabric with pictorial motifs and applique it over the bottom of the base fabric. Add the applique after stitching templates A to F in place. This way, you can hide their edges. It will be difficult to find the same hunting scene I have used, but you can choose from many wonderful prints that depict similar country scenes. Once you have added this large applique, you may wish to cut away the base fabric behind it.

applique in place until about the midway point. With a new needle, applique stem D in place, sewing over stem C and again stopping about midway. Applique Stem E in place, looping beneath stem C and over stem D. Continue with stem C, this time stopping about 2″ (5 cm) from top. Complete stems D, F, and C. If you wish, follow the directions in the sidebar to add a pictorial applique at the bottom of the background base.

Make three flowers, one bud

4. Using template A from *Mandarin* (see page 154), cut three flower pieces from each of two fabrics. Match one of each color together, right sides together, then sew them together around seam allowances, leaving a 1″ (2.5 cm) opening. Turn right side out. Blind stitch opening closed. Finger press seam.

5. Fold point A to center as shown and stitch to hold. Repeat until points B to H are stitched in place.

6. Gently open out the petals that form at the center so that more of the fabric shows. Make a single stitch at the tip of each petal to hold in place. Make a single stitch at each side of each petal to sew it to its neighbors.

7. Turn flower over. Gather-stitch around perimeter of hexagon. Pull threads to gather until hexagon measures about 1″ (2.5 cm). Backstitch twice to hold.

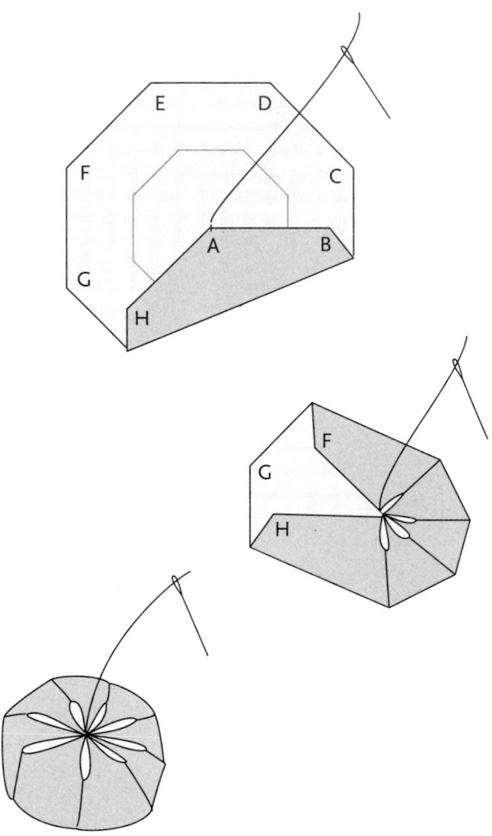

Step 5

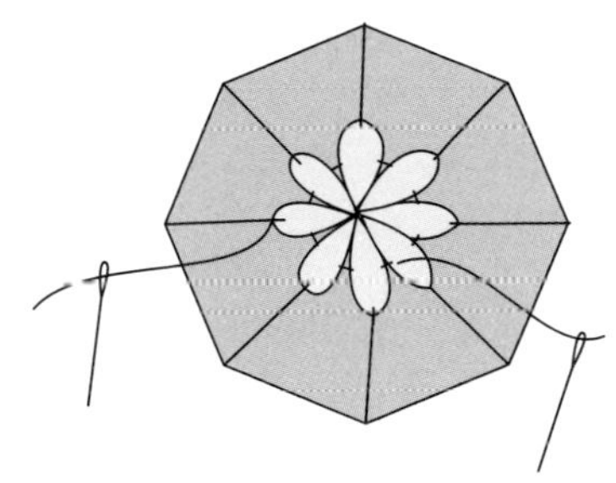

Step 6

8. Using template G, cut 1 bud. Fold along dotted lines and tuck to solid lines. Pin to hold. Turn under seam allowance and applique onto base.

Complete

9. Attach flowers and bud to base at ends of stems. Use small stitches to secure underside of each in place.

10. Wrong sides together, pin the quilt top (including batting) to the center of the backing/border fabric. Fold inwards ½″ (1.5 cm) seam allowances around all sides of backing/border piece. Folded-in seam allowance aligns with horizontal seam line marked on base in Step 1, ½″ (1.5 cm) in from raw edge. Pin in place.

11. Fold bottom edge of backing inwards by 1½″ (4 cm); turn bottom edge of quilt top in by ½″ (1.5 cm). Blind stitch bottom edge of quilt top in place on top of backing to create narrow bottom border.

12. Fold sides of backing/border fabrics inwards by 1½″ (4 cm). Folded over seam allowance will meet line marked on base in Step 1. Pin in place.

13. Fold in top corners as shown. Fold again along dotted line. Folded-over seam allowance will meet line marked on base in Step 1. Pin in place.

14. Blind stitch around all three borders.

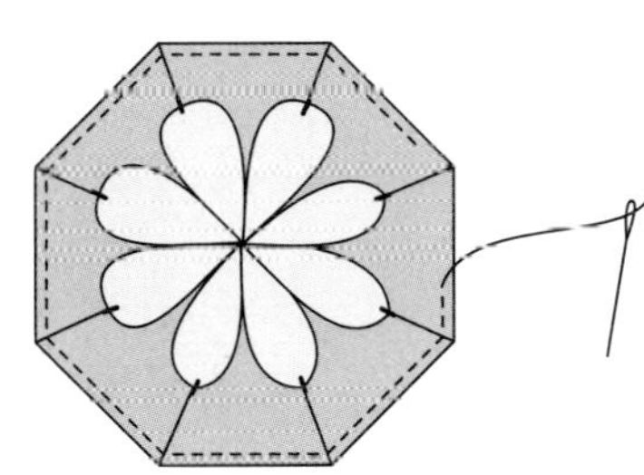

Step 7

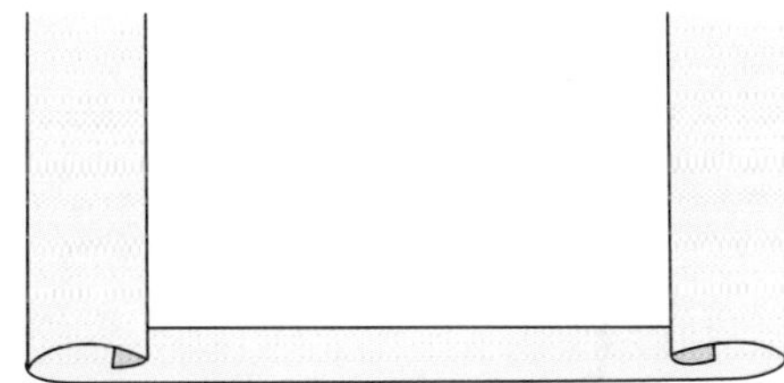

Step 12

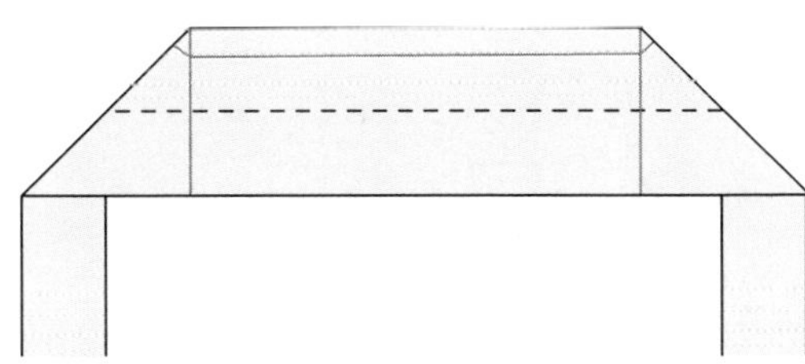

Step 13

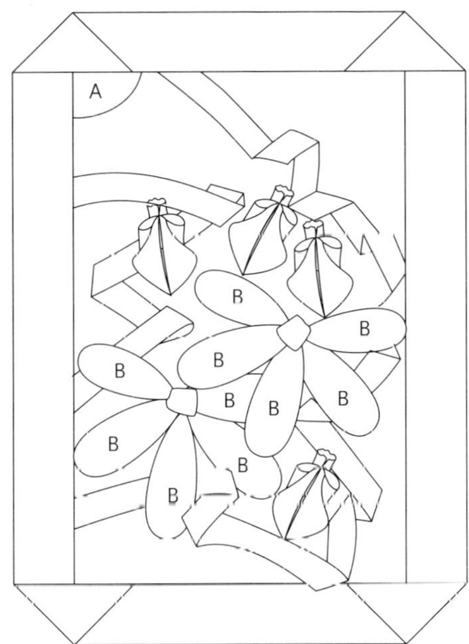

Vanda

The Vanda orchid, admired for its ability to bloom throughout the year, is a symbol of strength and resilience. Its tubular leaves encase an exotic flower of exquisite beauty.

See templates and on page 157. Use ⅛" (0.4 cm) seam allowance, unless noted otherwise.

Prepare block

1. Cut base rectangle of background fabric measuring 12" × 18" (30 cm × 45 cm). Mark a seam line ½" (1.5 cm) inwards from all raw edges, so that background base onto which you will applique measures 11" × 17" (27 cm × 42 cm). Cut batting to measure 15" × 21" (37 cm × 52 cm) and backing/border fabric to measure 20" × 26" (50 cm × 66 cm). Baste batting onto wrong side of base.

2. For stems, pin silk ribbon to base, folding as in photograph. The quilt shown uses three lengths of ribbon measuring 19" (47 cm) for top stem, 23" (57 cm) for left stem, and 28" (70 cm) for bottom right stem. Use herringbone stitch and embroidery floss to sew onto base.

3. Using templates A and B, cut one moon and ten leaves from a variety of fabrics. Applique onto base, covering rib-

YOU WILL NEED

Base: ½ yd (45 cm)

Flower fabrics: ¼ yd (25 cm), each of two fabrics or of variety of fabrics

For leaves, moon, and flower centers: Scraps, variety

For stems, 1" (2.5 cm) plain silk ribbon: 2 yds (180 cm)

For bud centers, 1" (2.5 cm) plain silk ribbon: Scraps

Backing/border: ¾ yd (70 cm)

Batting: ½ yd (45 cm)

Step 4

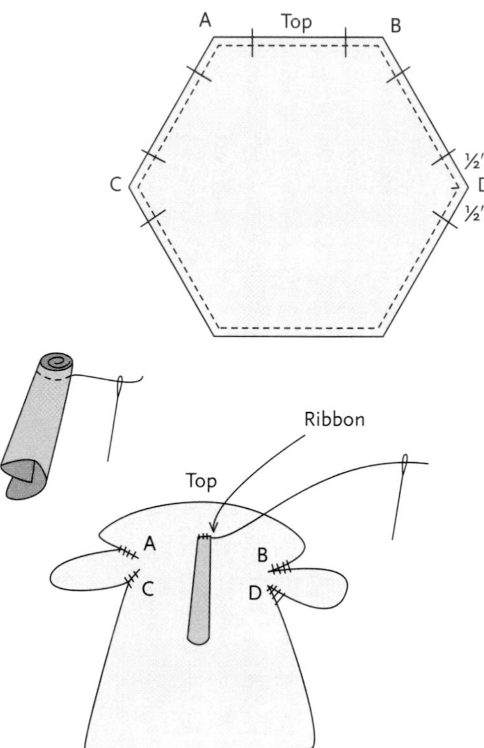

Step 6

bon as desired. If you wish, vary the sizes of the leaves a little by simply adjusting the seam allowance.

4. To make two flower centers, cut two strips of fabric measuring 1″ × 3″ (2.5 cm × 8 cm). Turn under long edges by ⅛″ (0.4 cm) and press in place. Join short ends to create loop. Turn right side out. Manipulate with fingers to create three smaller loops. Blind stitch along top of each. Blind stitch in place at onto base with sewn tips facing up.

Make four buds

5. Using template J from *Calypso* (see page 138), cut four bud pieces from each of two fabrics (one light, one dark). Use a variety of fabrics, if desired. Matching light to dark and with right sides together, stitch around seam allowances, leaving a 1″ (2.5 cm) opening. Turn right side out. Blind stitch opening closed. Finger press seam.

6. Mark each side of hexagon ½″ (1.5 cm) on either side of angles A to D. Fold and pin each angle so that marks on either

side of it are aligned. Blindstitch edges together. Take a 1″ × 1½″ (2.5 cm × 4 cm) strip of brightly colored silk ribbon and gather stitch one short edge. Roll ribbon to create shape shown in diagram and pull thread to gather. Blindstitch to hold. Position at center of each flower as shown. Pin then stitch in place.

7. Make a single gather stitch at each of points A to D. Pull thread tight to draw all points to center. Backstitch twice to hold. Gather-stitch around top of center loop as shown. Pull thread lightly so that this loop is slightly puckered. Backstitch twice to hold.

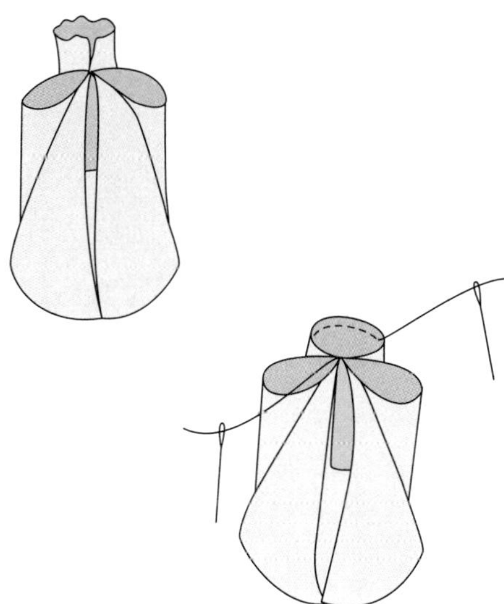

Step 7

Complete

8. Arrange completed buds along stems as desired. Using small stitches at underside, stitch each onto base.

9. To add backing and 2″ (5 cm) border, see page xviii.

NOVEMBER

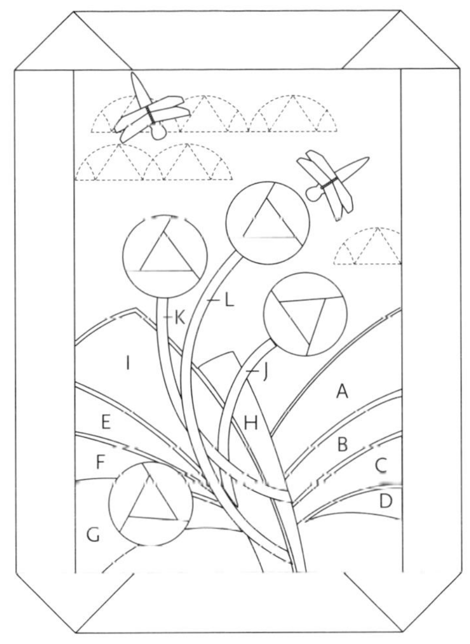

China Aster

A queen among flowers in the Autumn garden, the name China Aster derives from the Greek and means "beautiful crown." In lovely pastels—rose pink, lilac, violet, and lavender—her graceful blossoms sway in the falling leaves.

See templates on pages 158–160. Use ⅛" (0.4 cm) seam allowance, unless noted otherwise.

YOU WILL NEED

Base: ½ yd (45 cm)

Flower and stem fabrics: Scraps, variety

For leaves: ¼ yd (25 cm) each of two fabrics

For edging of leaves, ¾" (2 cm) plain silk ribbon: ½ yd (45 cm) each of four colors

For dragonflies: Scraps, variety

Backing and border: ¾ yd (70 cm)

Batting: ¼ yd (25 cm)

Quilting thread

Small decorative beads

Prepare block

1. Cut base rectangle of background fabric measuring 12" × 18" (30 cm × 45 cm). Mark a seam line ½" (1.5 cm) inwards from all raw edges, so that background base onto which you will applique measures 11" × 17" (27 cm × 42 cm). Cut batting to measure 15" × 21" (37 cm × 52 cm) and backing/border fabric to measure 20" × 26" (50 cm × 66 cm). Baste batting onto wrong side of base.

2. Using templates A to I, cut out leaf pieces. Matching lengths to the lengths of the upper edges of each leaf template, cut strips of ribbon. Allow a little extra ribbon in case of error. Fold in half lengthwise. Applique leaves A to I onto base in alphabetical order, inserting silk ribbon beneath them so that about ⅛" (0.4 cm) shows. Stitch through all layers, appliquing both ribbon and leaves onto base.

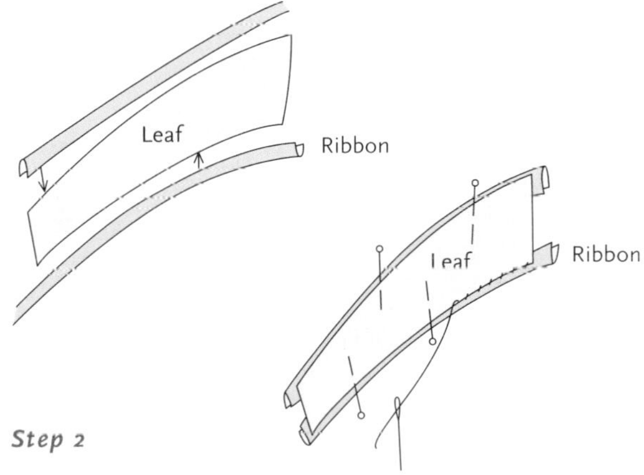

Step 2

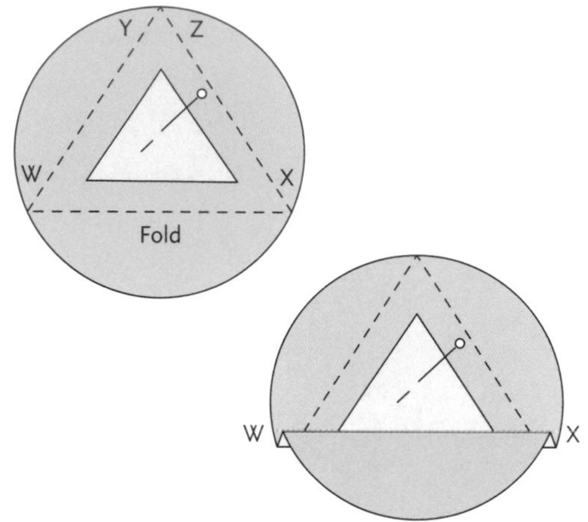

Step 4

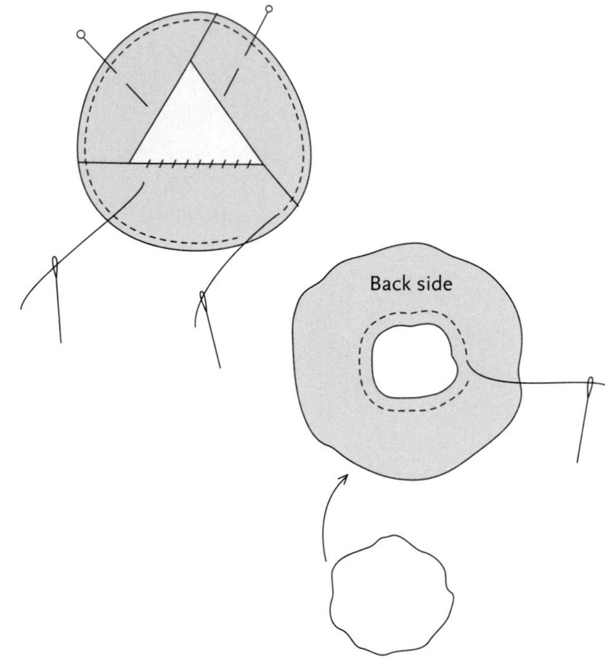

Step 5

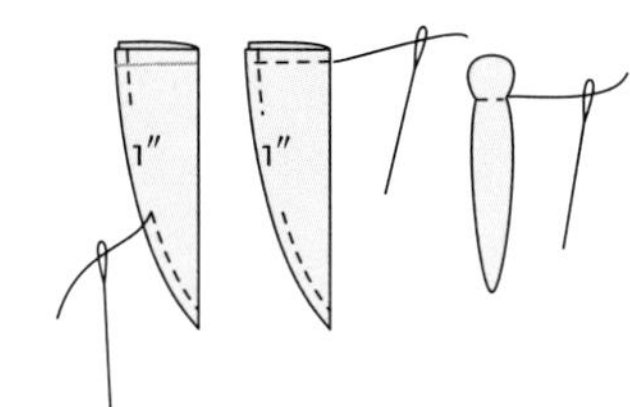

Step 7

3. Using templates J to L, cut out stems. Applique onto base in alphabetical order.

Make four flowers

4. Set compass to 3½″ (9 cm) radius to draw circle measuring 7″ (18 cm) in diameter. This includes ⅛″ (0.4 cm) seam allowance. Cut four from a variety of fabrics. Using template M, cut four triangles. Pin a triangle to center of a circle. Fold along line W-X, then align fold line with bottom side of triangle to make a tuck. Pin in place. Blindstitch fold line to bottom side of triangle, hiding seam allowance in fold. Repeat, folding along line X-Y, then line W-Z.

5. Gather-stitch around perimeter of circle. From back, stuff with batting, pulling thread to close gathering stitches. Backstitch twice to hold.

Make two dragonflies

6. Using templates N and O, cut out two body pieces from red fabric and four wings from complementary fabrics.

7. Fold body piece in half lengthwise, right side in, and stitch along curved edge as shown, leaving a 1″ (2.5 cm) opening. Gather-stitch top edge, leaving tail of thread at *right side* of fabric. Do not pull thread yet. Turn right side out and stuff firmly with batting. Pull thread taut to gather, creating head. Backstitch to hold. Blindstitch opening closed.

8. Fold wings in half lengthwise, right side in, and stitch along curved edge as shown, leaving a 1″ (2.5 cm) opening.

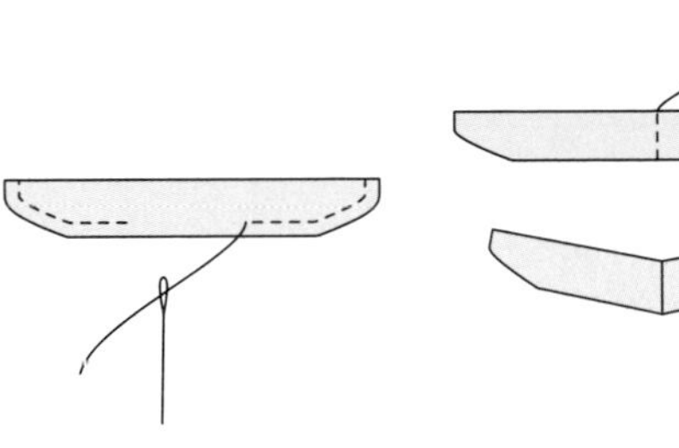

Step 8 Step 9

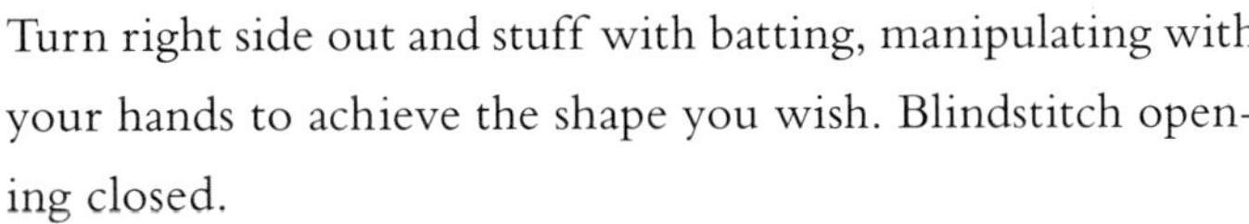

Turn right side out and stuff with batting, manipulating with your hands to achieve the shape you wish. Blindstitch opening closed.

9. Gather stitch across the center of each wing. Pull thread to create wing shapes. Backstitch to hold.

10. With small stitches, attach bottom wing about ½″ (1.5 cm) below head. Attach top wing so that its bottom edge slightly overlaps first wing.

11. Thread about 10 small beads onto a length of embroidery floss or onto a safety pin. Stitch in place or secure the pin through the body so that the beads sit along the center of the wings. Sew on two small beads for the eyes.

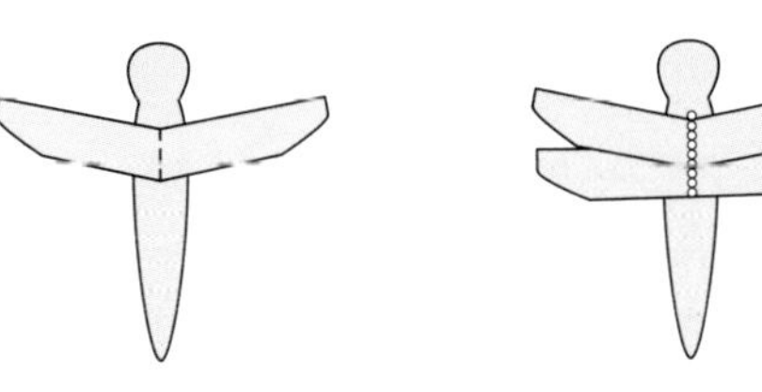

Step 10 Step 11

Complete

12. Arrange flowers, leaves, and dragonflies on base as desired. Use small stitches to secure underside of each flower or leaf in place. Stitch decorative beads onto base as desired.

13. To add backing and 2″ (5 cm) border, see page xviii.

14. Using stencil below, mark sashiko pattern. Stitch as shown.

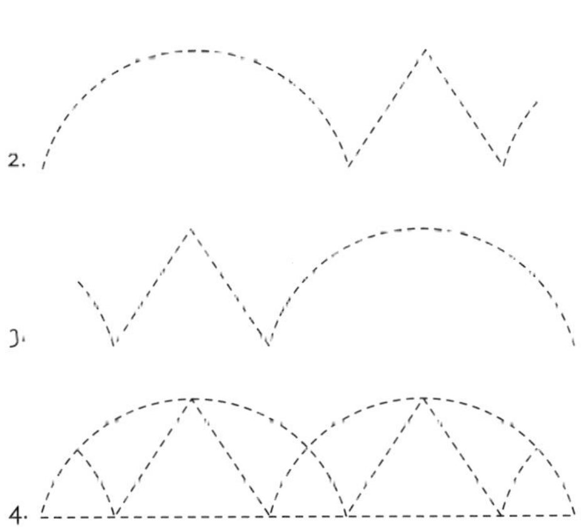

Step 14

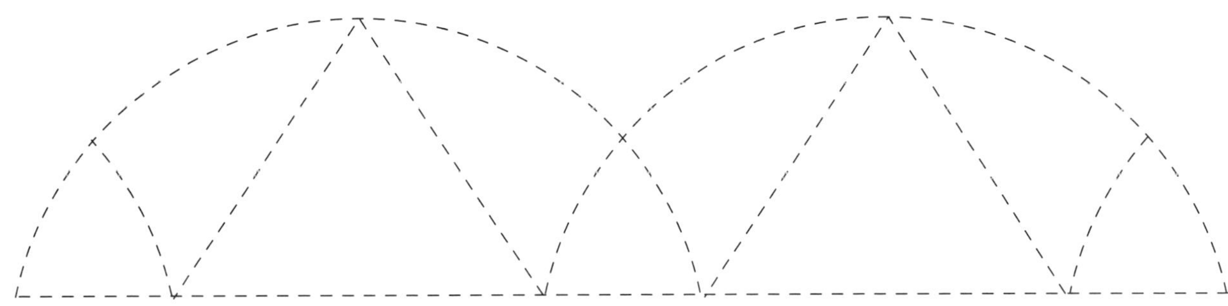

Sashiko stencil

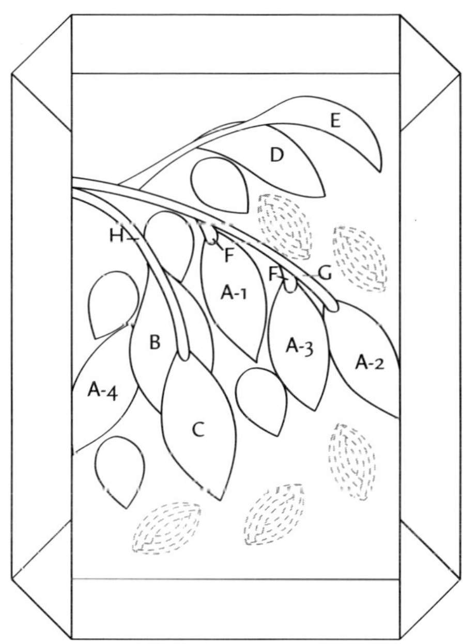

Waratah

Australia's most admired flower, the Waratah—brilliant in color—brings a ray of Summer sunshine to the crisp days of Autumn.

See templates on pages 161–163. Use ⅛" (0.4 cm) seam allowance, unless noted otherwise.

Prepare block

1. Cut base rectangle of background fabric measuring 12" × 18" (30 cm × 45 cm). Mark a seam line ½" (1.5 cm) inwards from all raw edges, so that background base onto which you will applique measures 11" × 17" (27 cm × 42 cm). Cut batting to measure 15" × 21" (37 cm × 52 cm) and backing/border fabric to measure 20" × 26" (50 cm × 66 cm). Baste batting onto wrong side of base.
2. Using templates A to E, cut out leaves. Applique onto base in following order: A-1, A-2, A-3, A-4, B, C, D, and E.
3. Using templates F to H, cut out stems. Applique onto base in alphabetical order.

Make five buds

4. Cut five squares of fabric measuring 7½" × 7½" (19.5 cm × 19.5 cm). On right side, mark solid and dotted vertical lines as

YOU WILL NEED

Base: ½ yd (45 cm)

Flower fabric: ¼ yd (25 cm), two or more fabrics

For leaves and stems: Scraps, variety

Backing/border: ¾ yd (70 cm)

Batting: ½ yd (45 cm)

Quilting thread

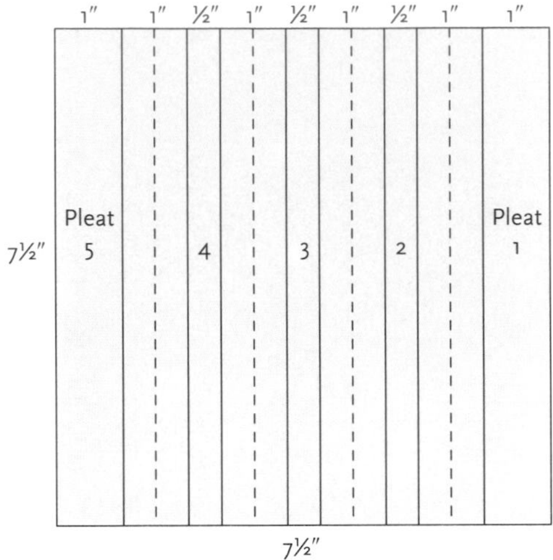

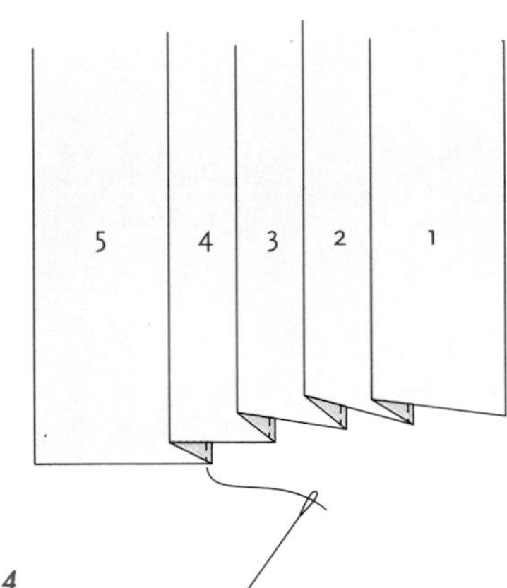

Step 4

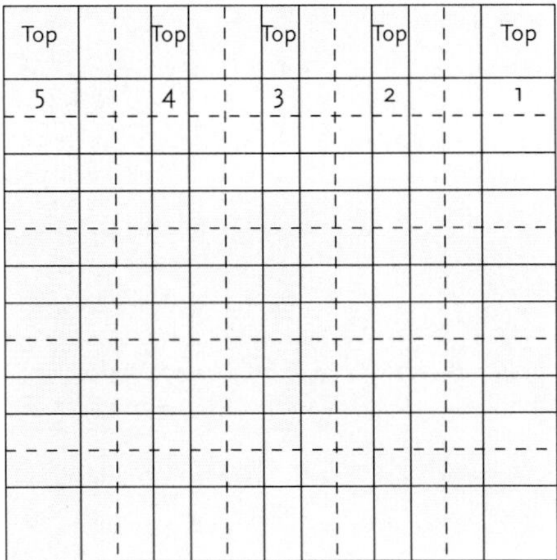

Step 5

shown in diagram. Fold along dotted lines so that pleat 2 aligns with pleat 1, pleat 3 aligns with pleat 2, pleat 4 aligns with pleat 3, and pleat 5 aligns with pleat 4. Turn the fabric over, then take a running stitch at ⅛″ (0.4 cm) inwards from each fold, from top to bottom.

5. Mark solid and dotted horizontal lines on right side of fabric as shown. Fold along dotted lines as in step 4 to create pleats. Turn the fabric over, then take a running stitch ⅛″ (0.4 cm) in from each fold, from left to right. Pin then baste around perimeter of resulting square. Using template I, trace bud design onto fabric.

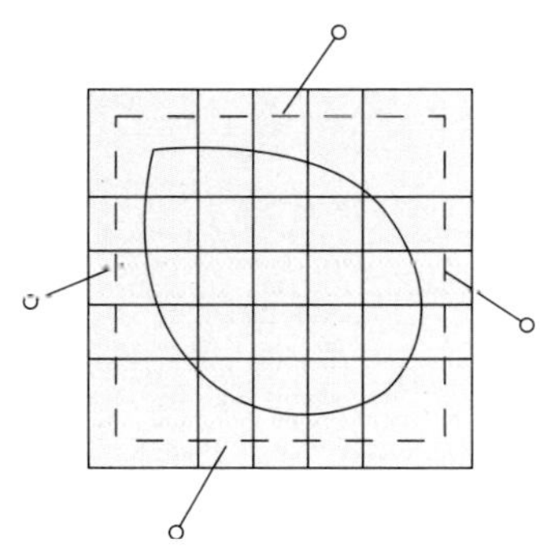

Step 5

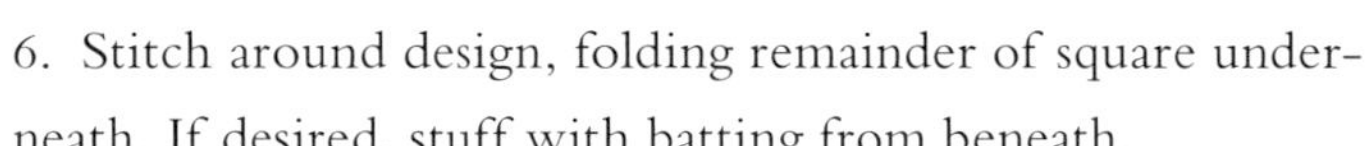

6. Stitch around design, folding remainder of square underneath. If desired, stuff with batting from beneath.

Complete

7. Arrange buds on base as desired. Use small stitches to secure underside of each in place.
8. To add backing and 2″ (5 cm)border, see page xviii.
9. Using leaf stencil below, mark then quilt or sashiko leaves onto base. Follow the sequence shown for making the sashiko design.

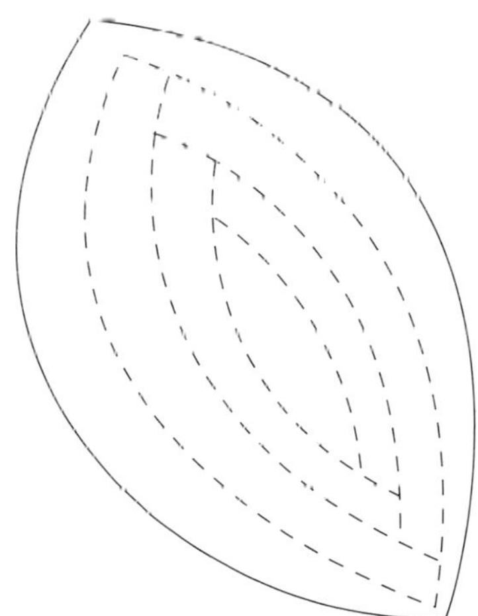

Sashiko stencil

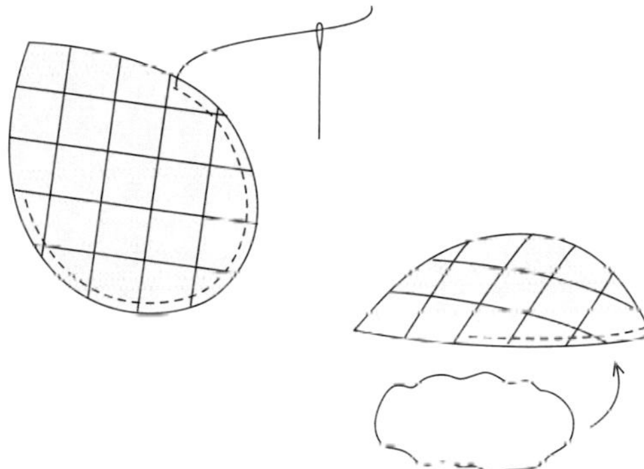

Step 6

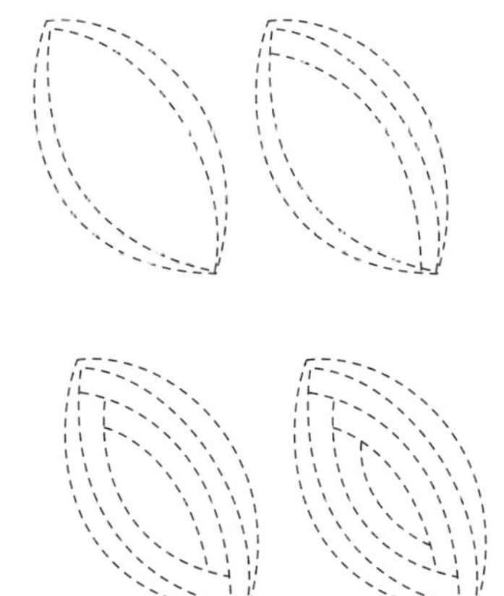

Step 9

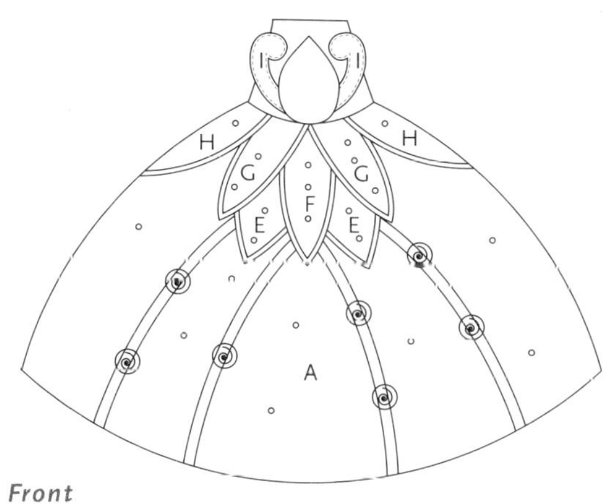

Front

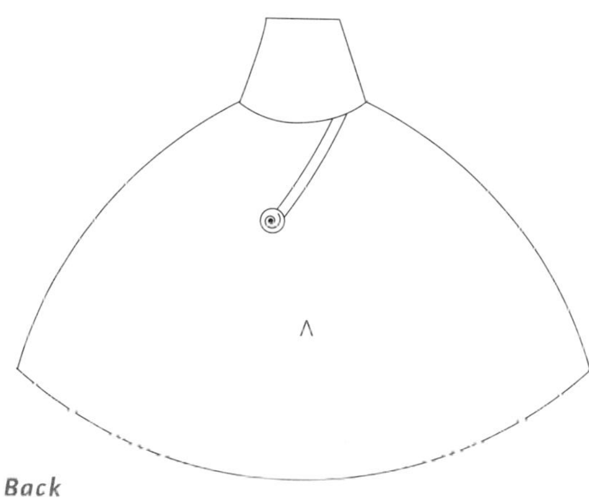

Back

Autumn Glory

Inspired by the vibrant red blossoms of the Waratah, this little purse is perfect for Autumn outings. Take it with you on an evening stroll to view the harvest moon or to collect the brilliant red, gold, and yellow leaves of Autumn.

See templates on pages 164–166. Use ⅛" (0.4 cm) seam allowance, unless noted otherwise

1. Join two template A pieces to create full template. Adding ½" (1.5 cm) seam allowance, cut two each from fabric, lining, and batting. Baste batting to wrong side of fabric for front and back of purse. Trim batting to scant ⅛" (0.4 cm).
2. Using templates C and D, cut four long and one short strip from felt. Do not add seam allowance. Use a running stitch and contrasting thread to sew the felt strips onto the front and back of purse, as shown in photograph. Stitch out to the raw edges of the purse fabric so that ends of felt can later be enclosed in seam allowance.
3. Using templates E to H, cut leaves from felt and fabric. Add ⅛" (0.4 cm) seam allowance to all pieces (finished felt leaves will be slightly larger than fabric leaves, since felt seam allowance will not be turned under). Use a running stitch and

YOU WILL NEED

Purse fabric: ½ yd (45 cm) or less
Lining fabric: ½ yd (45 cm) or less
Flower fabric: ¼ yd (25 cm) or less
For buds and strips: Felt scraps
Thin batting: ½ yd (45 cm) or less
Tiny beads for embellishment

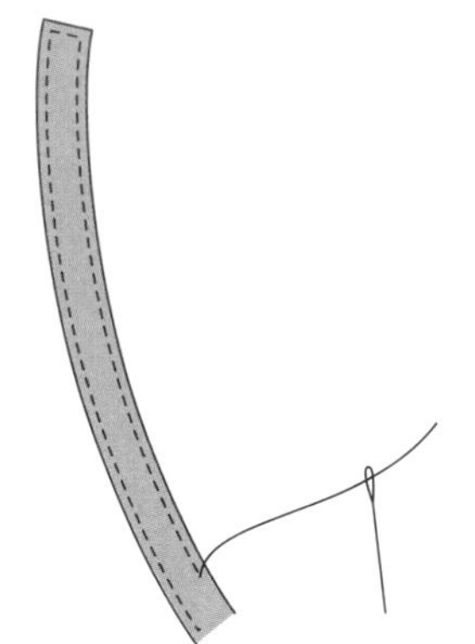

Step 2

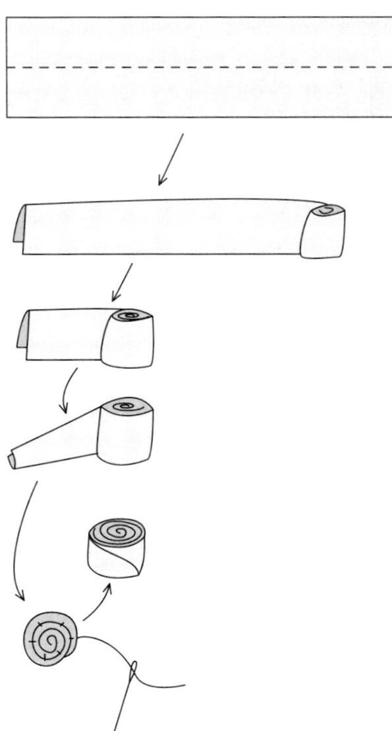

Step 4

contrasting thread to sew felt leaves in place. Applique fabric leaves on top of felt leaves.

4. Cut eight strips of felt measuring 1″ × 4″ (2.5 cm × 10 cm). Fold in half lengthwise. Roll from one end to other, shifting fabrics so that layers show. Stitch bottom of rolled bud as shown to hold in place. Use small stitches to attach completed buds to purse.

5. Right sides together and using ½″ (1.5 cm) seam allowance, sew front and back of purse together, leaving top open. Do not turn right side out. Repeat for lining.

6. Wrong sides together, position lining on top of purse and pin in place, aligning center bottom of lining with center bottom of purse. Make two or three small stitches through all layers at center bottom to secure lining to purse. Repeat at about 2″ (5 cm) at either side of first set of stitches. Remove pins. Turn purse right side out, with lining falling in place inside. Fold under top edge of purse by a ¾″ (2 cm). Press to hold. Blindstitch folded seam to lining.

7. Using template B and adding ½″ (1.5 cm) seam allowance, cut two handle pieces from fabric and one from batting. Baste batting to one of fabric pieces. Trim batting to scant ⅛″ (0.4 cm). Right sides together, sew handle pieces together along long sides. Turn right side out. Turn under seam allowances at each end of handle and press to hold. Position one

Back view

end of handle around curve at top of purse front, inserting purse top between fabric and lining of handle. Blind stitch in place. Repeat to attach other end of handle to back of purse.

8. Follow steps 5 to 7 of *Waratah* to make one flower. Using template I, cut four petals from felt. Use a running stitch to sew two of them together. Add tiny beads for embellishment. Repeat for second petal. Sew flower and petals to purse as shown in photograph.

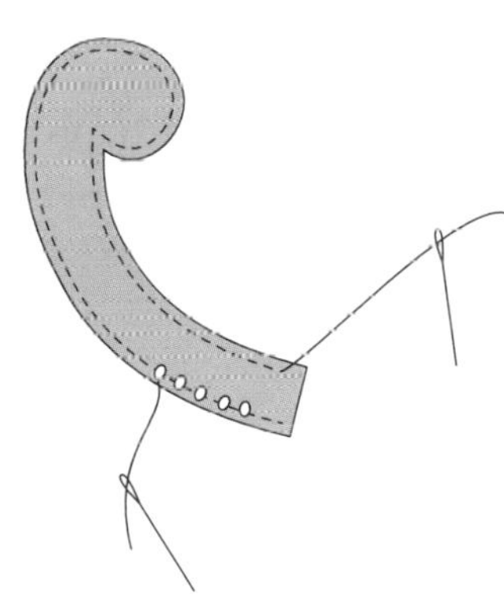

Step 8

Winter

As Autumn wanes and the chorus of crickets fades, so do the flowers that enriched the landscape. Yet even as Winter takes hold, the tea garden is alive with color. Gentle waves of green are dotted with the pinks and whites of Winter kale. As we prepare to celebrate the New Year, flower shops are abloom with Winter flora. One of my favorites is the Adonis plant, whose yellow flowers burst like sunshine over the snow. Temple bells ring in the New Year and we decorate the doors of our homes with branches of pine, bamboo, and cherry, symbolizing hope. Tea ceremonies are held in temples, amid the falling snow. Looking out through the temple gates, there are few sights as beautiful as the bright red seeds of the *Nandin* tree or dark pink of the Camellia against a background of deep white snow.

I recall the Camellia trees that grew around the shrine near my aunt's home in the mountains. Their branches, adorned with brilliant red flowers, surrounded the shrine. Watching the petals fall to the ground, I would feel as though I were in a secret garden. I would gather the scattered petals and pretend they were rich jewels. I imagined the shiny green leaves were coins—how rich I was! Sweet memories like these still bloom for me deep inside Camellia flowers.

Kaantsubaki
Yuki no naka kara
Hi o tomoso

This elegant haiku describes the Camellia flower, ablaze with color in a field of snow.

DECEMBER

Holly Hock

The showy clusters of this classic heirloom flower have graced gardens for centuries. The Holly Hock is short-lived—a reminder that beauty is fleeting. Capture its brilliant colors in Winter ikebana arrangements or in your quilts.

See templates on pages 167–168. Use ⅛″ (0.4 cm) seam allowance, unless noted otherwise.

YOU WILL NEED

Base: ½ yd (45 cm)

Flower fabrics: ¼ yd (30 cm), each of two or more fabrics

For leaves and stems: Scraps, variety

For buds, lightweight fabric such as chiffon or silk ribbon: Scraps

#25 embroidery floss

Backing/border: ¾ yd (70 cm)

Batting: ½ yd (45 cm)

Prepare block

1. Cut base rectangle of background fabric measuring 12″ × 18″ (30 cm × 45 cm). Mark a seam line ½″ (1.5 cm) inwards from all raw edges, so that background base onto which you will applique measures 11″ × 17″ (27 cm × 42 cm). Cut batting to measure 14″ × 20″ (35 cm × 50 cm) and backing/border fabric to measure 18″ × 24″ (45 cm × 60 cm). Baste batting onto wrong side of base.
2. Using templates A to J, cut out leaves and stems. Join two pieces of template H before cutting fabric. Applique onto base in alphabetical order.
3. Threading two strands of #25 embroidery floss together, make decorative stitches following the stitch sequences shown. Note that the dotted lines indicate the position of the

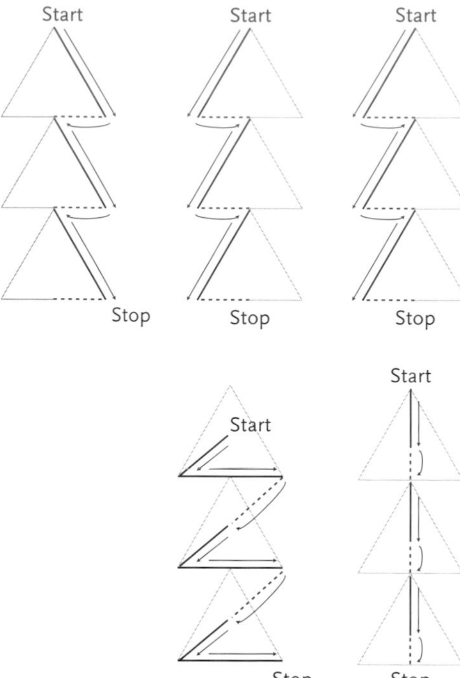

Step 3

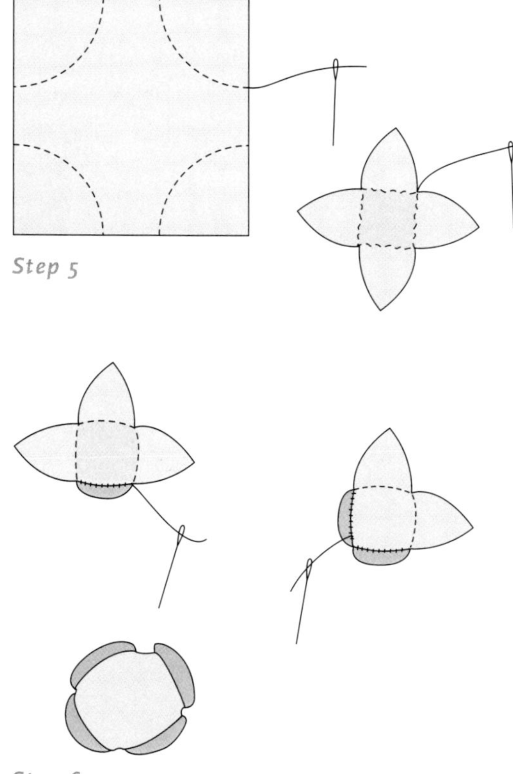

Step 5

Step 6

thread beneath the fabric. Diagrams show how to complete a vertical row of three triangles; make fewer or more triangles using the same stitch sequences, as desired. From left to right, the quilt photographed has rows of 3, 2, 2, 4, and 5 triangles.

Make five flowers

4. Cut five squares from each of two fabrics (one light, one dark), each measuring 5¾″ × 5¾″ (14.5 cm × 14.5 cm). This includes a ⅛″ (0.4 cm) seam allowance. Matching light to dark, right sides together, sew them together around seam allowances, leaving a 1″ (2.5 cm) opening. Turn right side out. Blind stitch opening closed. Finger press seam.
5. Gather-stitch arcs at corners as shown. Pull threads to gather and backstitch twice to hold.
6. Roll each petal from tip inwards towards center. Stitch to hold.
7. Overlap rolled edges as shown and stitch to hold.
8. Gather-stitch around center of flower, pushing fabric outward with your finger. Gently pull thread to gather. Backstitch to hold.

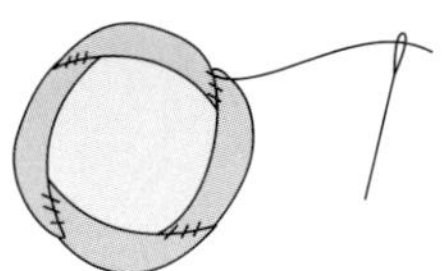

Step 7

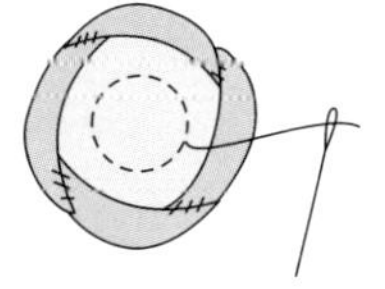

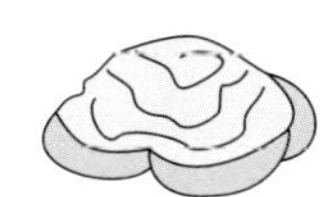

Step 8

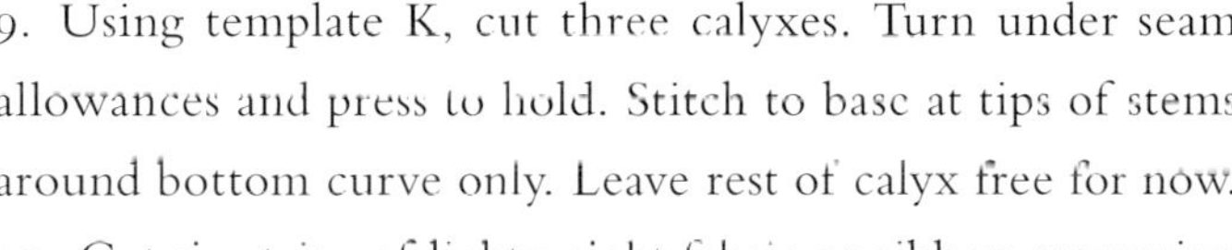

Make three buds

9. Using template K, cut three calyxes. Turn under seam allowances and press to hold. Stitch to base at tips of stems around bottom curve only. Leave rest of calyx free for now.

10. Cut six strips of lightweight fabric or ribbon measuring 1″ × 6″ (2.5 cm × 15 cm). Fold in half lengthwise, wrong side out. Stitch long edges together, leaving 1″ (2.5 cm) opening. Gather stitch both ends. Pull gathers tight and backstitch to hold. Turn right side out. Blindstitch opening closed.

11. Create three loops as shown. Weave one loop through others and stitch to hold.

12. Stuff ends of calyxes from Step 9, adding scraps of batting to stuff tightly. Stitch remainder of calyx to base, trapping bud in place.

Complete

13. Sew completed flowers onto base. Use small stitches to secure underside of each in place.

14. To add backing and 1½″ (4 cm) border, see page xviii.

Step 9

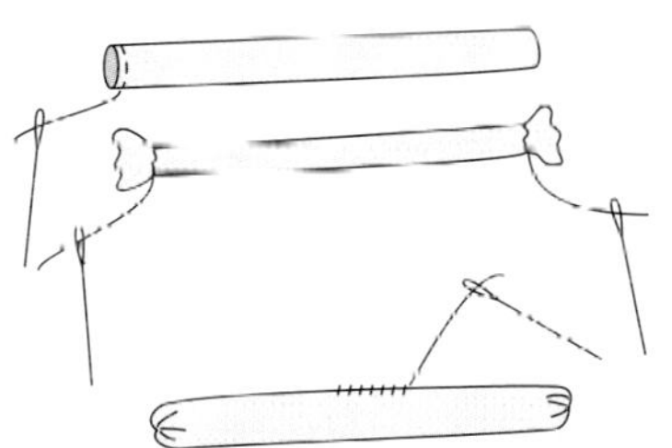

Step 10

Step 11

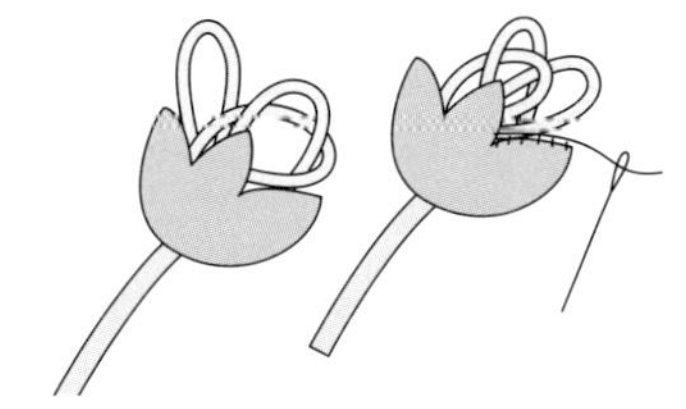

Step 12

Sea Holly

Let these brilliant blue flowers and colorful blossoms brighten a long Winter day. The vibrant colors of this long-lasting thistle makes it a perfect choice for Winter flower arrangements.

Use ⅛" (0.4 cm) seam allowance, unless noted otherwise.

YOU WILL NEED

Base: ½ yd (45 cm)

Flower fabrics: ¼ yd (25 cm), each of two or more fabrics

For buds, 1½" (2.5 cm) wired silk ribbon: 1¼ yds (115 cm)

Batting: ½ yd (45 cm)

Backing/border: ¾ yd (70 cm)

Prepare block

1. Cut base rectangle of background fabric measuring 12" × 18" (30 cm × 45 cm). Mark a seam line ½" (1.5 cm) inwards from all raw edges, so that background base onto which you will applique measures 11" × 17" (27 cm × 42 cm). Cut batting to measure 15" × 21" (37 cm × 52 cm) and backing/border fabric to measure 20" × 26" (50 cm × 66 cm). Baste batting onto wrong side of base.

Make three flowers

2. Set compass to 2¾" (7 cm) radius to draw circle measuring 5½" (14 cm) in diameter. This includes ⅛" (0.4 cm) seam allowance. Cut eight from a variety of light and dark fabrics. Matching light to dark and with right sides together, sew two circles together around seam allowances, leaving a 1" (2.5 cm)

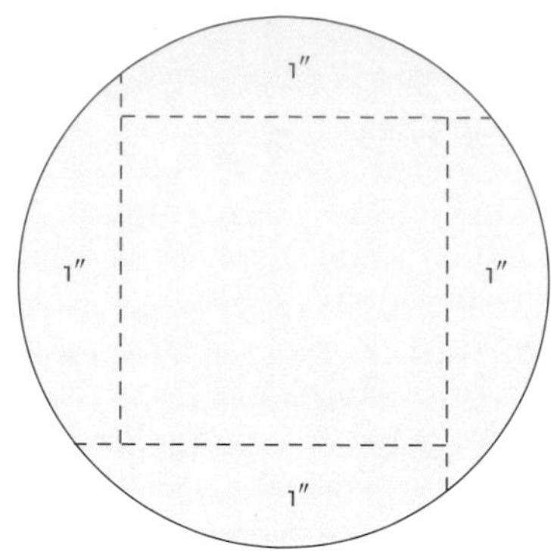

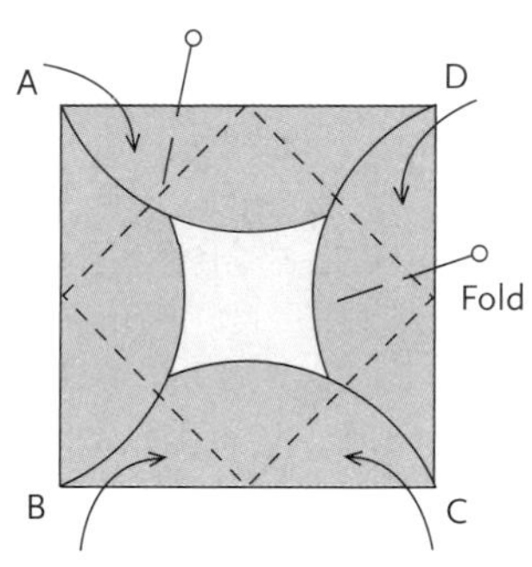

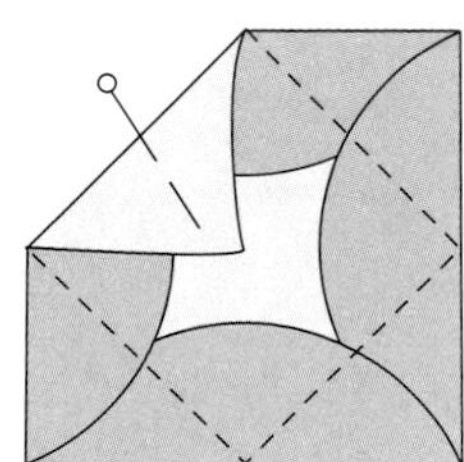

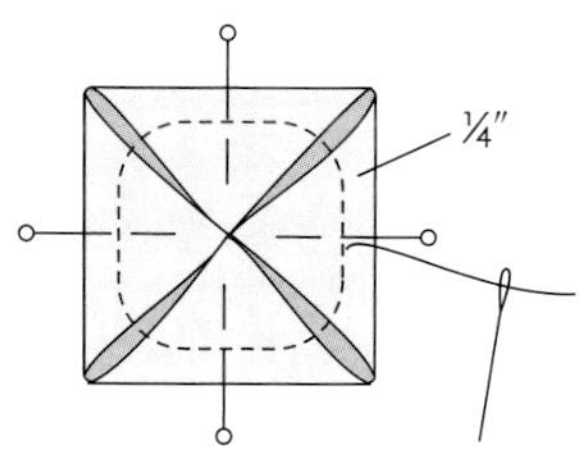

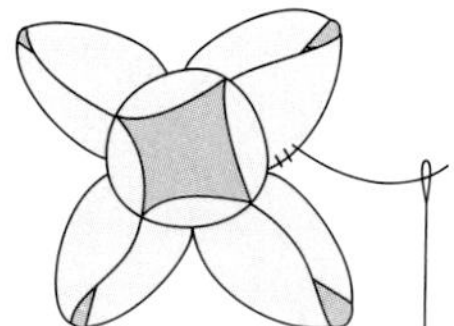

Step 3

opening. Turn right side out. Blind stitch opening closed. Finger press seam.

3. Fold in arcs of circle by 1″ (2.5 cm) to create a square. Pin to hold. Then fold corners A to D inwards to center to make a smaller square. Pin to hold. Gather-stitch around perimeter, ¼″ (0.75 cm) in from edge. Pull thread to create petals, arranging as desired. Backstitch to hold.

Make five buds

4. Cut five lengths of wired silk ribbon, each measuring 8″ (20 cm). Leaving 1½″ (4 cm) at either end unfolded, make pleats at every ½″ (1.5 cm) across the entire length. Gather-stitch across folds. Backstitch to hold.

5. Stitch ends of ribbon together, then turn right side out.

If you wish, cut additional motifs from leftover base fabric and applique them onto the border. The blue flowers overlapping the border in the quilt photographed are added in this way.

Complete

6. Arrange flowers and buds on base as desired. Use small stitches to secure underside of each in place. If you decide to allow one of the flowers to overlap the border, make sure you do not stitch that portion of the flower to the base.
7. To add backing and 2″ (5 cm) border, see page xviii.

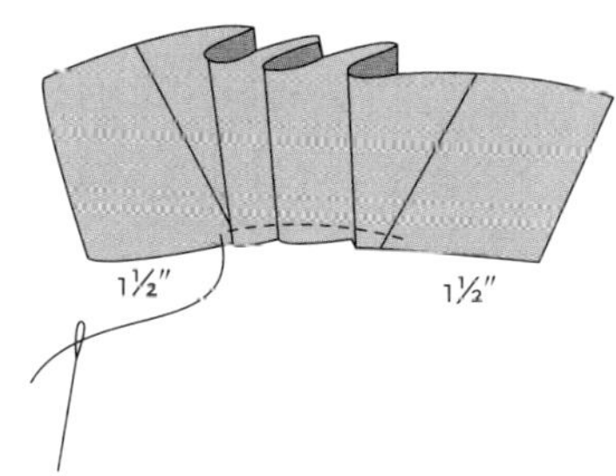

Step 4

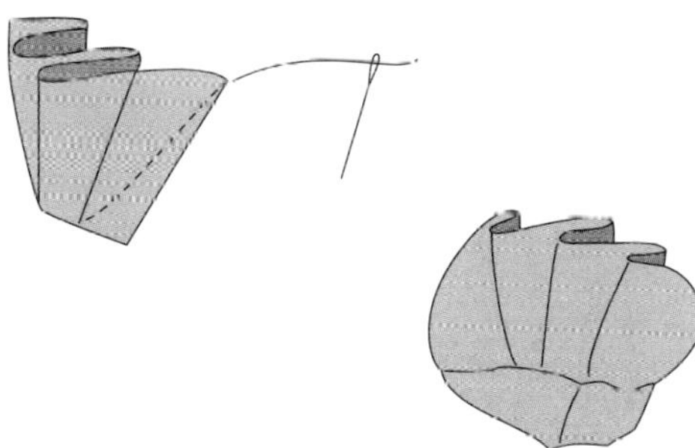

Step 5

JANUARY

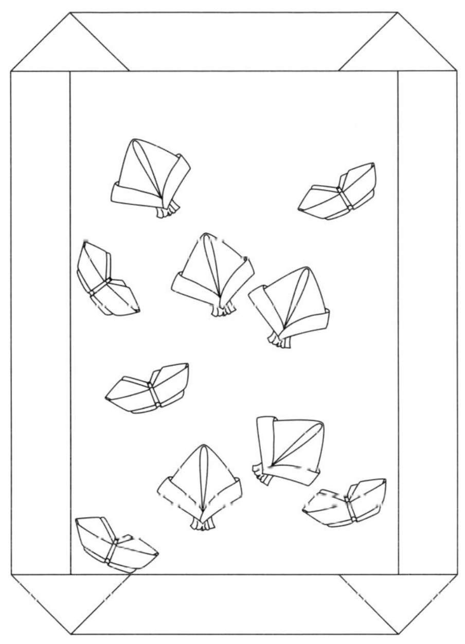

Cathedral Bell

At the stroke of midnight on New Years Eve, temple bells ring out to banish the old year and welcome the new. Create these pretty flowers in fabric to remind you that the turn of the year heralds a fresh beginning.

Use ⅛" (0.4 cm) seam allowance, unless noted otherwise.

YOU WILL NEED

Base: ½ yd (45 cm)

Flower fabrics: ¼ yd (25 cm), each of two fabrics

For butterflies, 1½" (4 cm) wired silk ribbon: 1¼ yds (120 cm)

Backing/border: ¾ yd (70 cm)

Batting: ½ yd (45 cm)

Prepare block

1. Cut base rectangle of background fabric measuring 12" × 18" (30 cm × 45 cm). Mark a seam line ½" (1.5 cm) inwards from all raw edges, so that background base onto which you will applique measures 11" × 17" (27 cm × 42 cm). Cut batting to measure 15" × 21" (37 cm × 52 cm) and backing/border fabric to measure 20" × 26" (50 cm × 66 cm). Baste batting onto wrong side of base.

Make five flowers

2. Set compass to 3" (7.5 cm) radius to draw circle measuring 6" (15 cm) in diameter. This includes ⅛" (0.4 cm) seam allowance. Cut five from each of two fabrics. Match one of each color together, right sides together, then sew them

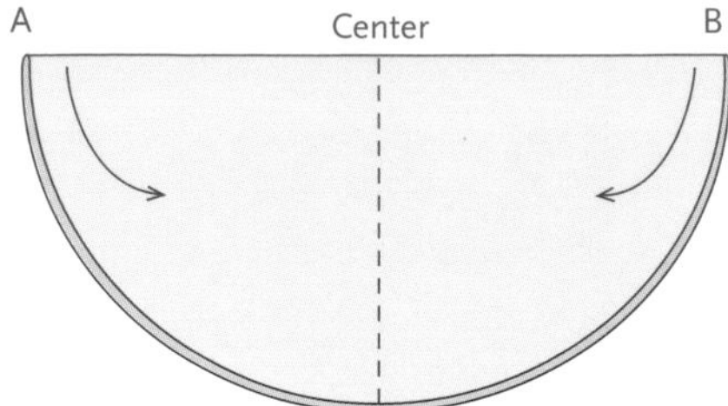

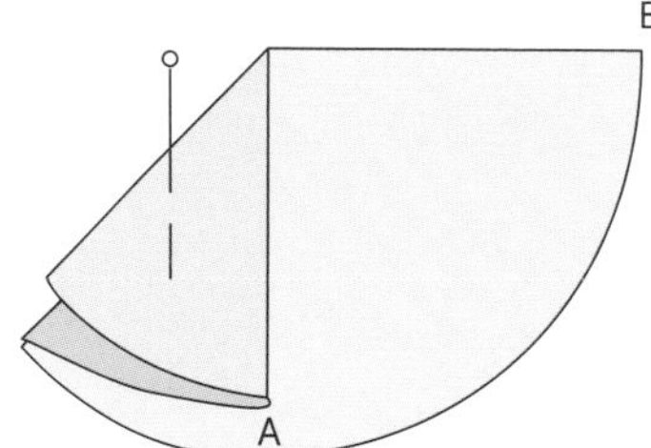

Step 3

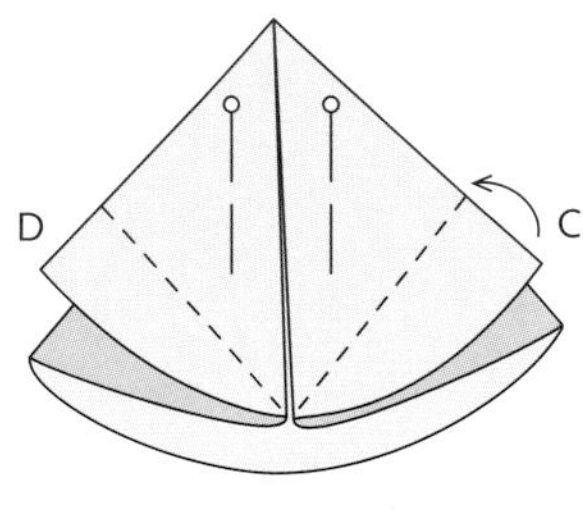

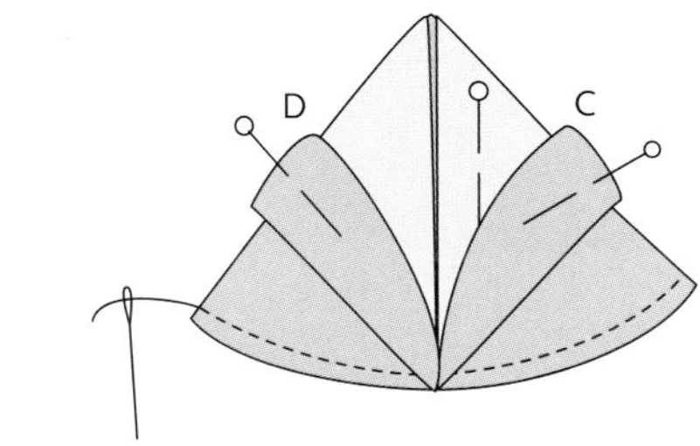

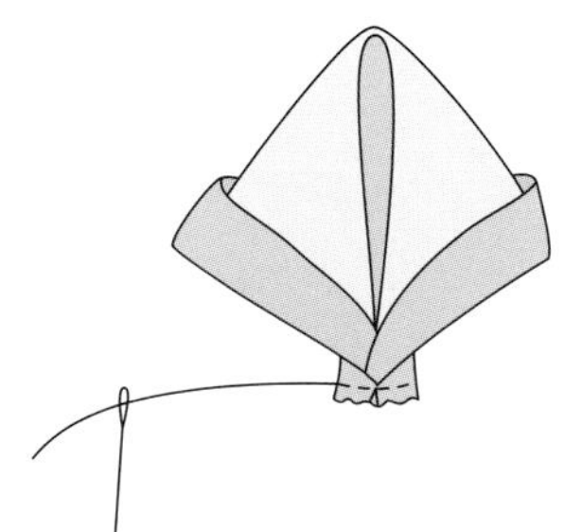

Step 4

together around seam allowances, leaving a 1″ (2.5 cm) opening. Turn right side out. Blind stitch opening closed. Finger press seam.

3. Fold completed circle in half. Fold A and B to center line. Pin in place.

4. Fold C and D inwards, along marked line. Pin in place. Gather-stitch around unfolded base as shown. Pull thread to gather. Backstitch twice to hold.

Make five butterflies

5. Cut five lengths of 1½″ (4 cm) wired silk ribbon, each measuring 8″ (20 cm). Fold bottom edge in lengthwise by ½″ (1.5 cm)

Step 5

6. Fold in raw ends diagonally as shown to create triangle tips. Make fold 2″ (5 cm) from center. Twist ribbon so that tip A meets center, as shown. Pin in place.

7. Repeat Step 6 to create second wing, tucking tip under tip A.

8. Fold in half, aligning wings. Gather-stitch ¼″ (0.75 cm) from folded line.

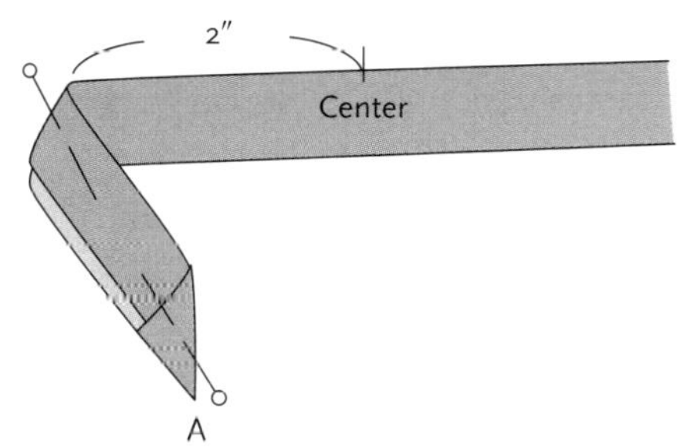

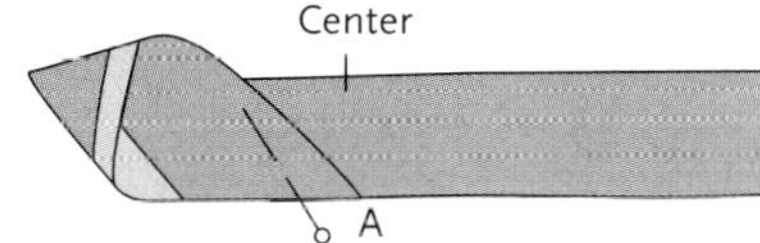

Step 6

Complete

9. Arrange flowers and butterflies on base as desired. Use small stitches to secure underside of each flower or butterfly in place.

10. To add backing and 2″ (5 cm) border, see page xviii.

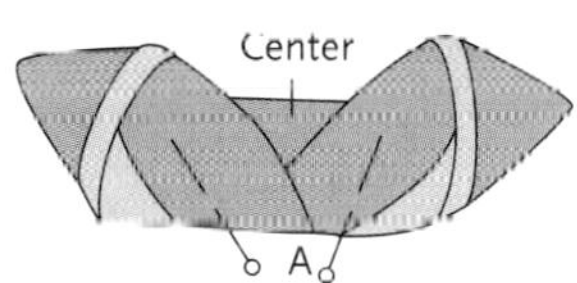

Step 7

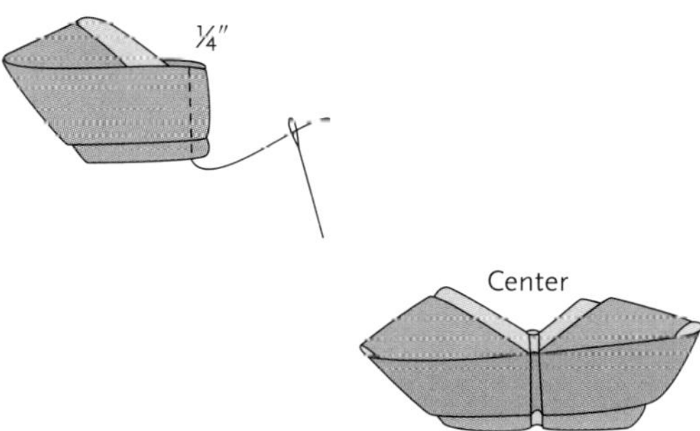

Step 8

Kalanchoe of Africa

The glowing pink blooms of the Kalanchoe or Coral Bell bring joie de vivre to the dreariest Winter days. Grow this plant in any sunlit window and it will reward you with its showy bursts of color all Winter long.

See templates on page 168. Use ⅛" (0.4 cm) seam allowance, unless noted otherwise.

YOU WILL NEED

Base: ½ yd (45 cm)

Circle fabric: Scraps

Leaf fabric: ¼ yd (25 cm) or less

Flower fabrics: ¼ yd (25 cm) or less, each of three fabrics

Backing and border: ¾ yd (70 cm)

Batting: ½ yd (45 cm)

Prepare block

1. Cut base rectangle of background fabric measuring 12" × 18" (30 cm × 45 cm). Mark a seam line ½" (1.5 cm) inwards from all raw edges, so that background base onto which you will applique measures 11" × 17" (27 cm × 42 cm). Cut batting to measure 15" × 21" (37 cm × 52 cm) and backing/border fabric to measure 20" × 25" (50 cm × 65 cm). Baste batting onto wrong side of base.
2. Set compass to 2" (5 cm) to draw circle measuring 4" (10 cm) in diameter. Cut 2. Adjust compass to 1¼" (3.2 cm) to draw circle measuring 2½" (6.4 cm). Cut 3. Adjust compass again to ¾" (2 cm) to draw circle measuring 1½" (4 cm). Cut 2, using same fabric as mid-sized circle. Turning under by ⅛" (0.4 cm), applique all circles to base.

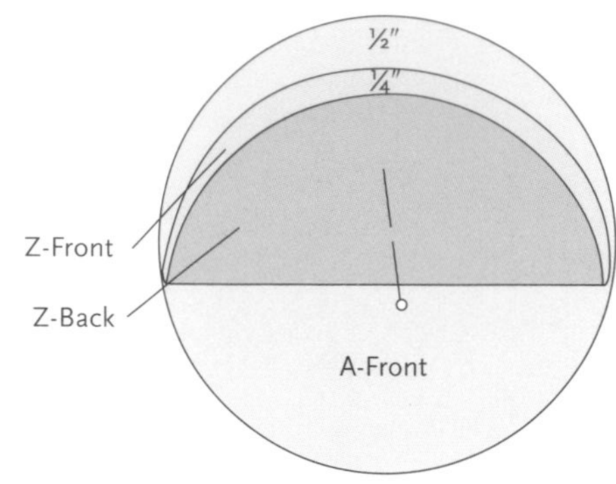

Step 5

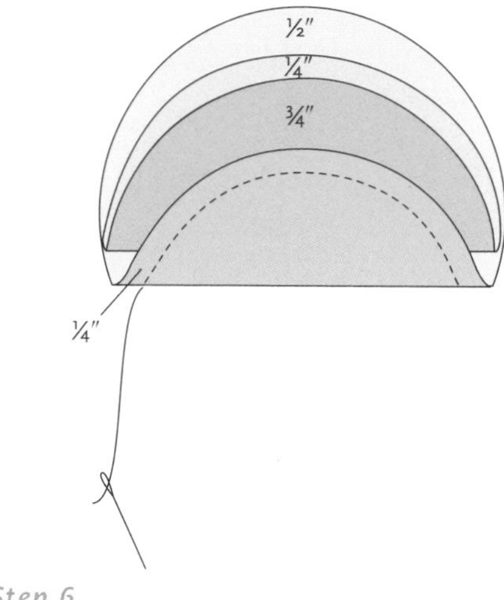

Step 6

3. Using template A, cut eight. Fold in half lengthwise, wrong side out. Sew around curve, leaving 1″ (2.5 cm) opening. Turn right side out. Blind stitch opening closed. Finger press seam. Make eight and set aside.

Make three flowers

4. Set compass to 2⅜″ (6 cm) radius to draw circle measuring 4¾″ (12 cm) in diameter. This includes ⅛″ (0.4 cm) seam allowance. Cut six from fabric 1, three from fabric 2, and three from fabric 3. Place fabric 1 circles, right sides together, then sew them together around seam allowances, leaving 1″ (2.5 cm) opening. Turn right side out. Blind stitch opening closed. Finger press seam. Repeat with fabrics 2 and 3, this time pairing unmatched fabrics together. You will now have three double-sided circles made out of a single fabric (circle Y) and three made out of unmatched fabrics (circle Z)

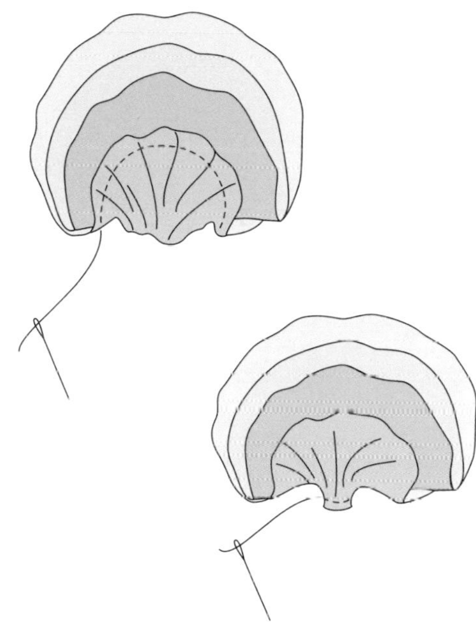

Step 7

5. Position Z on top of Y so that there is a ½″ (1.5 cm) gap between the center top of Y and the center top of Z, as shown. Fold center bottom of Z upwards, leaving a gap of ¼″ (1.5 cm) at center top.

6. Fold center bottom of Y upwards, leaving 3/4″ (2 cm) of Z showing at center top. Gather-stitch ¼″ (0.75 cm) in from the curve line of Y, stitching through all layers.

7. Pull thread slowly to gather. Backstitch twice to hold.

Complete

8. Arrange leaves and flowers as desired. Use small stitches to secure underside of each flower in place. Applique leaves in place, sewing around about a third of each leaf and leaving the rest free. Add beads as desired and stitch to base.

9. To add backing and 2″ (5 cm) border, see page xviii.

FEBRUARY

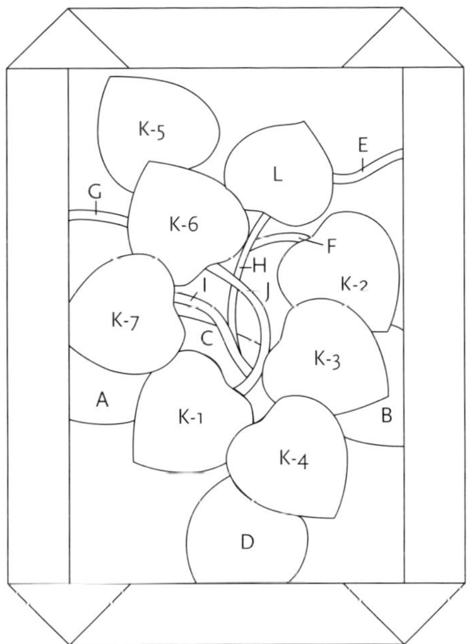

Qualup Bell

The bell-like blossoms of this colorful Australian flower bring a welcome reminder of Summer to the coldest Winter days. Create the flower in striking fabrics and on a brilliantly colored background.

See templates on pages 168–169. Use ⅛" (0.4 cm) seam allowance, unless noted otherwise.

Prepare block

1. Cut base rectangle of background fabric measuring 12" × 18" (30 cm × 45 cm). Mark a seam line ½" (1.5 cm) inwards from all raw edges, so that background base onto which you will applique measures 11" × 17" (27 cm × 42 cm). Cut batting to measure 15" × 21" (37 cm × 52 cm) and backing/border fabric to measure 20" × 26" (50 cm × 66 cm). Baste batting onto wrong side of base.

2. Cut templates A to K from various fabrics. Applique leaf pieces A to D onto base, then stem pieces E to J. Applique leaf pieces K-1 to K-5, L, then K-6 and K-7 onto base.

Make two flowers

3. Set compass to 2⅝" (6.7 cm) radius to draw circle measuring 5¼" (13.4 cm) in diameter. This includes ⅛" (0.4 cm) seam

YOU WILL NEED

Base: ½ yd (45 cm)

Leaf and stem fabrics: Scraps (variety)

Flower fabrics: Scraps (one striped print, two other prints)

Backing/border: ¾ yd (70 cm)

Batting: ½ yd (45 cm)

#30 and #50 heavy-duty thread or embroidery floss

If you wish to create a scene like mine in the foreground, search out a fabric with pictorial motifs and applique it over the bottom of the base fabric. It will be difficult to find the same fabric I have used, but you can choose from many wonderful prints that depict similar country scenes. Once you have added this large applique, you may wish to cut away the base fabric behind it.

allowance. Cut twelve from your own combination of striped and other fabrics, such as floral prints. (In the photo, stripes are used for the top and bottom layers). Matching two circles of your choice right sides together, sew them together around seam allowances, leaving a 1″ (2.5 cm) opening. Turn right side out. Blind stitch opening closed. Finger press seam. You will have six double-sided circles.

4. Choose three circles to make first flower. Stack them, then fold the stack in half as shown. Gather-stitch along center line, using #30 heavy-duty thread. Pull thread lightly to gather and backstitch twice to hold at point A.

5. Turn up side down. Sew the top layers together for about 1″ (2.5 cm), overlapping slightly as shown by about 1/8″

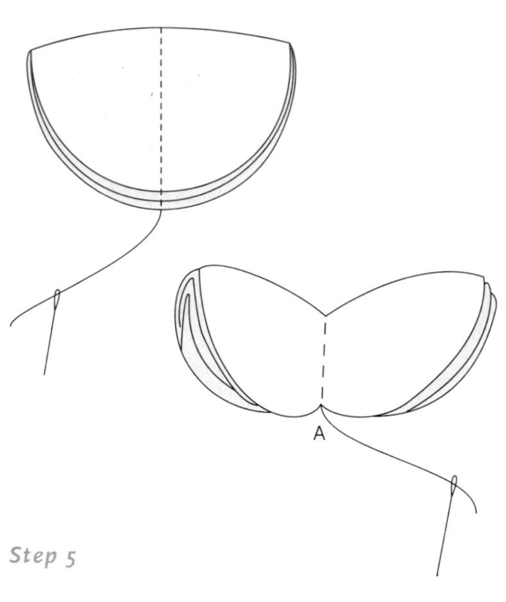

Step 5

Step 6

(0.4 cm). Pull the petals gently toward the center to shape as desired.

6. Knot a 36″ (90 cm) length of #50 thread or embroidery floss, then thread it through the center of the flower, coming out at point B. Loop as shown. Make a 1″ (2.5 cm) braid, using each half of the loop and the loose strand of thread. Make a stitch through the tip of the braid to hold securely in place. Leaving loop intact, use same threaded needle to sew the braid in place on the base so that the flower hangs freely from the stem.

7. Repeat Steps 3 to 6 to make second flower.

Complete

8. To add backing and 2″ (5 cm) border, see page xviii.

Step 6

Valentine Lily

There are few sights as delightful as early Lily blossoms peeking up through the snow, a sign that Spring is just around the corner. The Valentine Lily, recreated in pretty cottons or silks, makes an intimate gift on Valentine's day. It promises a new beginning as Spring approaches.

Use ⅛″ (0.4 cm) seam allowance, unless noted otherwise.

Prepare block

1. Cut base rectangle of background fabric measuring 12″ × 18″ (30 cm × 45 cm). Mark a seam line ½″ (1.5 cm) inwards from all raw edges, so that background base onto which you will appliqué measures 11″ × 17″ (27 cm × 42 cm). Cut batting to measure 15″ × 21″ (37 cm × 52 cm) and backing/border fabric to measure 20″ × 26″ (50 cm × 66 cm). Baste batting onto wrong side of base.

Make five flowers

2. From each of two fabrics (one light, one dark) cut five squares, each measuring 4½″ × 4½″ (11.5 cm × 11.5 cm). This includes a ¼″ (0.75 cm) seam allowance. Matching light to dark and right sides together, sew around all four sides using

YOU WILL NEED

Base: ½ yd (45 cm)

Flower fabrics: ¼ yd (25 cm), each of two fabrics

For leaves, 2″ (5 cm) wired silk ribbon: 1¼ yds (120 cm)

Backing/border: ¾ yd (70 cm)

Batting: ½ yd (45 cm)

Decorative beads

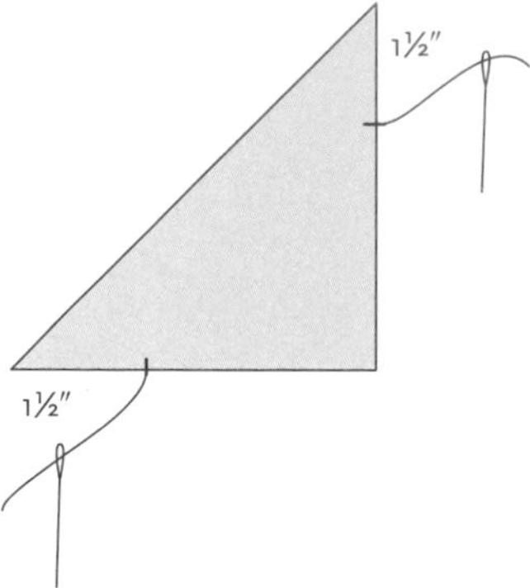

Step 3

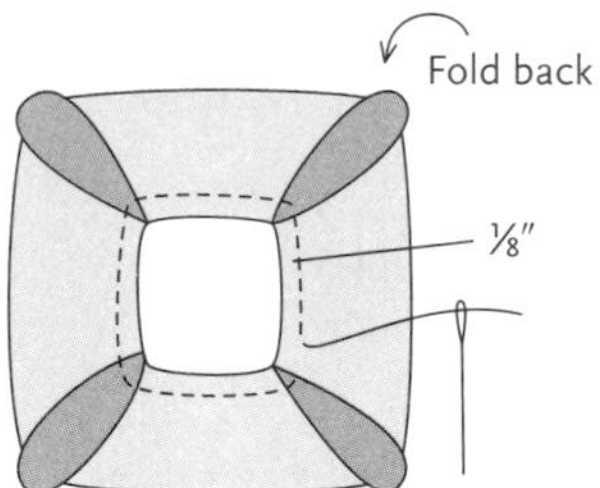

Step 4

Step 5

¼" (0.75 cm) seam allowance, leaving a 1" (2.5 cm) opening. Turn right side out. Blind stitch opening closed. Press.

3. Fold completed square in half diagonally to make triangle. Mark each short side of triangle 1½" (4 cm) away from acute angle, as shown. Make two small stitches to hold. Open out, back into square, then fold across other diagonal to form new triangle shape. Again, mark each short side 1½" (4 cm) away from acute angle and make two small stitches to hold. Open out.

4. Use your fingers to arrange the shape into a square, as shown. Gather-stitch around all sides, ⅛" (0.4 cm) in from edge. Pull thread to gather. Backstitch twice to hold.

5. Fold back each of four corner tips to allow more of inside fabric to show.

Make five leaves

6. Cut five lengths of wired ribbon, each measuring 9″ (20 cm). Fold in half, overlapping A with B, as shown. Fold edge of B upwards by about ⅓″ (0.8 cm). Wrap A over B and stitch through layers to hold, as shown.

Complete

7. Arrange flowers and leaves on base as desired. Use small stitches to secure underside of each flower or leaf in place. Add beads for embellishment.
8. To add backing and 2″ (5 cm) border, see page xviii.

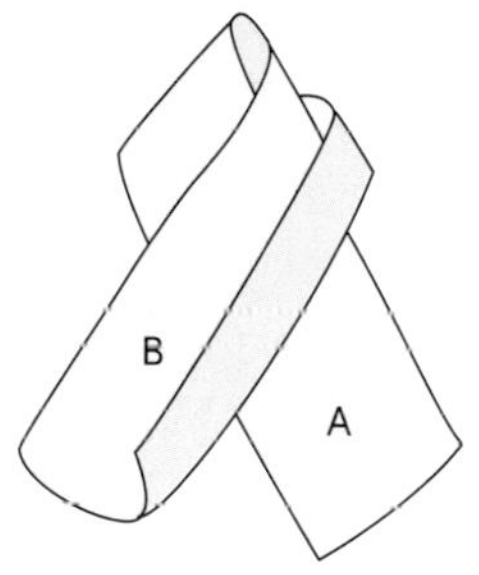

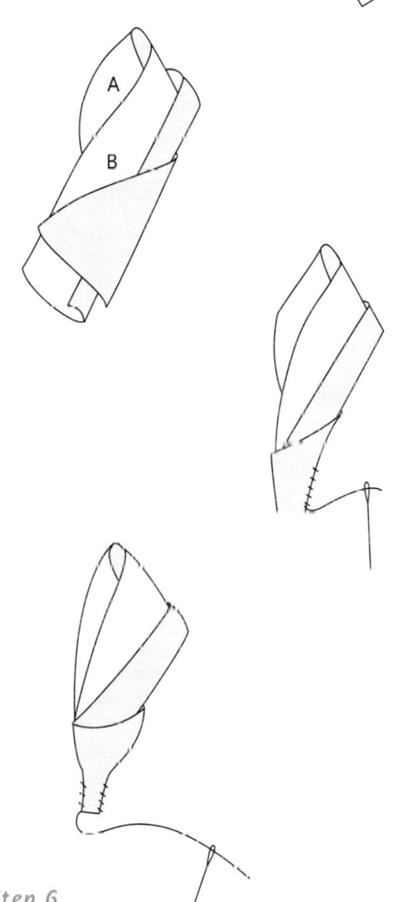

Step 6

A Valentine's Gift

The Valentine Lily decorates this simple yet elegant pochette. Use it to hold your Valentine tokens or make it as a special gift for Valentine's Day.

See template on page 170. Use ⅛" (0.4 cm) seam allowance, unless noted otherwise.

1. Join two template A pieces to create full template A. Adding ½" (1.5 cm) seam allowance, cut two each from fabric, lining, and batting. Baste batting to wrong side of fabric for front and back of purse. Trim batting to scant ⅛" (0.4 cm).
2. Cut two lengths of wired silk ribbon, each measuring 10" (25 cm). Starting at center, make tucks along the entire length of each ribbon. Shape each ribbon into a semi circle. Stitch in place at center of the purse, along the bottom, tucked edge of each ribbon. (See diagrams on page 126.)
3. Cut one more 10" (25 cm) length of wired silk ribbon. Tuck and gather as in Step 2, but pull gathers lightly to create a full circle. Backstitch to hold. Stitch ends of ribbon together. Sew onto back of purse. Add button at center.
4. From each of two fabrics (one light, one dark) cut two squares, each measuring 5½" × 5½" (11.5 cm × 11.5 cm). Fol-

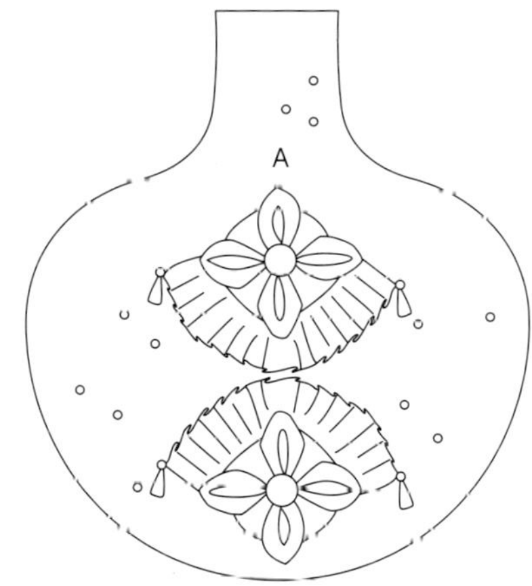

Front

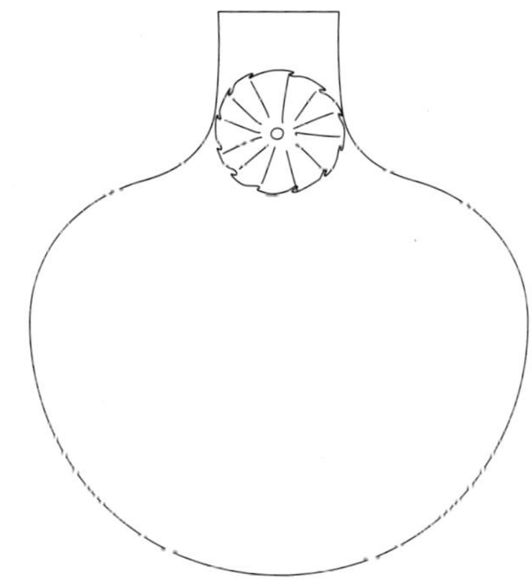

Back

YOU WILL NEED

Purse fabric: ½ yd (45 cm) or less

Lining fabric: ½ yd (45 cm) or less

Flower fabrics: ¼ yd (30 cm), each of two fabrics

For fan, 1½" (4 cm) wired silk ribbon: 1 yd (90 cm)

Thin batting: ½ yd (45 cm) or less

Beads for embellishment

Three decorative buttons

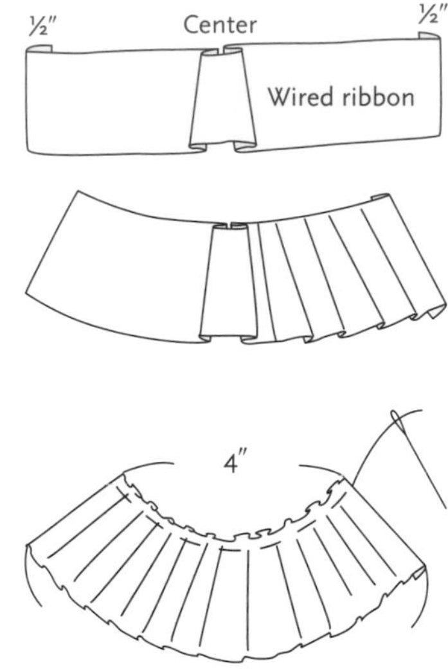

Step 2

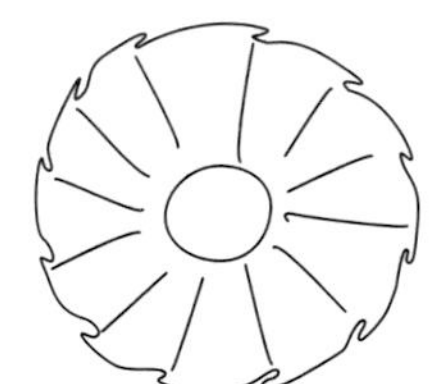

Step 3

Step 5

low Steps 2 to 5 of *Valentine Lily* to complete two flowers. In Step 3, make marks at 2″ (5 cm) away from each acute angle.

5. Arrange the flowers on the purse, covering the bottom, tucked edge of each ribbon. Sew a decorative button to center of each flower. Add beads for embellishment.

6. Right sides together, sew front to back, using ½″ (1.5 cm) seam allowance. Leave top open as shown on template A. Clip curves, if necessary, and press seams open. Repeat with lining front and lining back. Turn under seam allowance around handles and purse top and baste in place. Repeat with lining.

7. Wrong sides together, sew across top of handle pieces. Repeat for lining.

8. Wrong sides together, position lining on top of purse and pin in place, aligning center bottom of lining with center bottom of purse and aligning handles pieces. Make two or

Back view

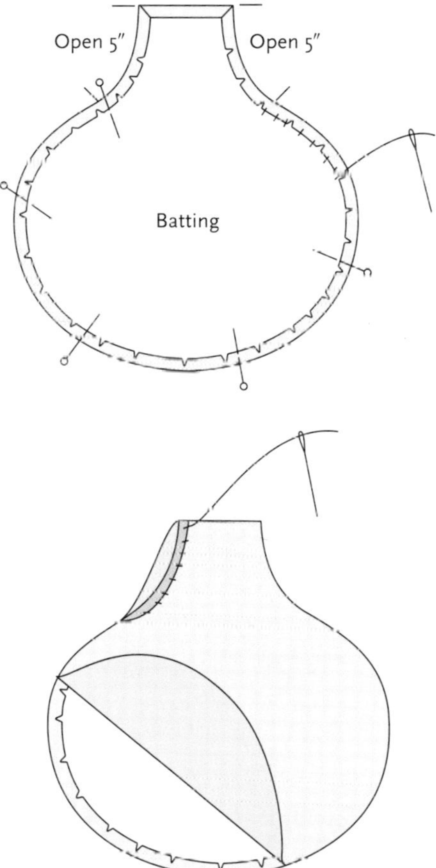

Step 8

three small stitches through all layers at center bottom to secure lining to purse. Repeat at about 2″ (5 cm) at either side of first set of stitches. Remove pins. Turn purse right side out, with lining falling in place inside. Blindstitch lining to purse around handles and top. You may need to adjust the seam allowances so that purse fabric overlaps the lining fabric a little. Remove all basting stitches.

Templates

Cockscomb

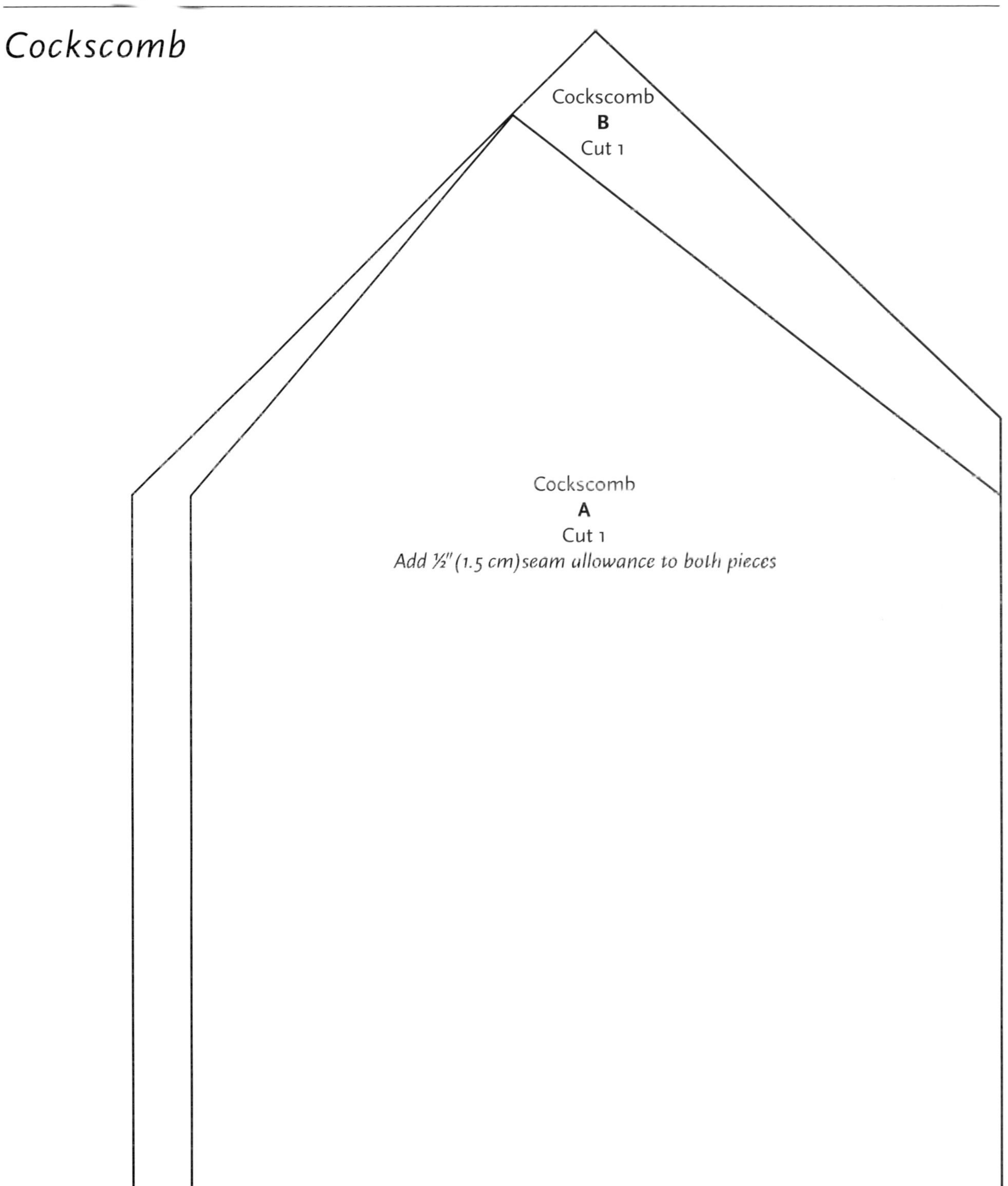

Passion Flower/ Maypop Sachet

Add ⅛" (0.4 cm) seam allowance unless otherwise indicated
Do not add seam allowance to batting or felt pieces

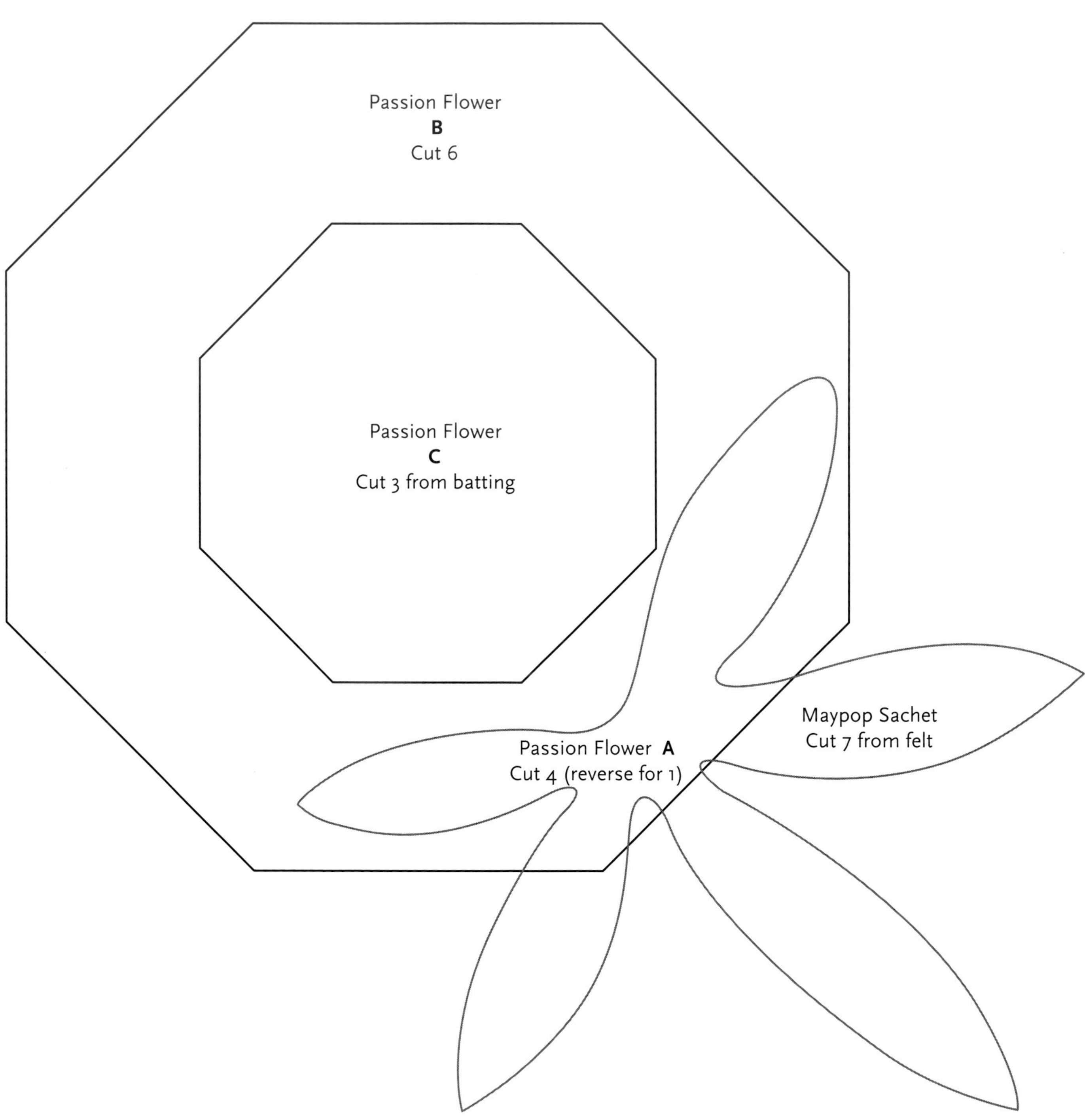

Maypop Sachet

Add ⅛" (0.4 cm) seam allowance unless otherwise indicated

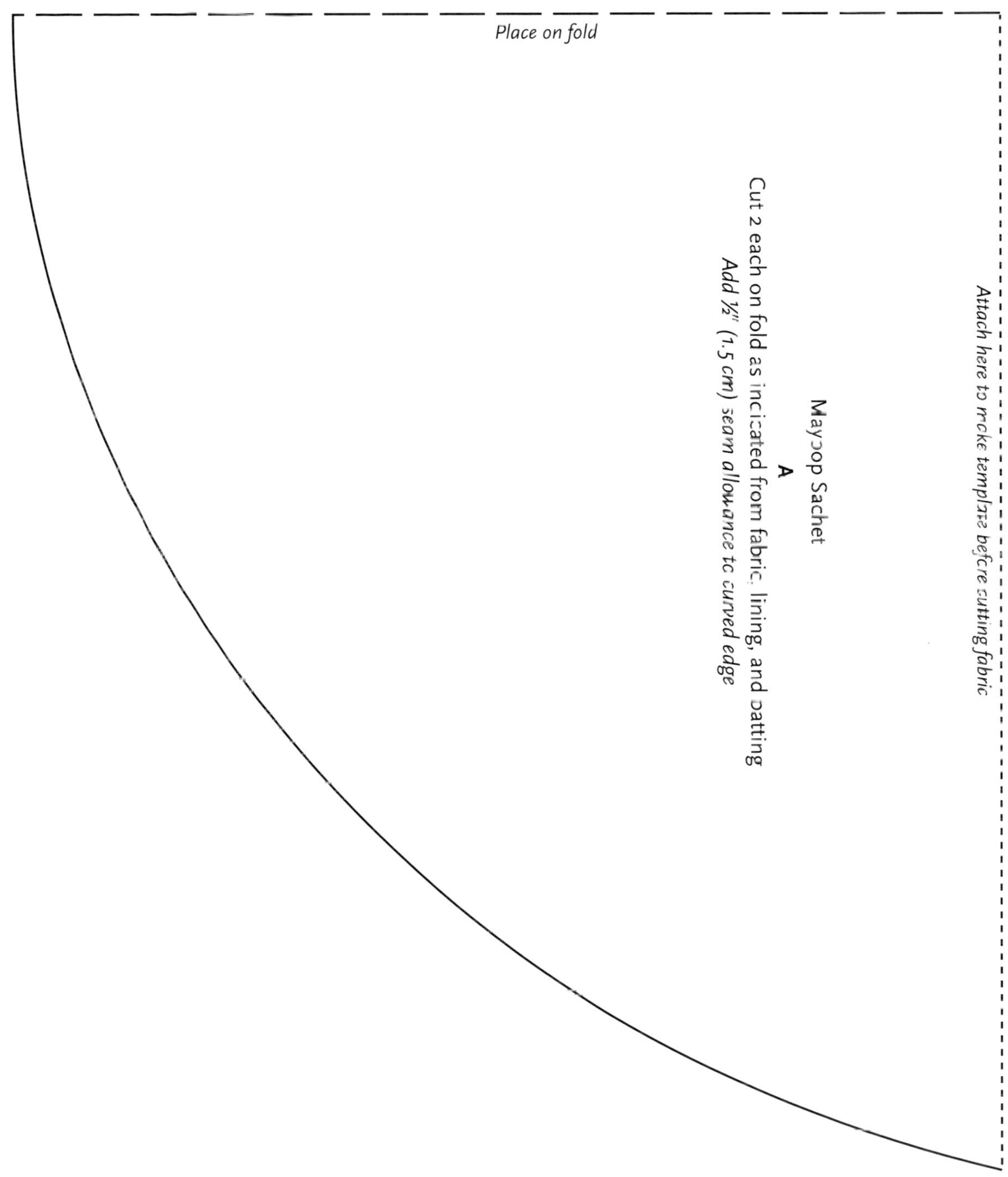

Maypop Sachet

continued

Place on fold

Attach here to make template before cutting fabric

Maypop Sachet

A

Cut here for batting only

Cut here for lining only

Cut here for fabric only

Maypop Sachet

continued

Add ⅛" (0.4 cm) seam allowance unless otherwise indicated
Do not add seam allowance to batting or felt pieces

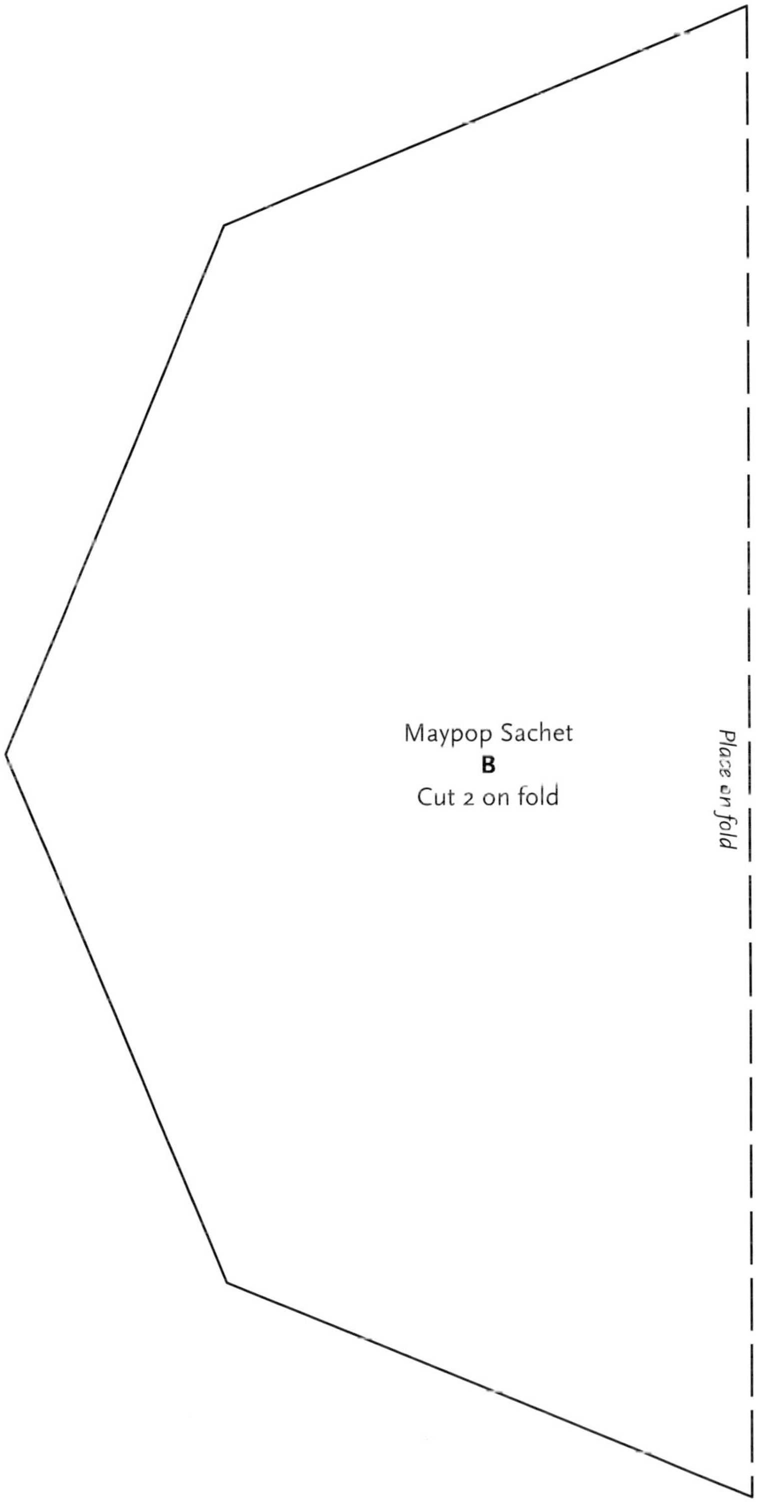

Maypop Sachet
B
Cut 2 on fold

Place on fold

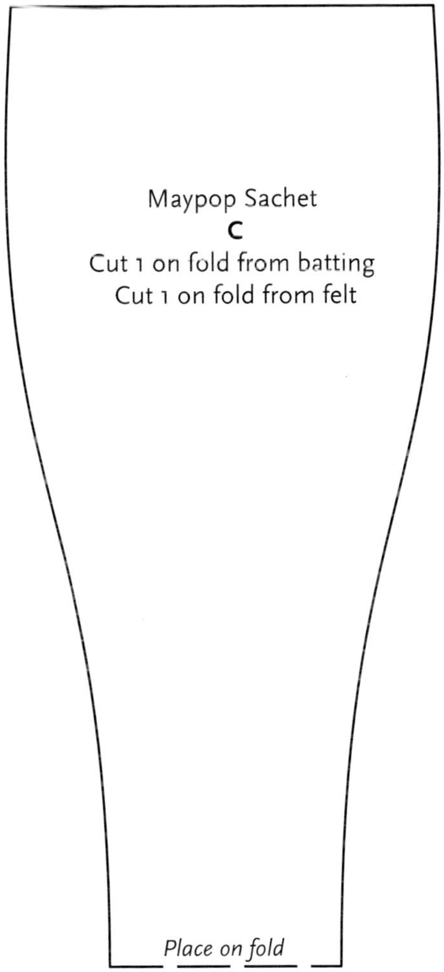

Maypop Sachet
C
Cut 1 on fold from batting
Cut 1 on fold from felt

Place on fold

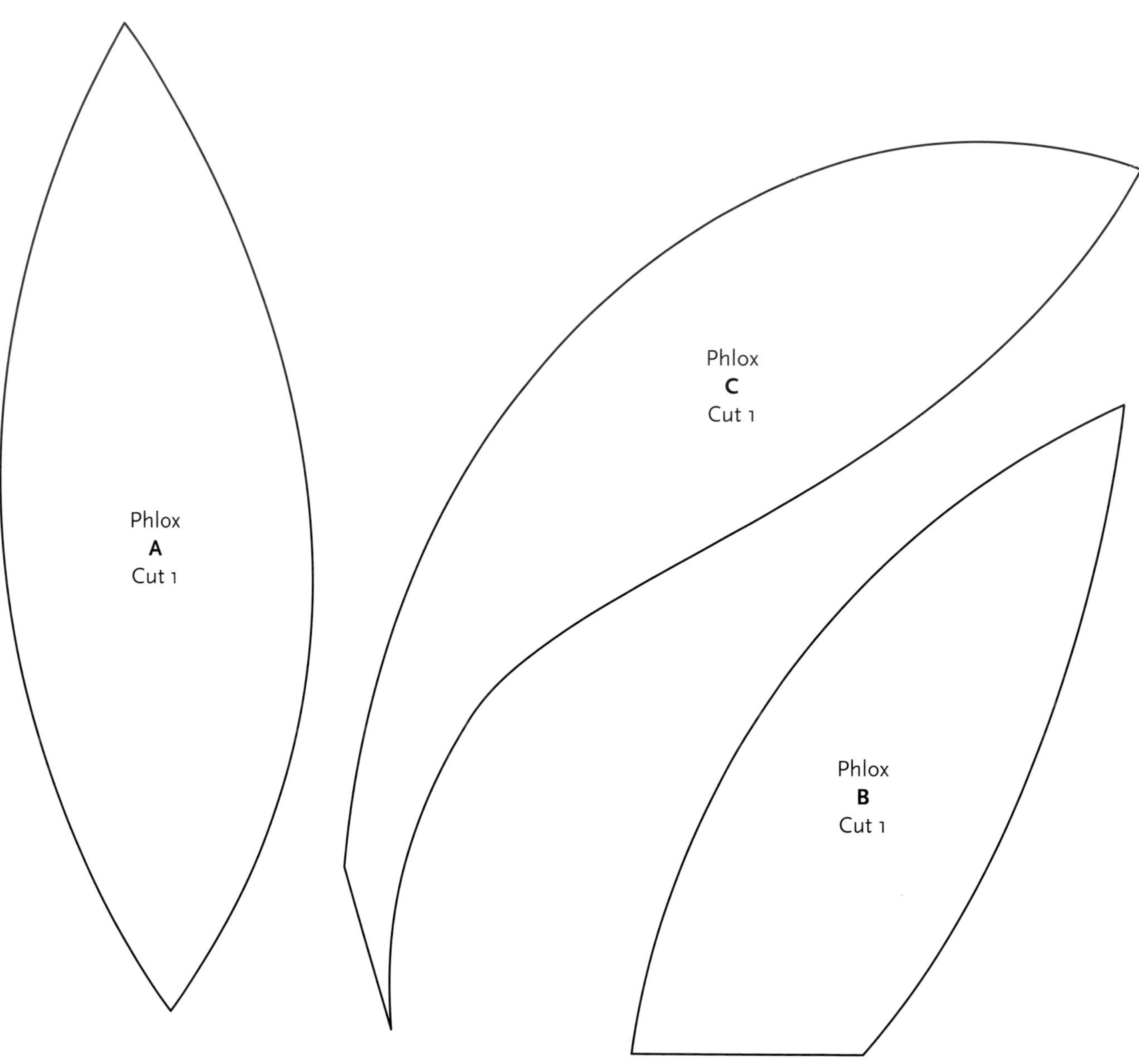

Phlox
A
Cut 1
Phlox
C
Cut 1
Phlox
B
Cut 1

Phlox

continued

Add ⅛" (0.4 cm) seam allowance unless otherwise indicated

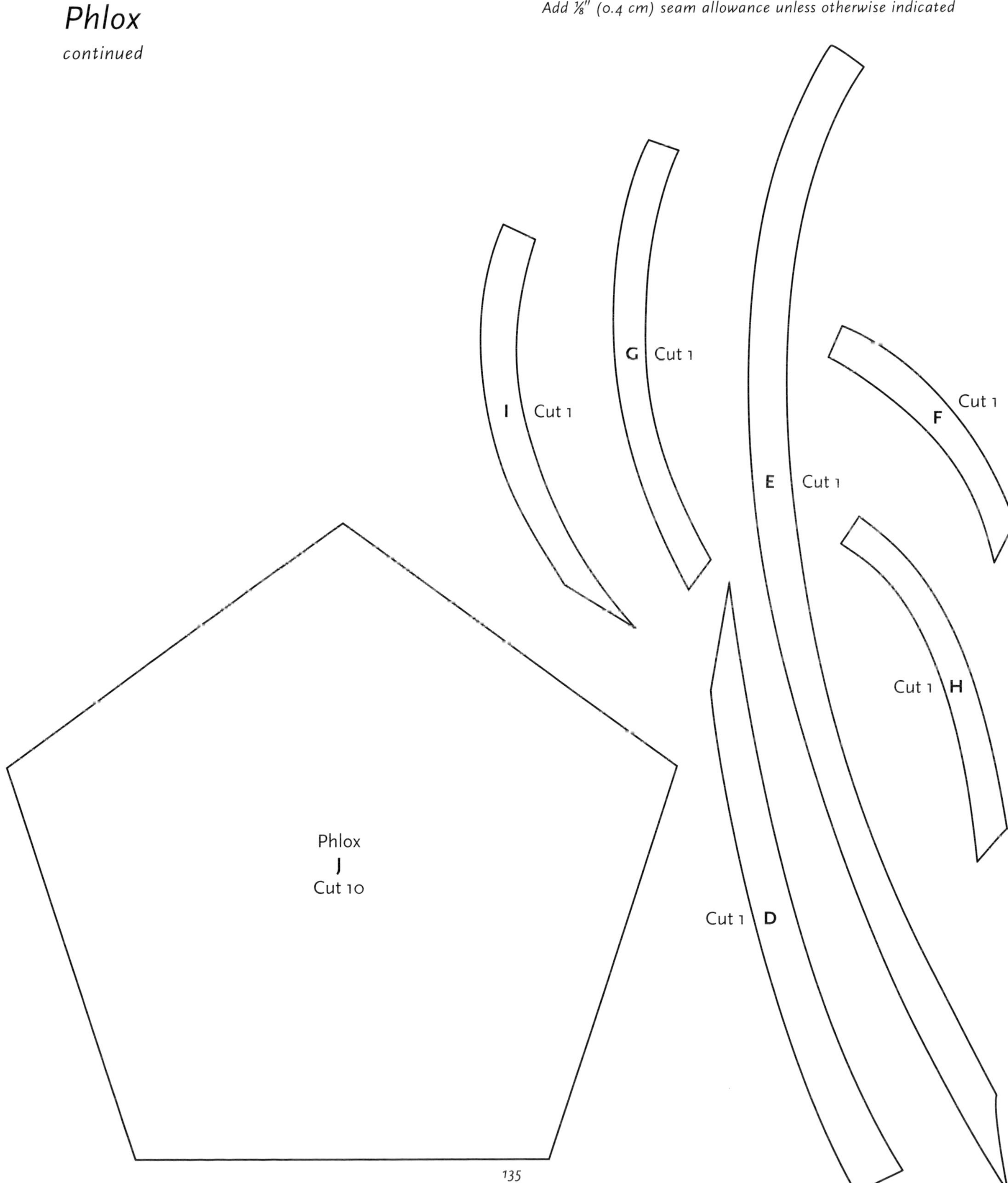

Calypso

Add ⅛" (0.4 cm) seam allowance unless otherwise indicated

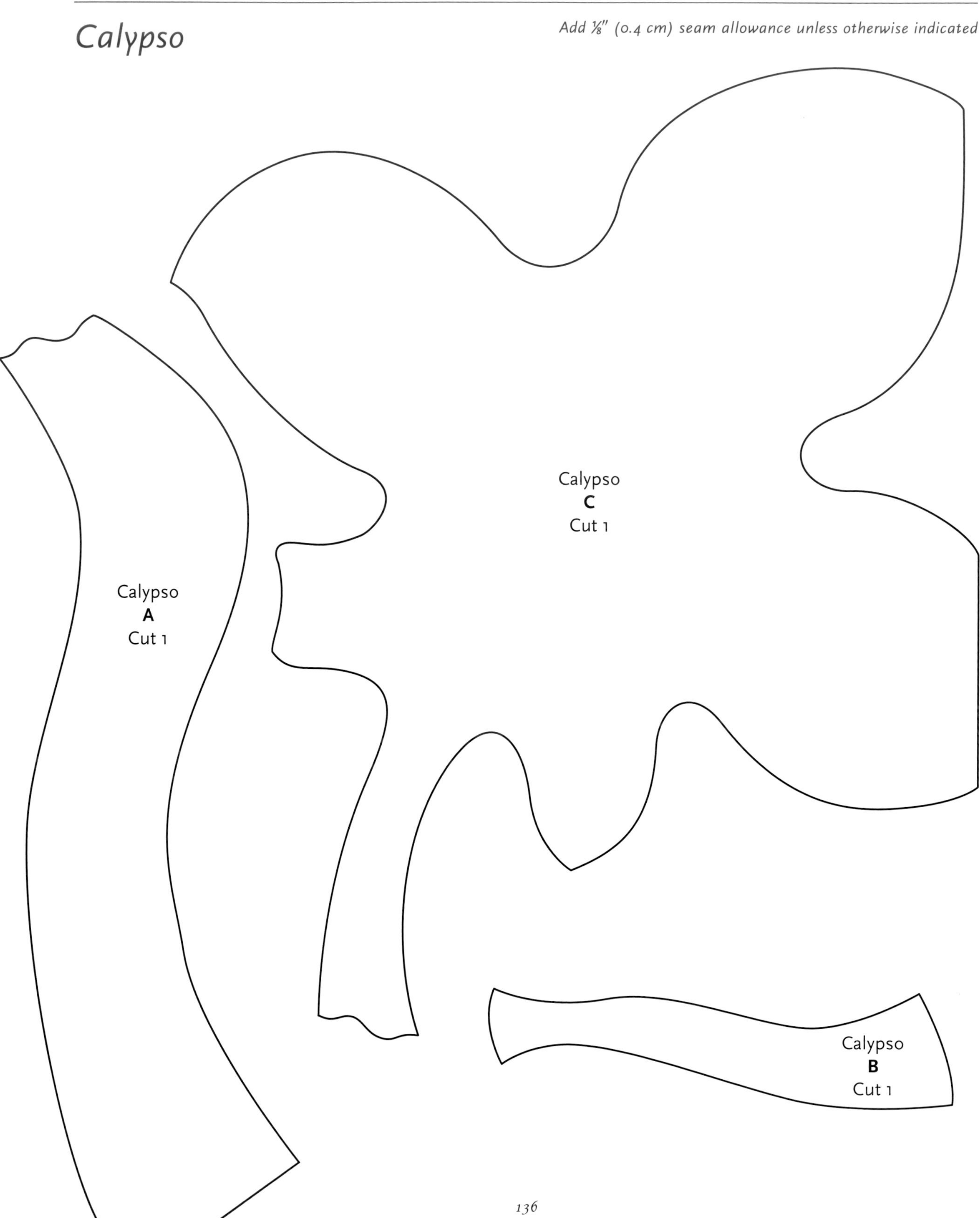

Calypso

continued

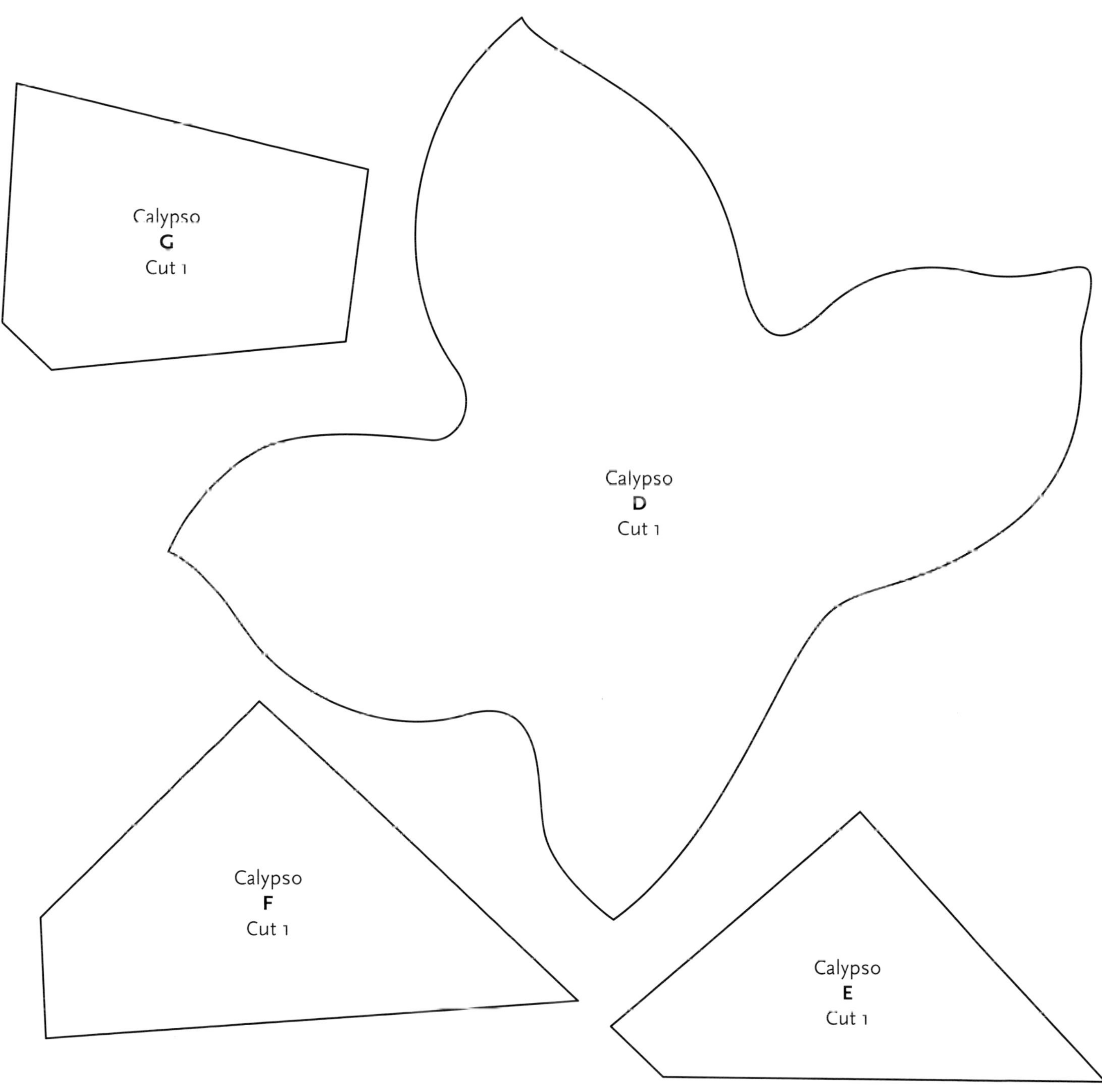

Calypso

continued

Add ⅛" (0.4 cm) seam allowance unless otherwise indicated

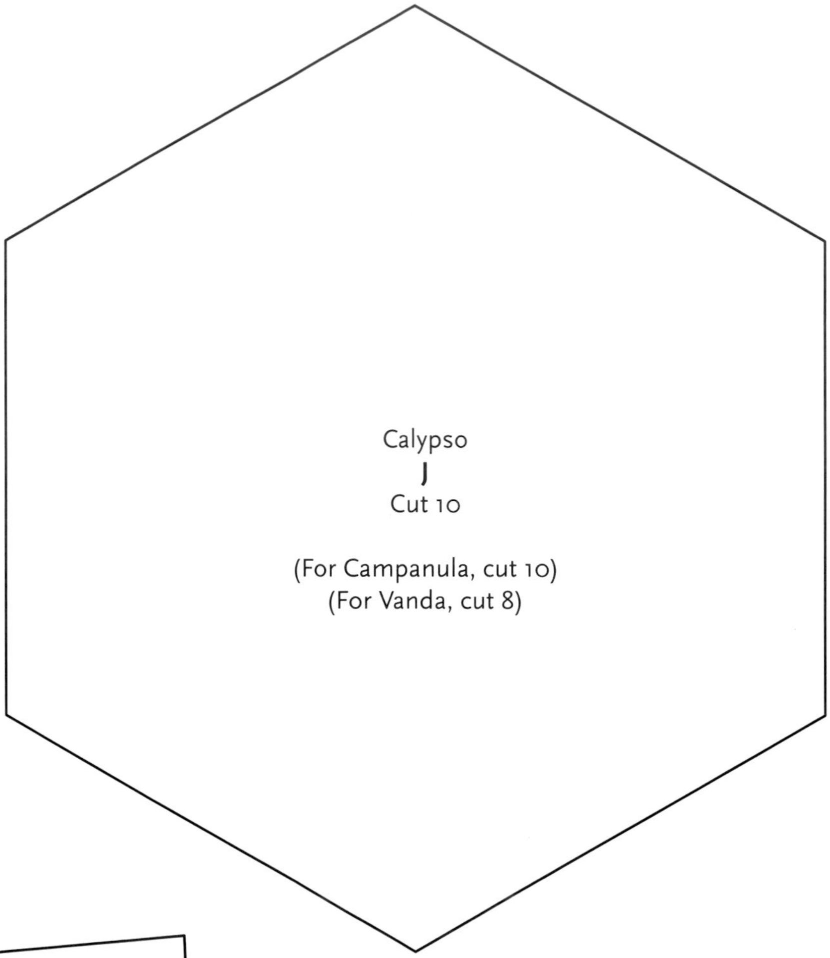

Calypso
J
Cut 10

(For Campanula, cut 10)
(For Vanda, cut 8)

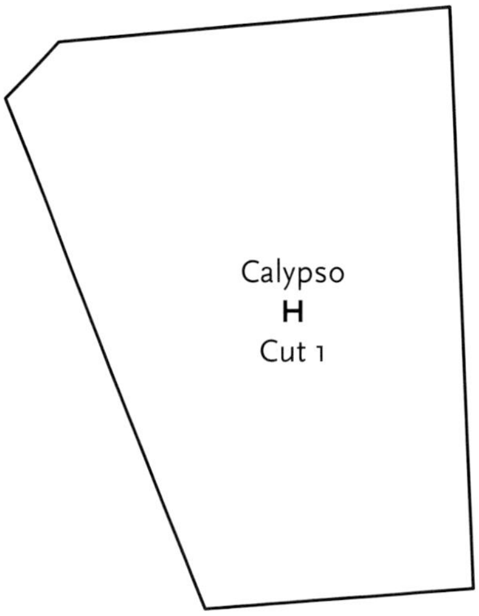

Calypso
H
Cut 1

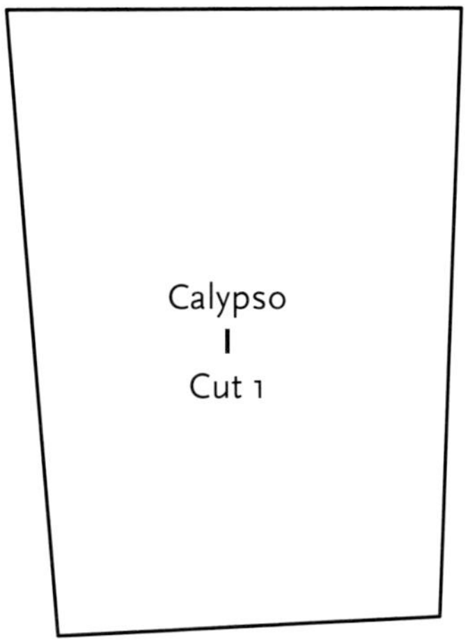

Calypso
I
Cut 1

Summer Surprise

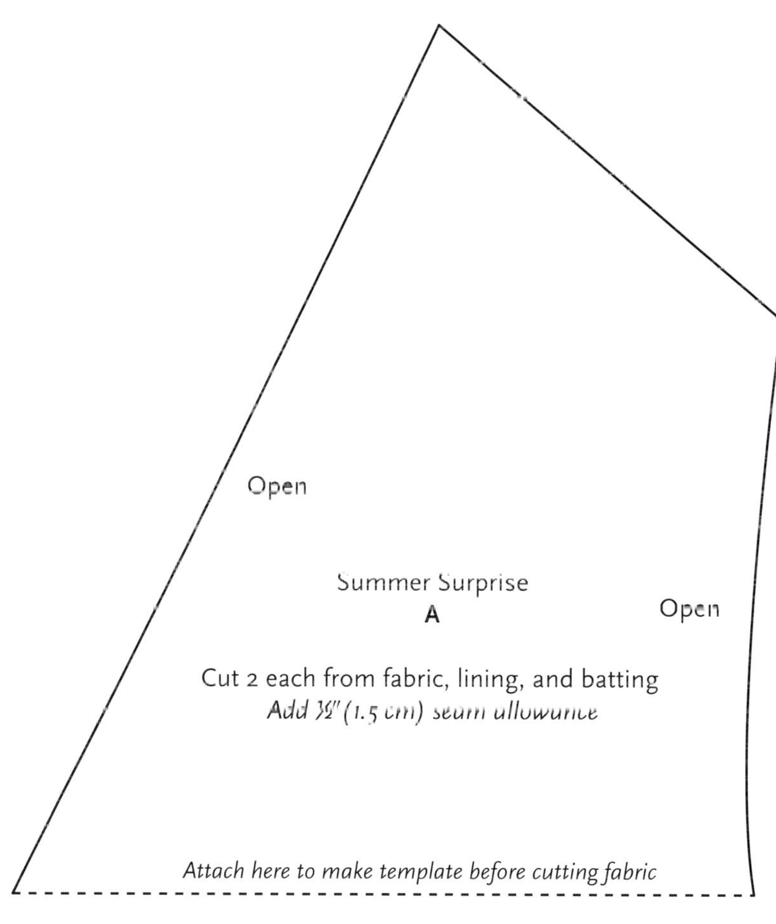

Summer Surprise

continued

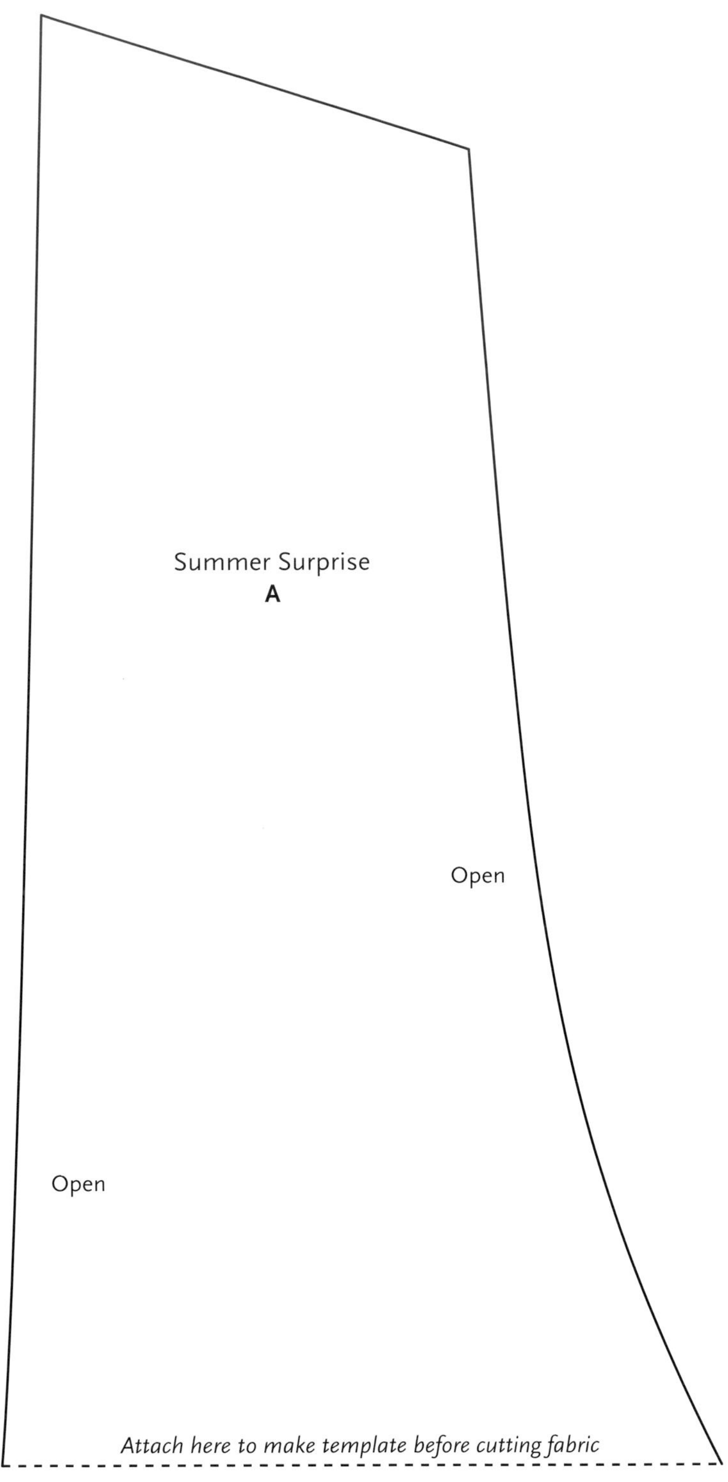

Summer Surprise

continued

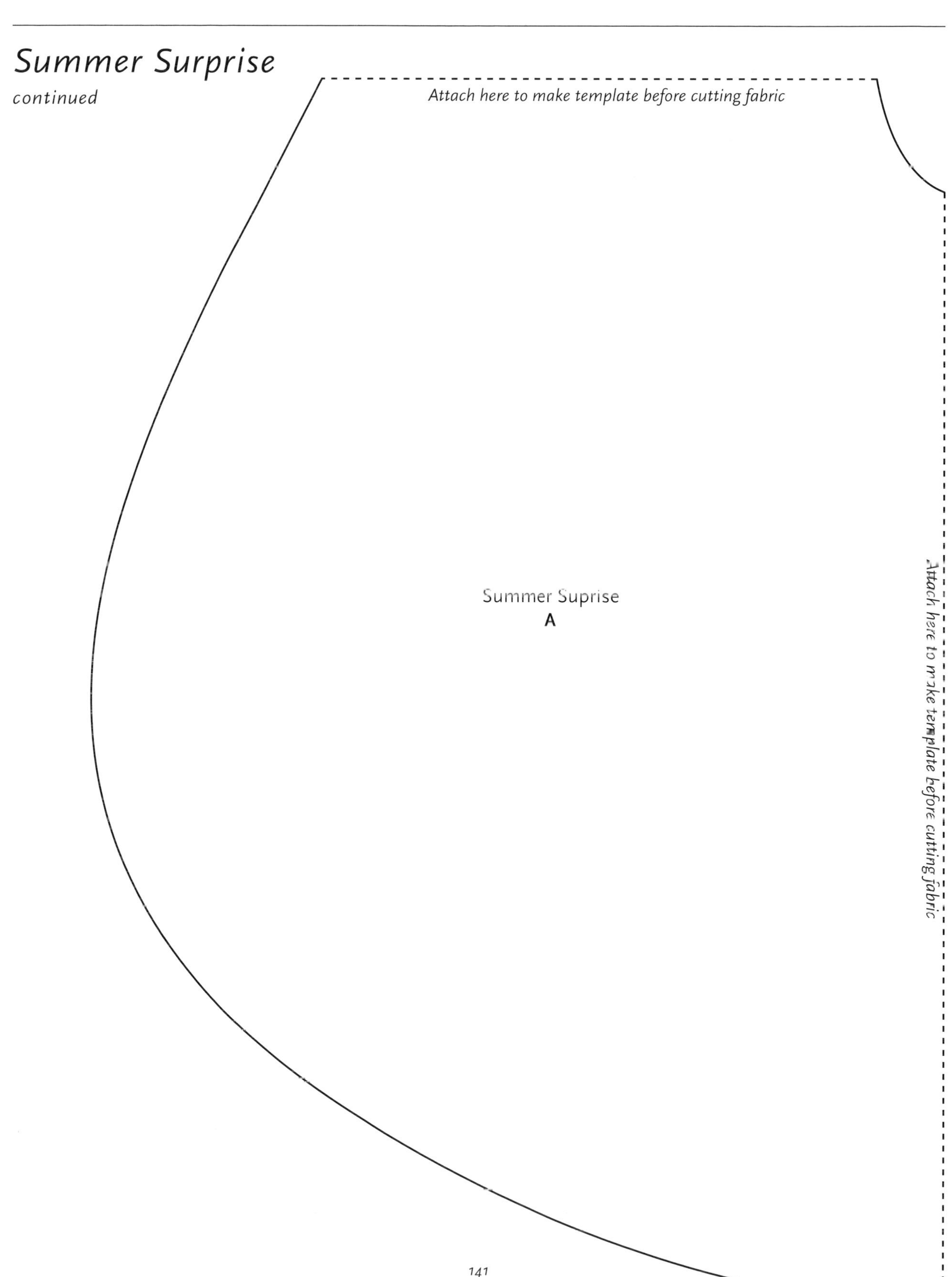

Summer Surprise

continued

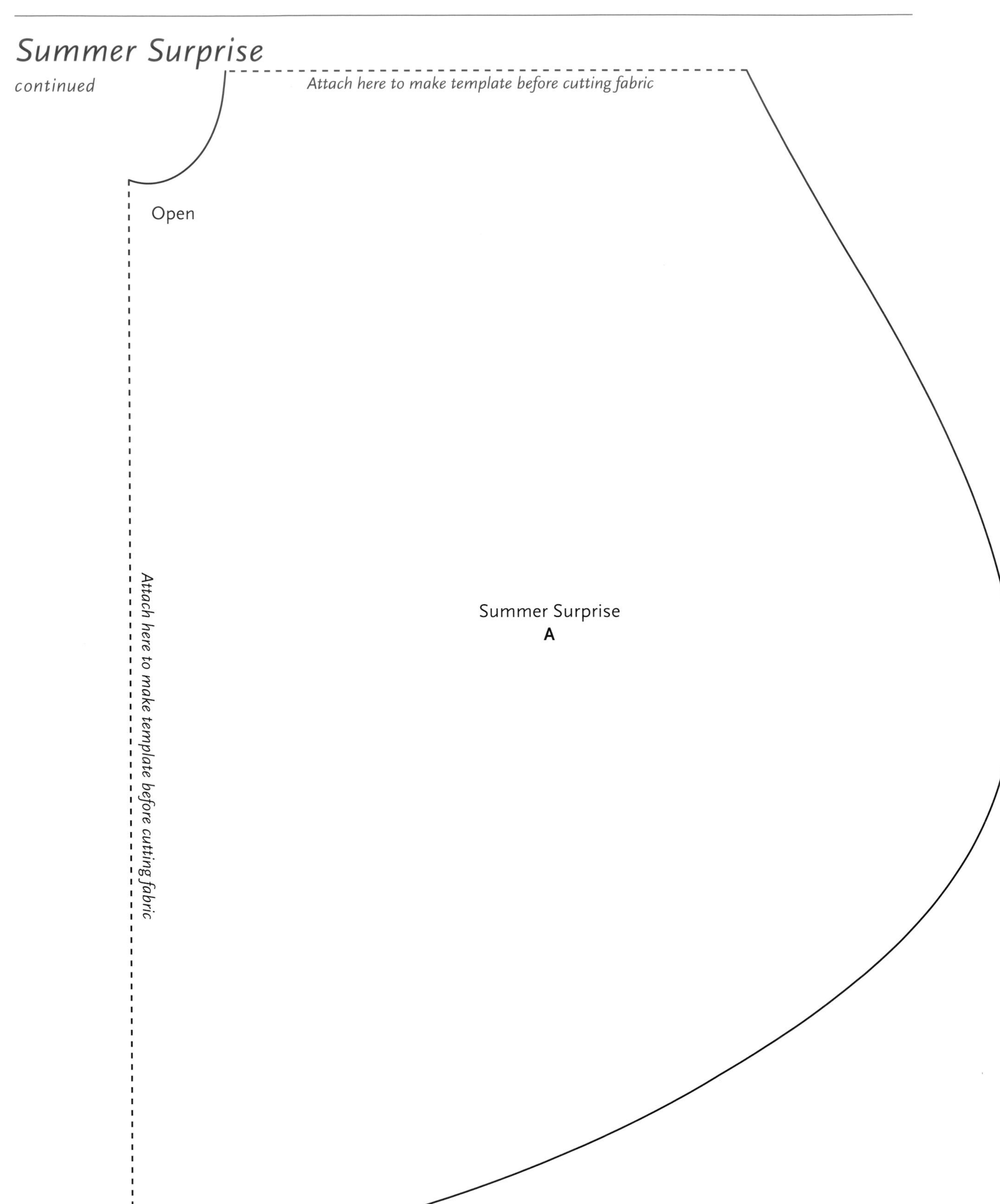

Protea

Add ⅛" (0.4 cm) seam allowance unless otherwise indicated

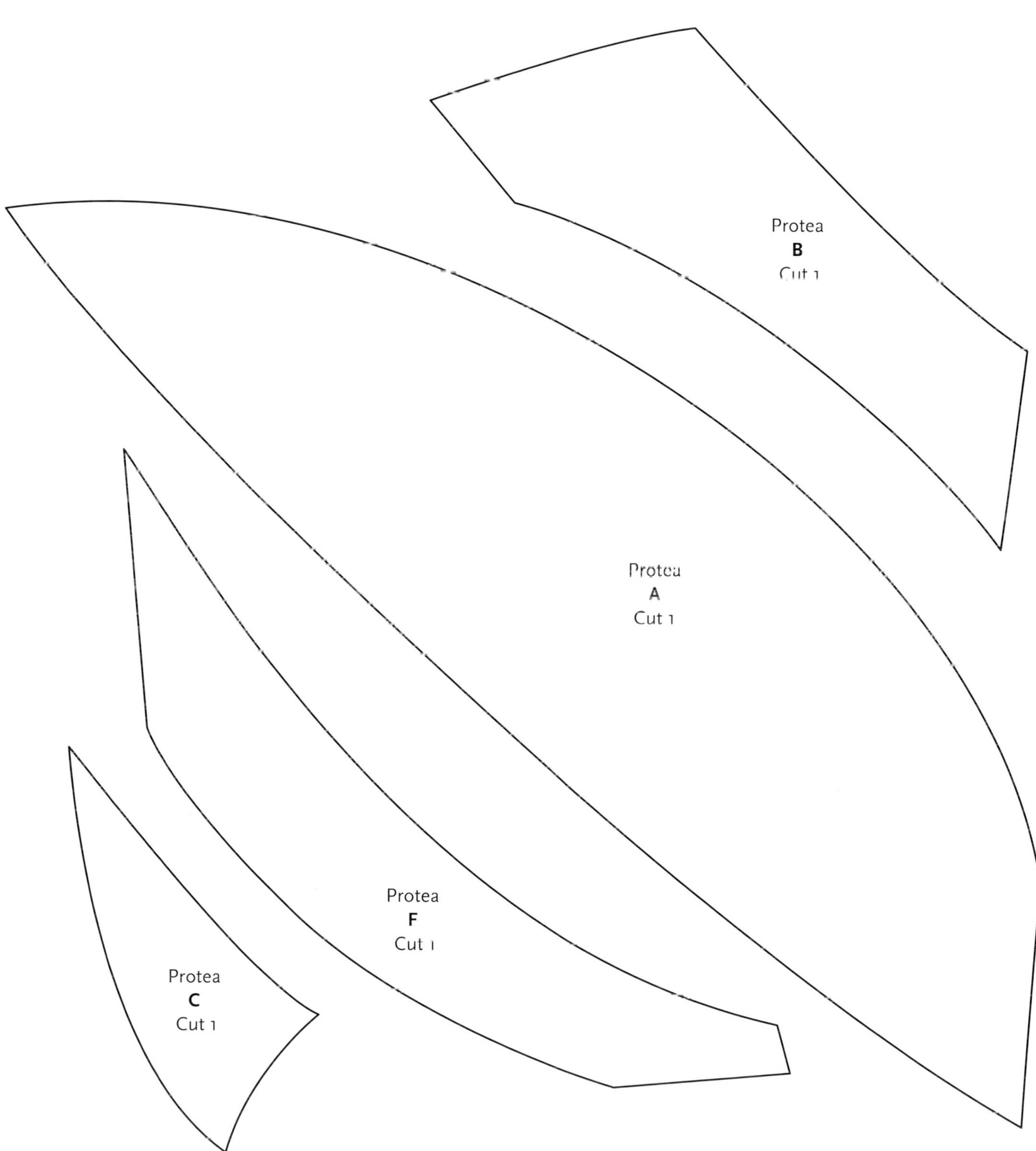

Protea

continued

Add ⅛″ (0.4 cm) seam allowance unless otherwise indicated

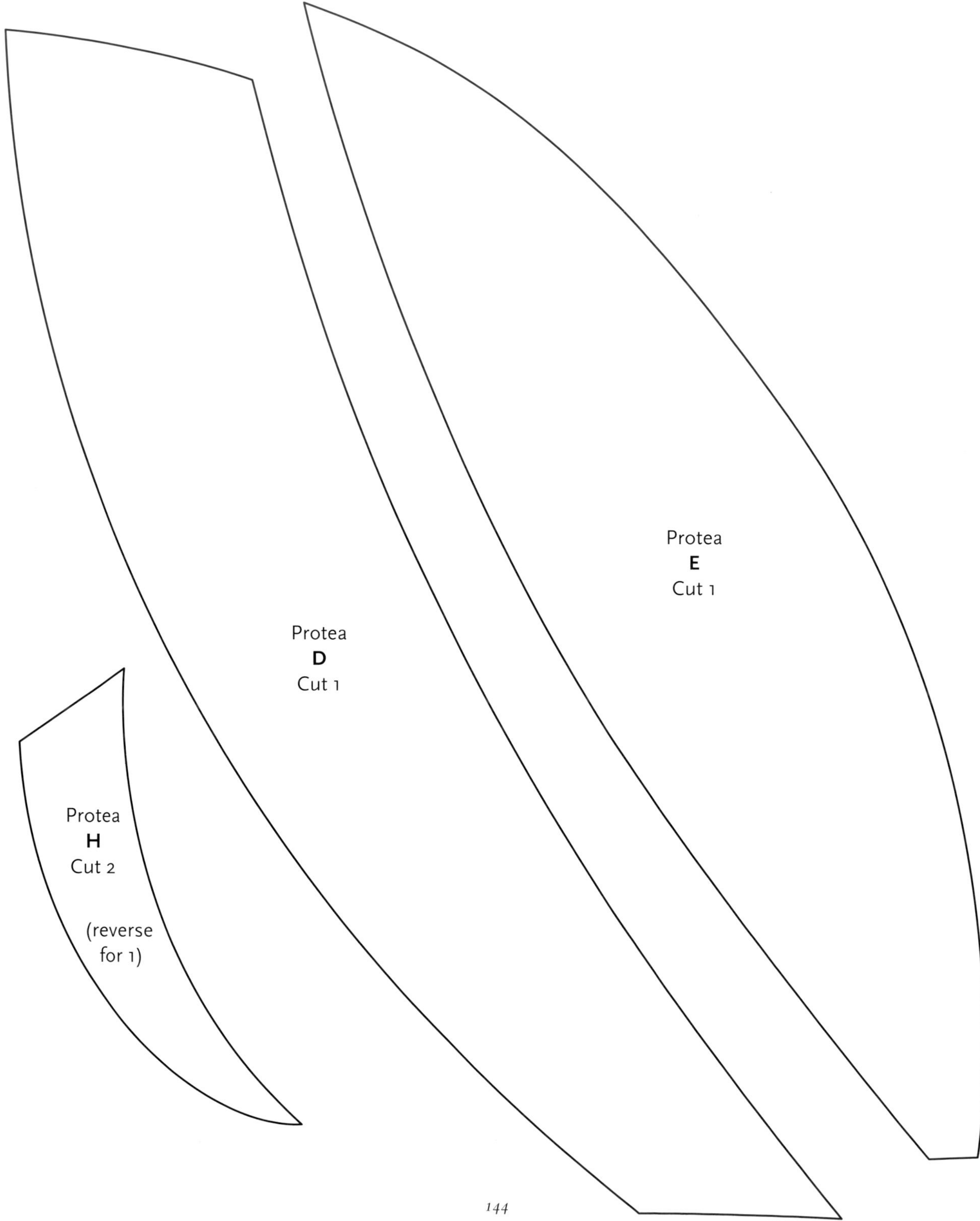

Protea

continued

Add ⅛″ (0.4 cm) seam allowance unless otherwise indicated

Protea
I
Cut 1

Protea
J
Cut 1

K
Cut 1

Protea
G
Cut 1

Protea

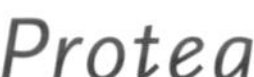

continued

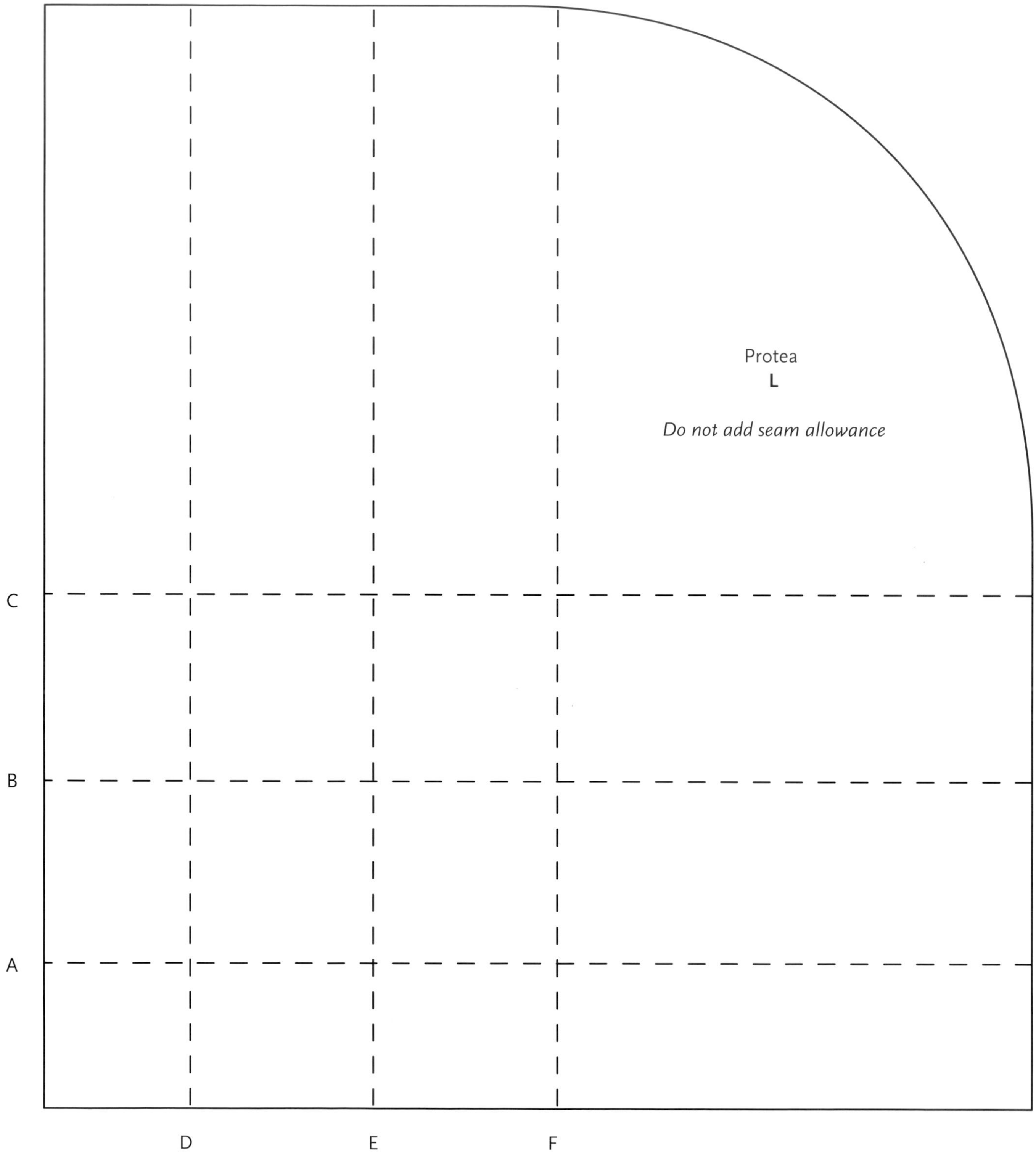
Protea
L
Do not add seam allowance
C
B
A
D
E
F

Lantern Flower

Add ⅛" (0.4 cm) seam allowance unless otherwise indicated

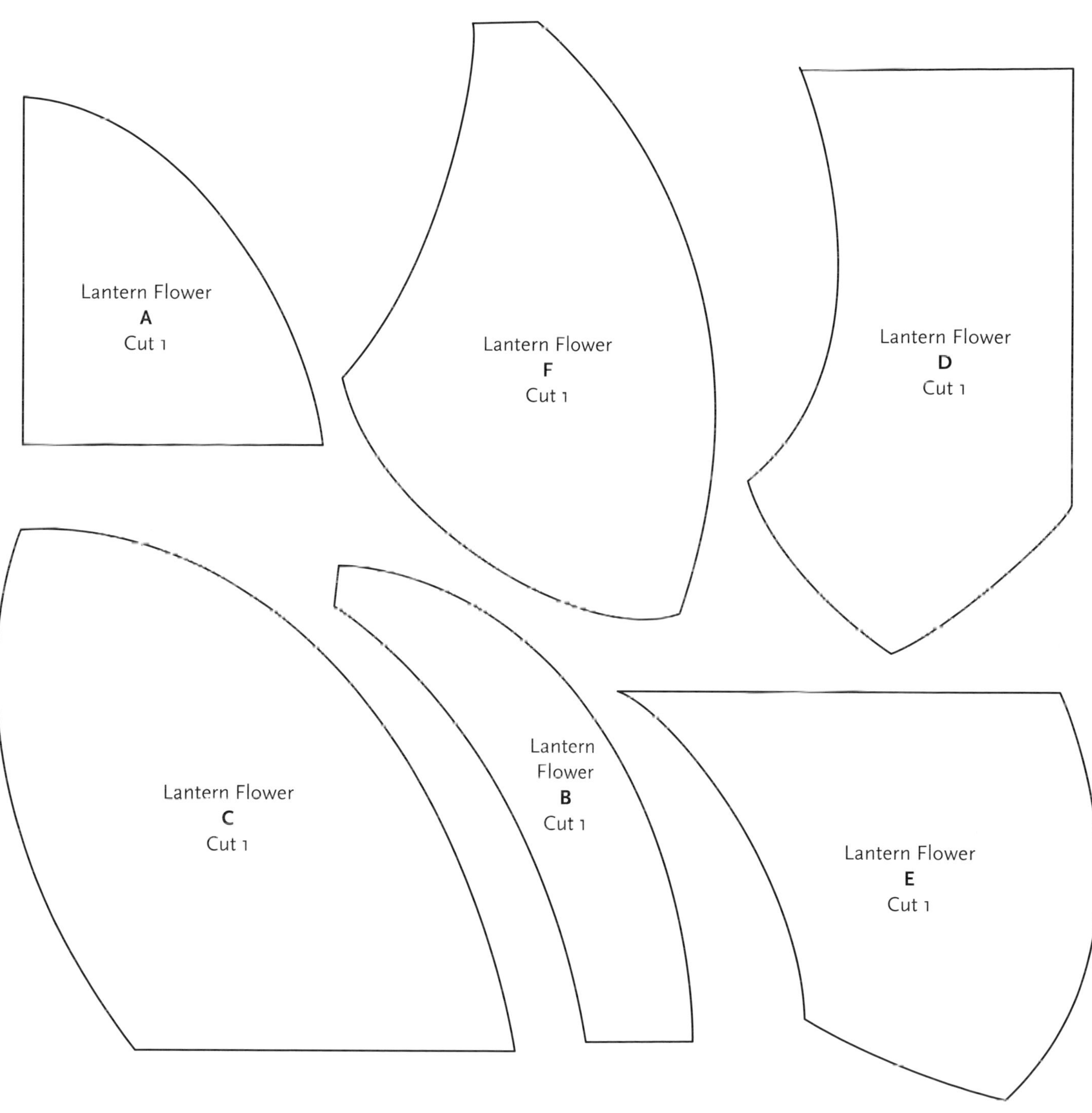

Lantern Flower

continued

Add ⅛" (0.4 cm) seam allowance unless otherwise indicated

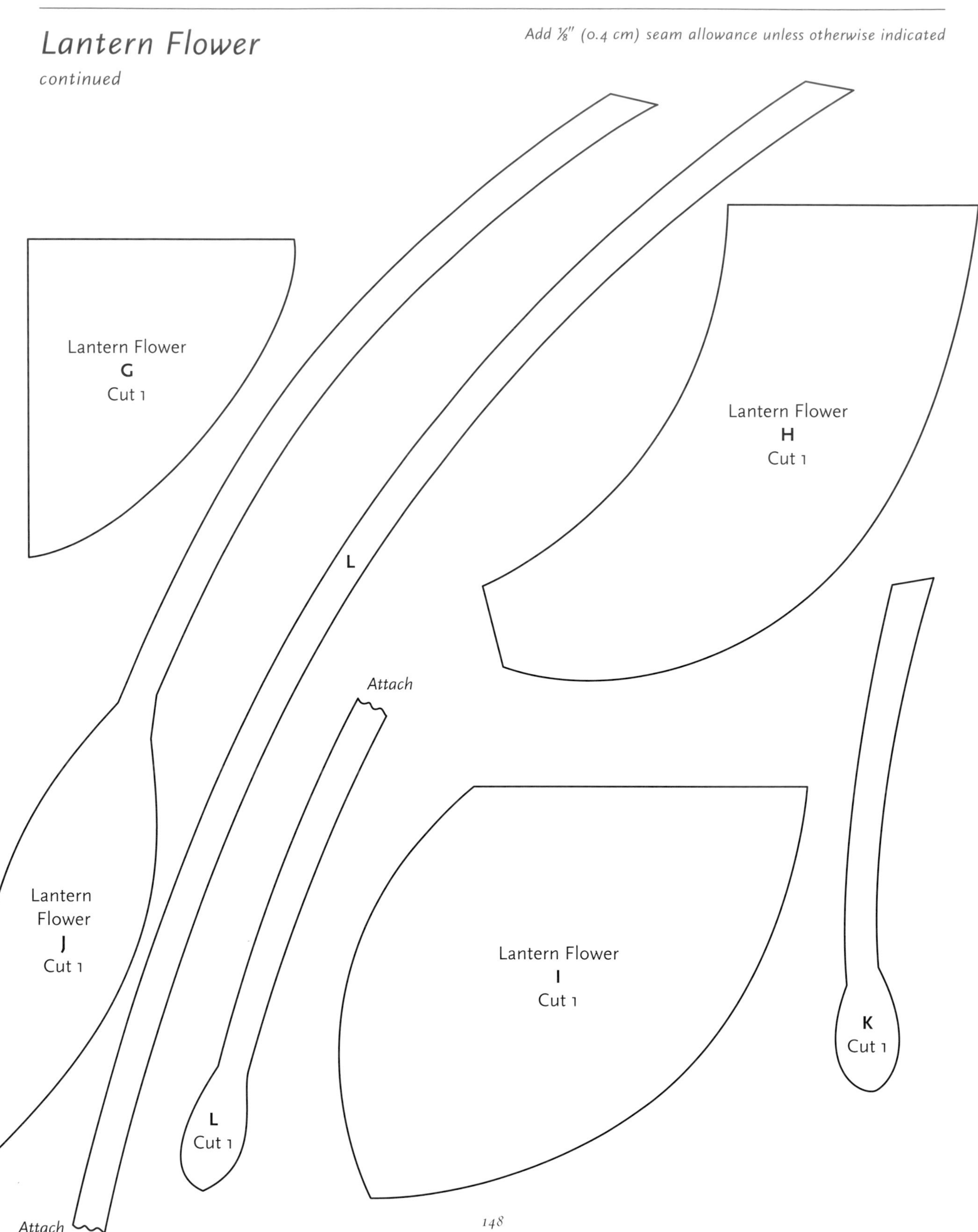

Lantern Flower

continued

Add ⅛" (0.4 cm) seam allowance unless otherwise indicated

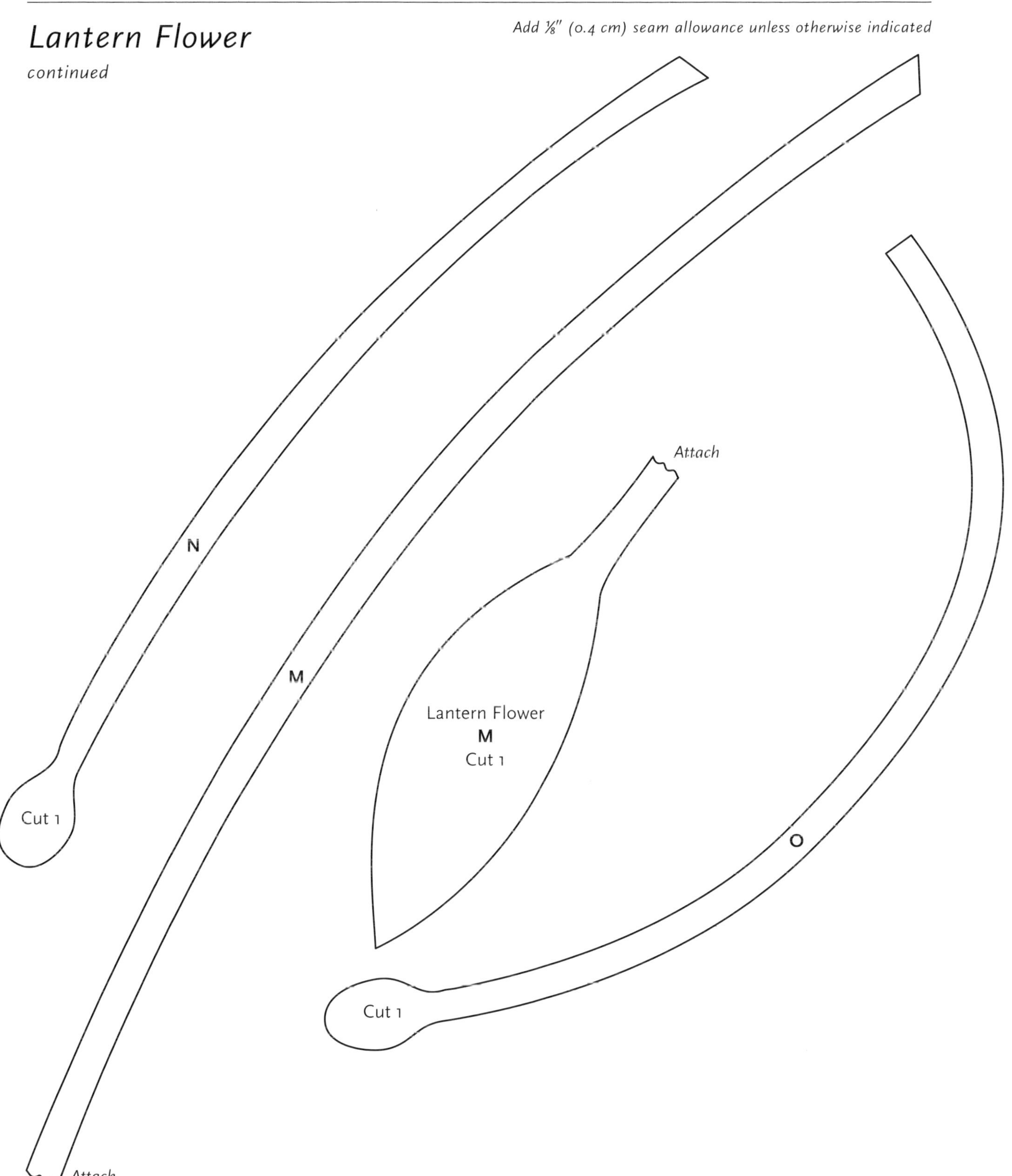

Lantern Flower

continued

Add ⅛" (0.4 cm) seam allowance unless otherwise indicated

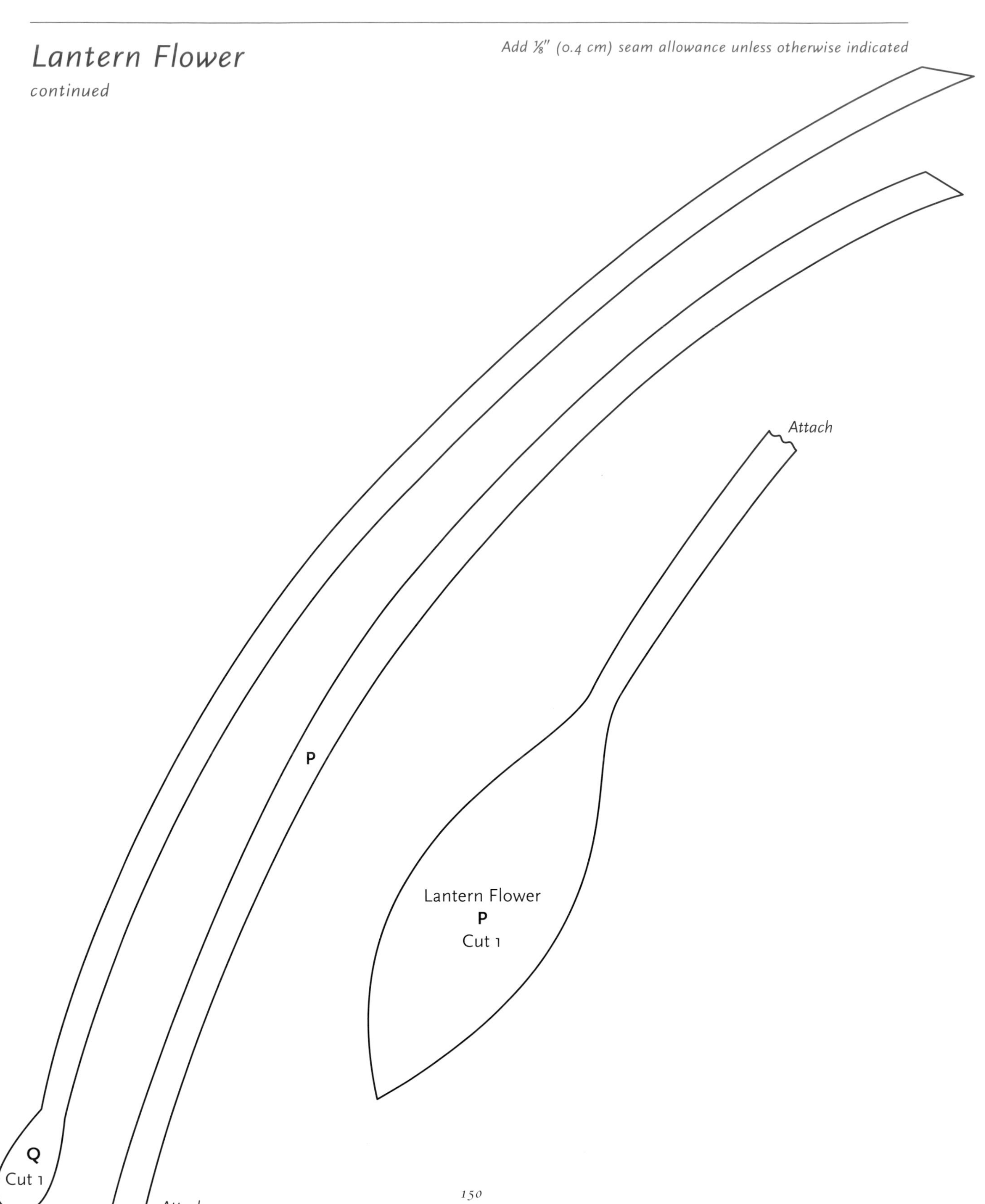

Hozuki

Add ⅛" (0.4 cm) seam allowance unless otherwise indicated
Do not add seam allowance to felt pieces

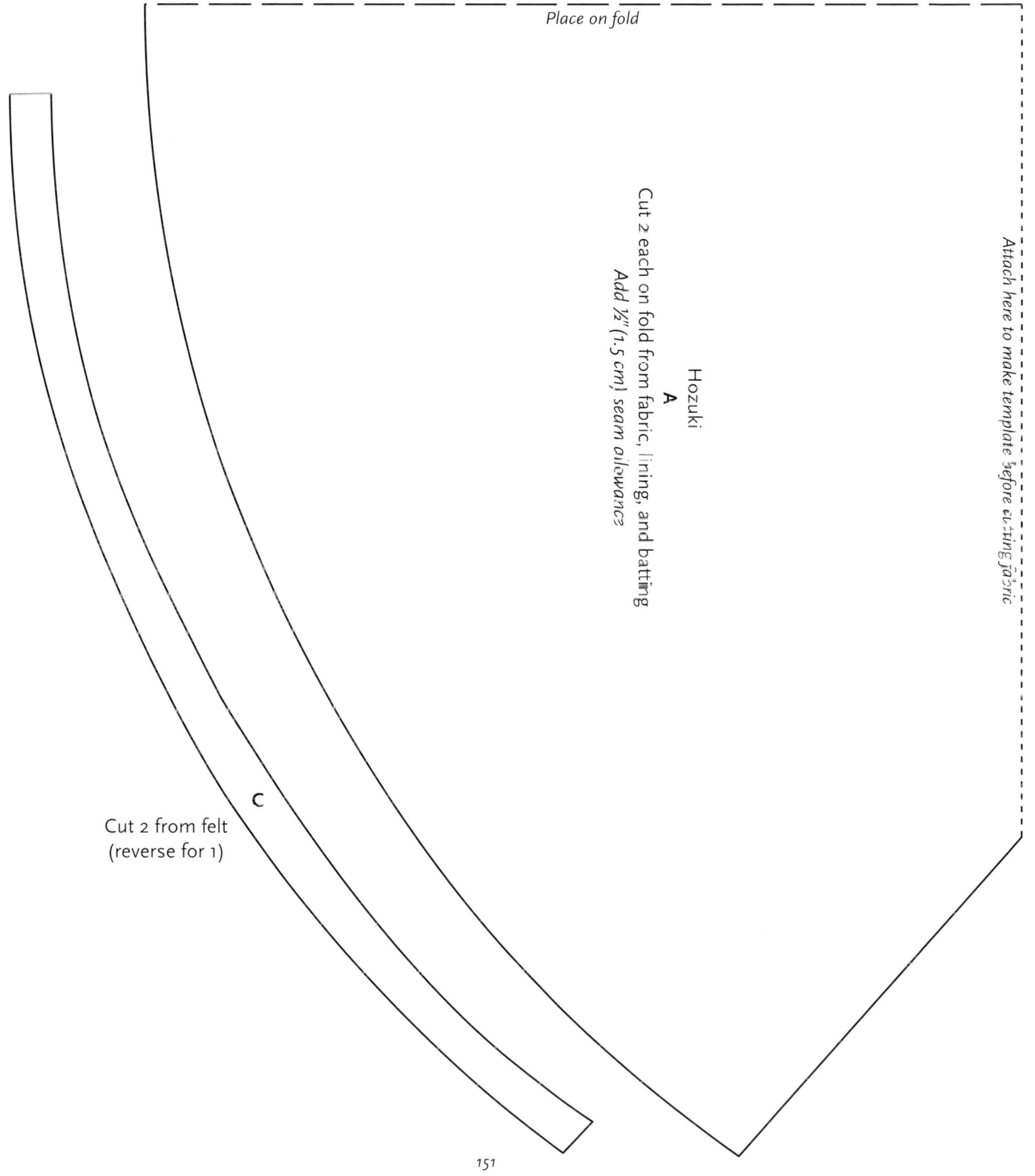

Hozuki
continued

Add ⅛" (0.4 cm) seam allowance unless otherwise indicated
Do not add seam allowance to felt pieces

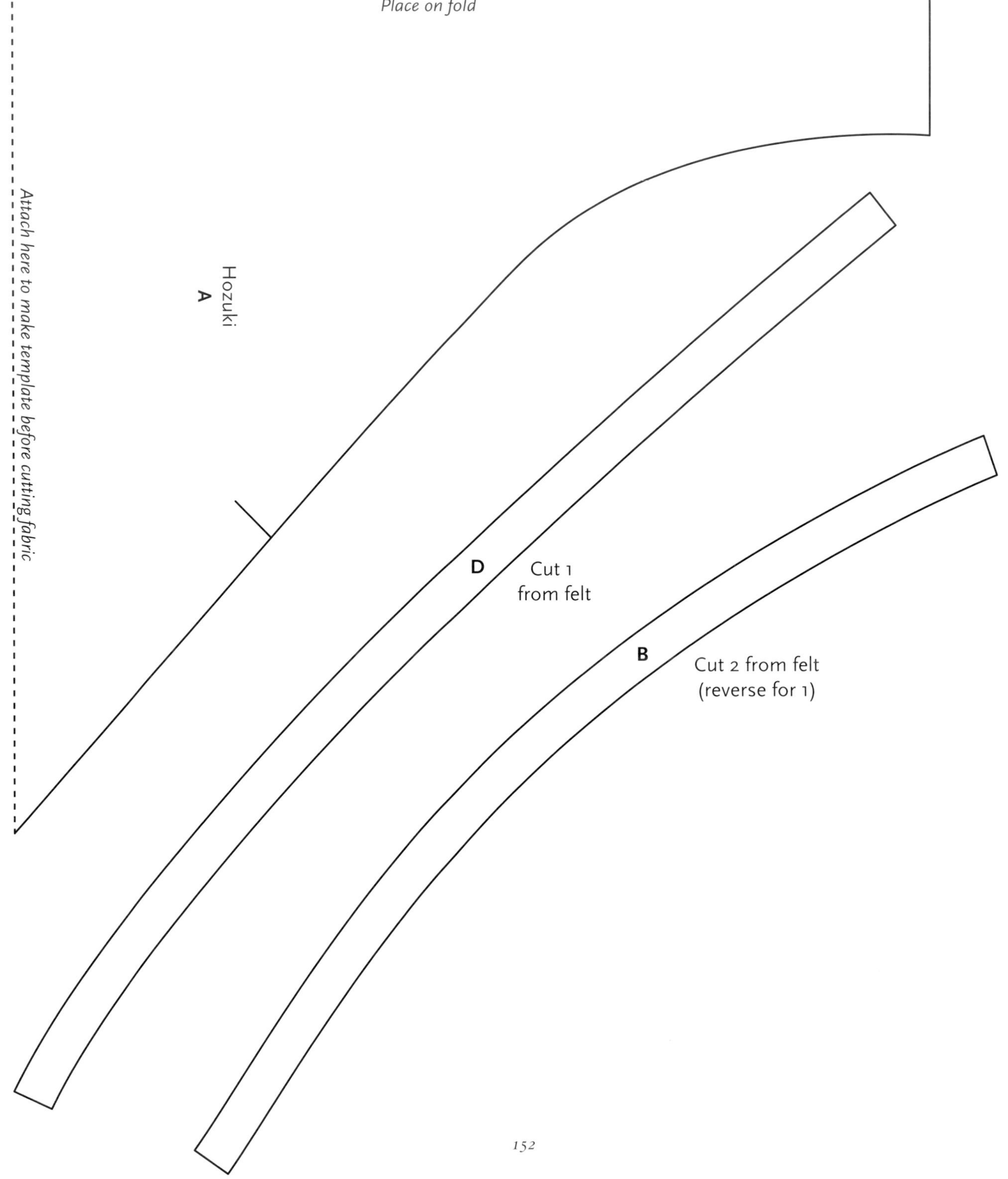

Add ⅛" (0.4 cm) seam allowance unless otherwise indicated
Do not add seam allowance to felt pieces

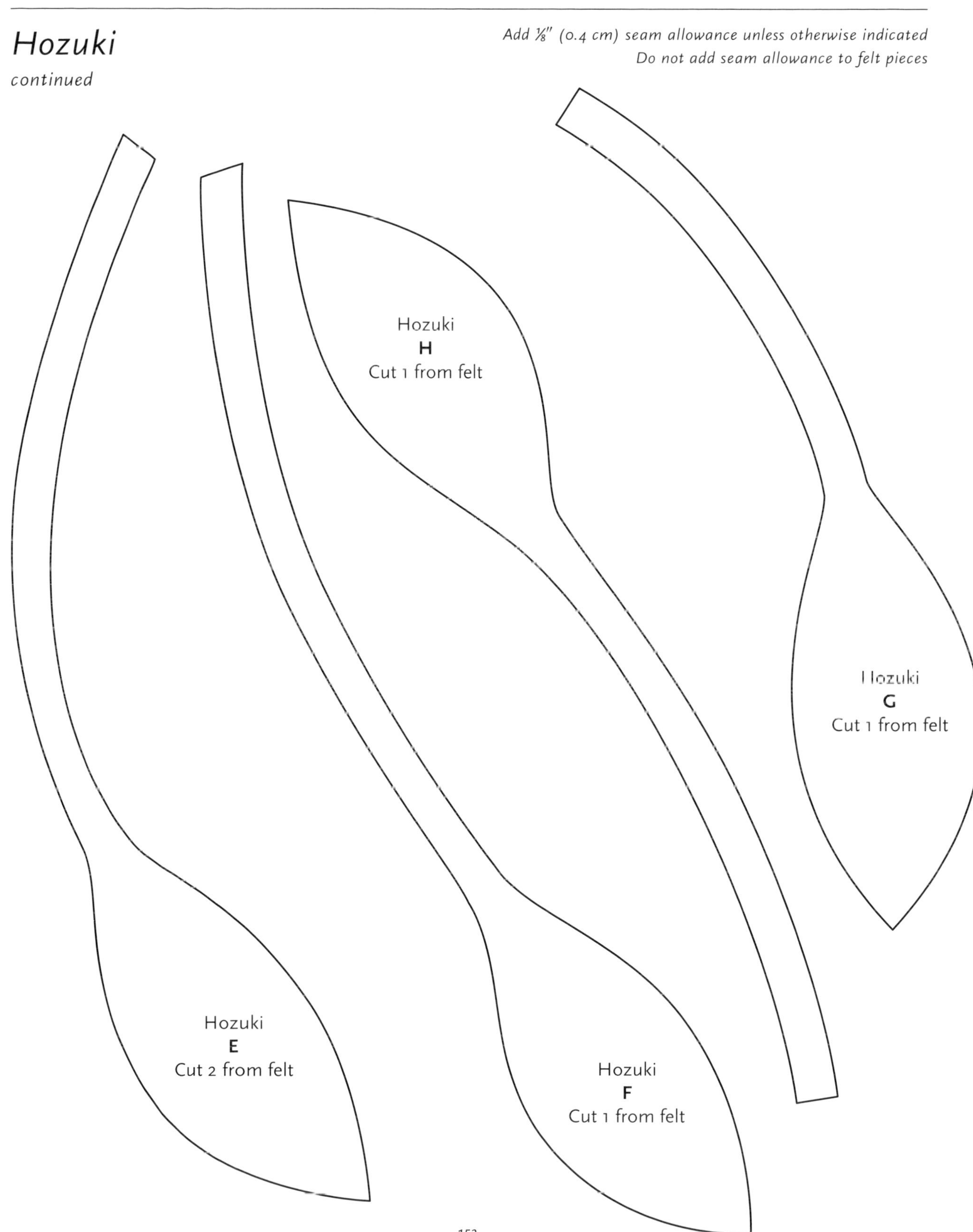

Mandarin

Add ⅛" (0.4 cm) seam allowance unless otherwise indicated
Do not add seam allowance to batting pieces

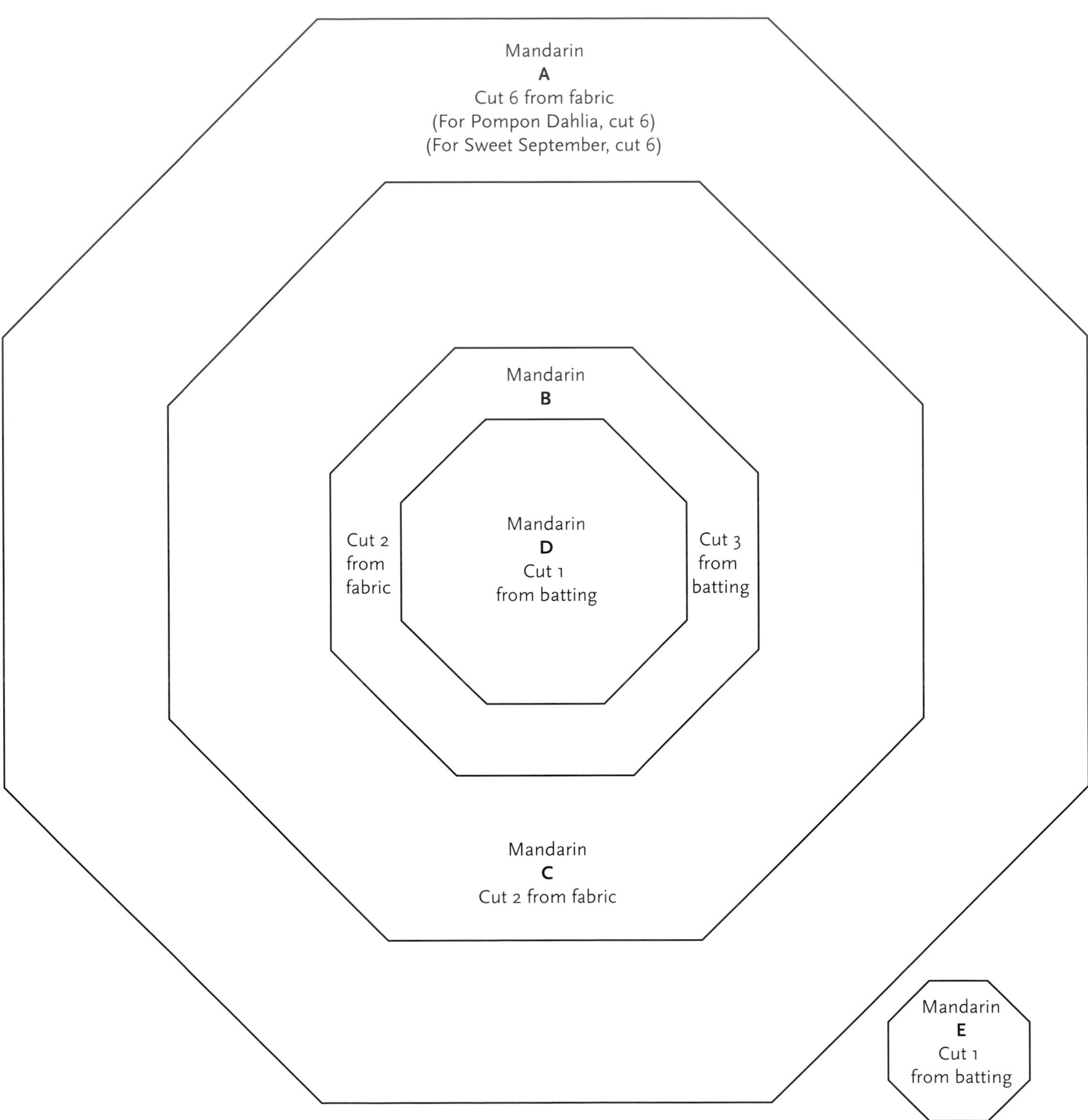

Sweet September

Add ⅛" (0.4 cm) seam allowance unless otherwise indicated
Do not add seam allowance to felt pieces

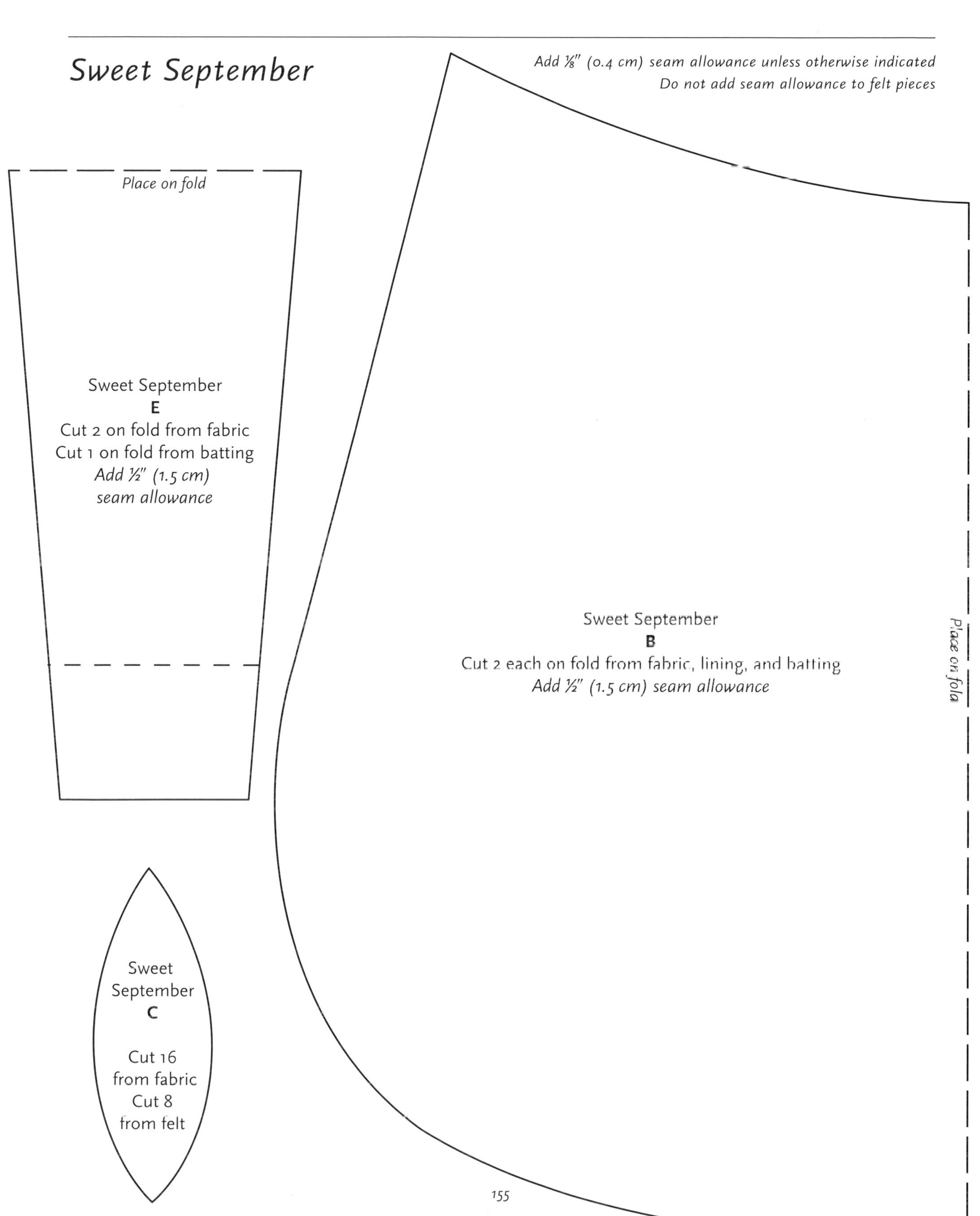

Sweet September continued/ *Pompon Dahlia*

Add ⅛" (0.4 cm) seam allowance unless otherwise indicated
Do not add seam allowance to batting pieces

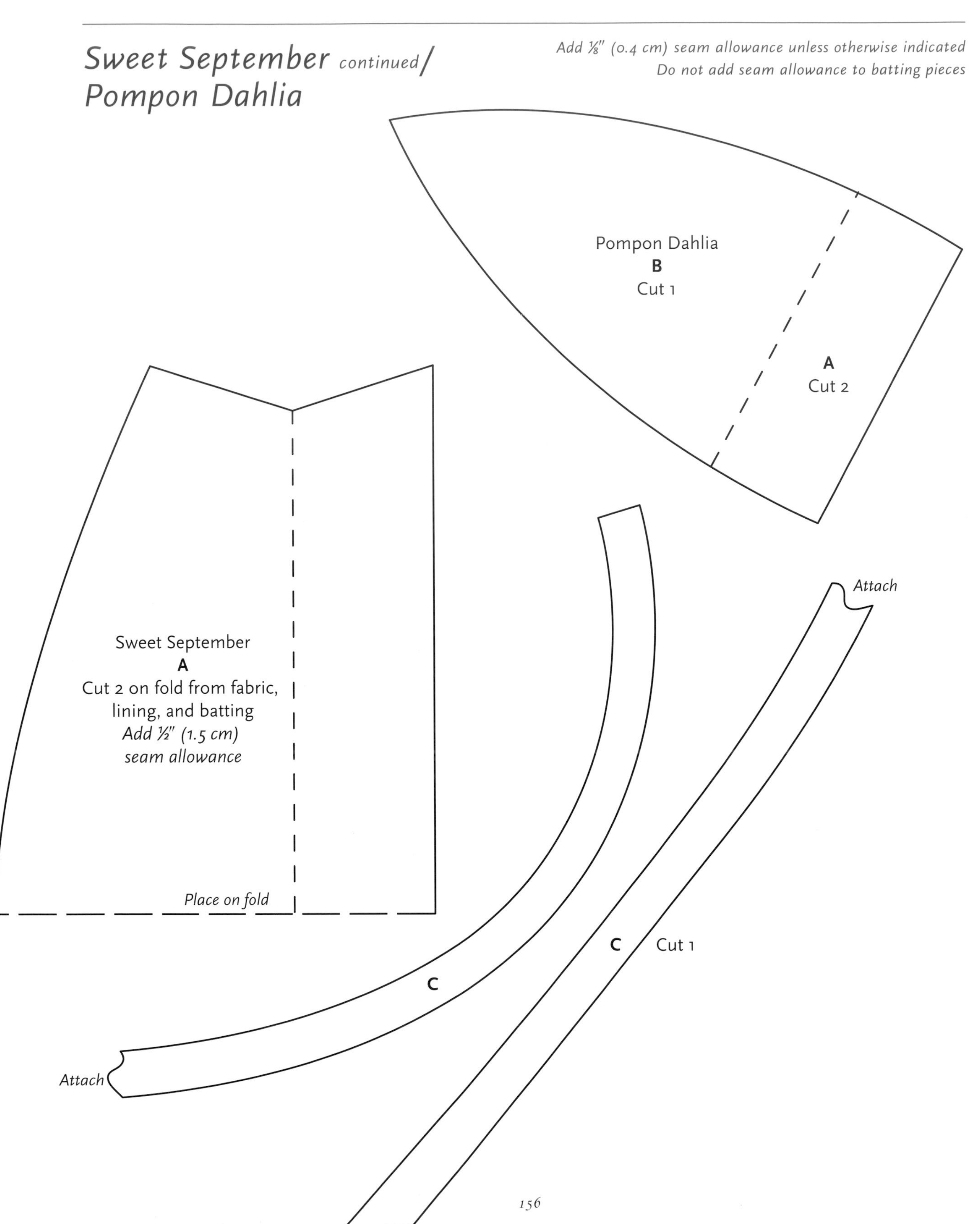

Pompon Dahlia *continued*/ *Vanda*

Add ⅛" (0.4 cm) seam allowance unless otherwise indicated

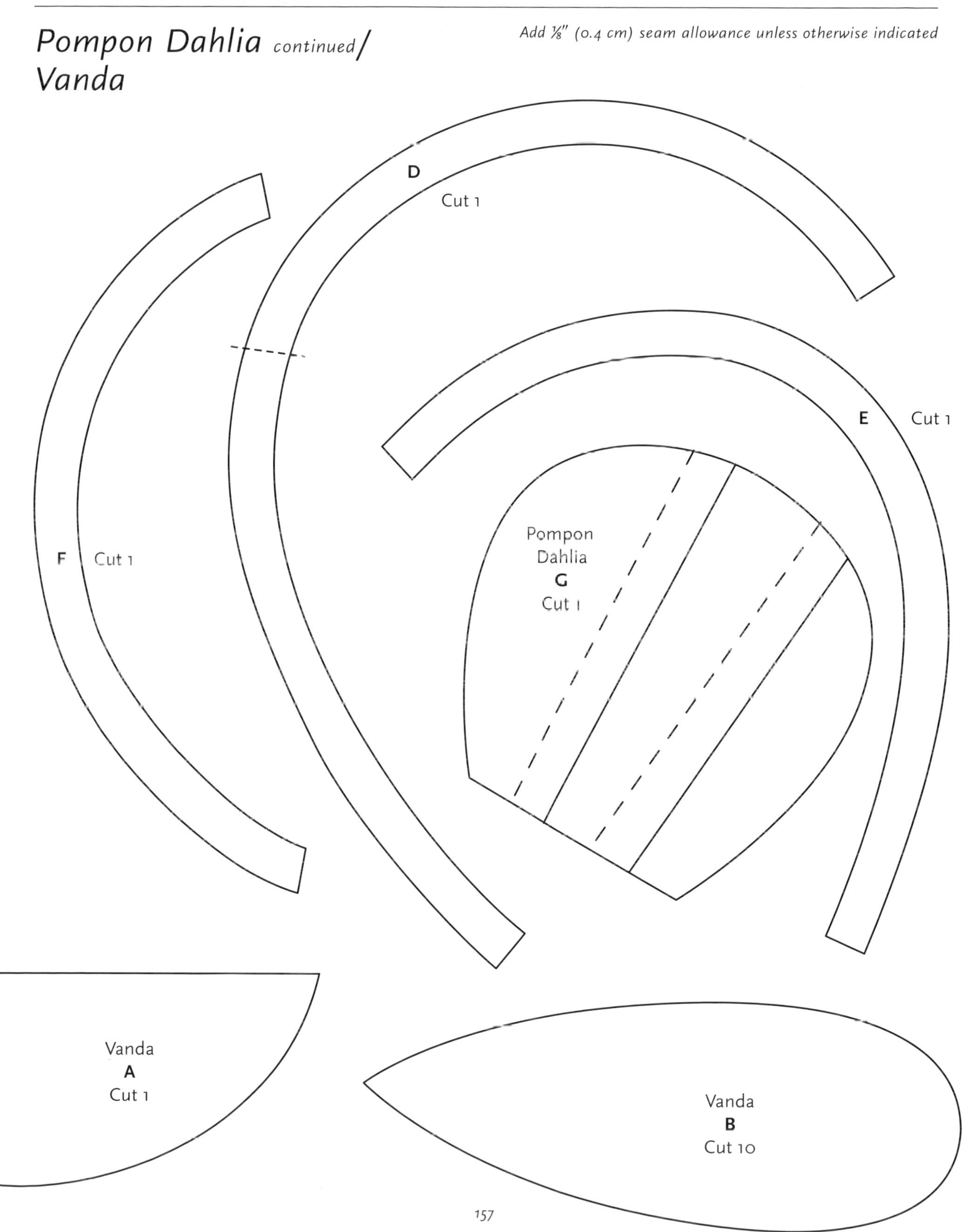

China Aster

Add ⅛" (0.4 cm) seam allowance unless otherwise indicated

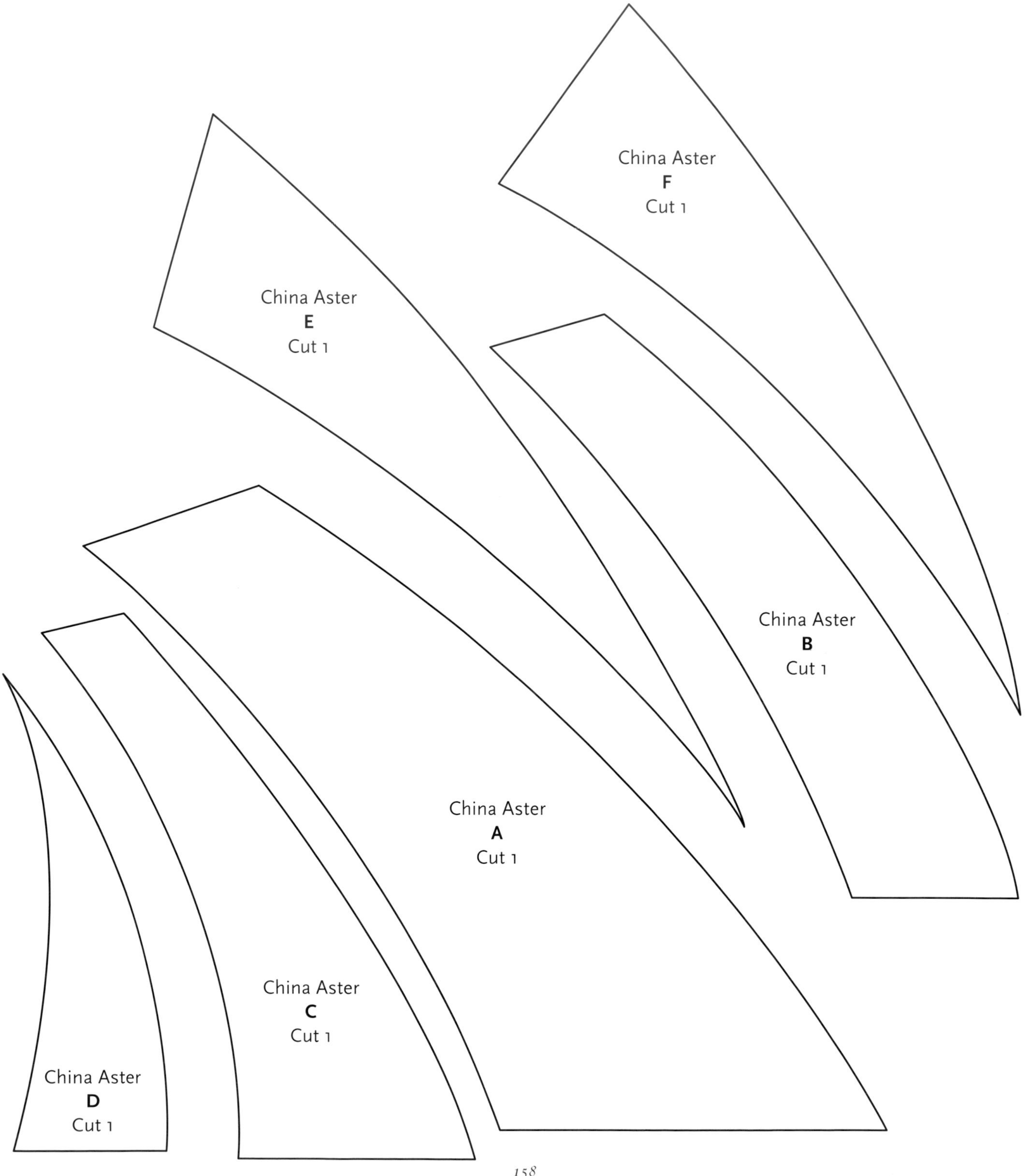

China Aster

continued

Add ⅛" (0.4 cm) seam allowance unless otherwise indicated

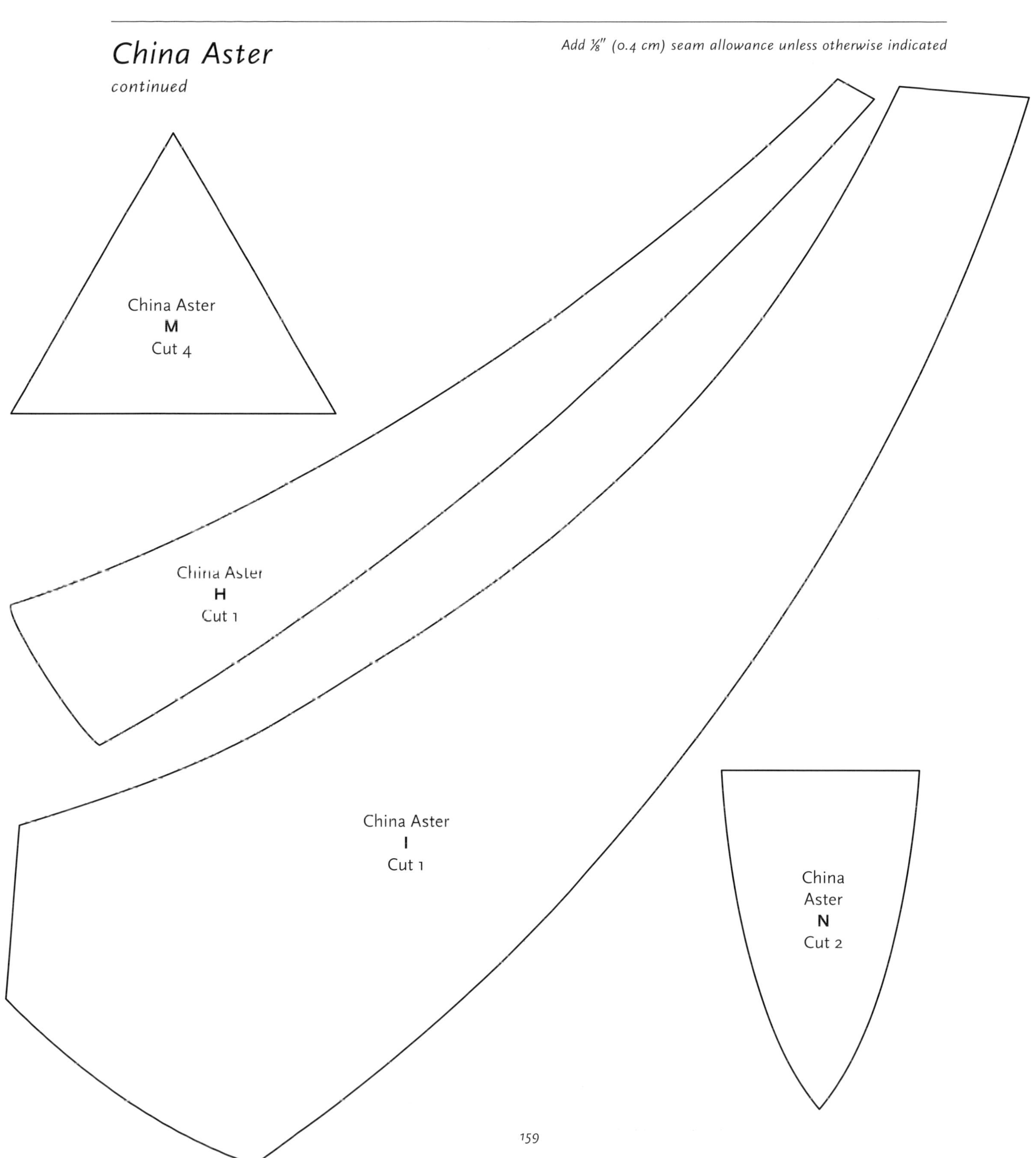

Add ⅛" (0.4 cm) seam allowance unless otherwise indicated

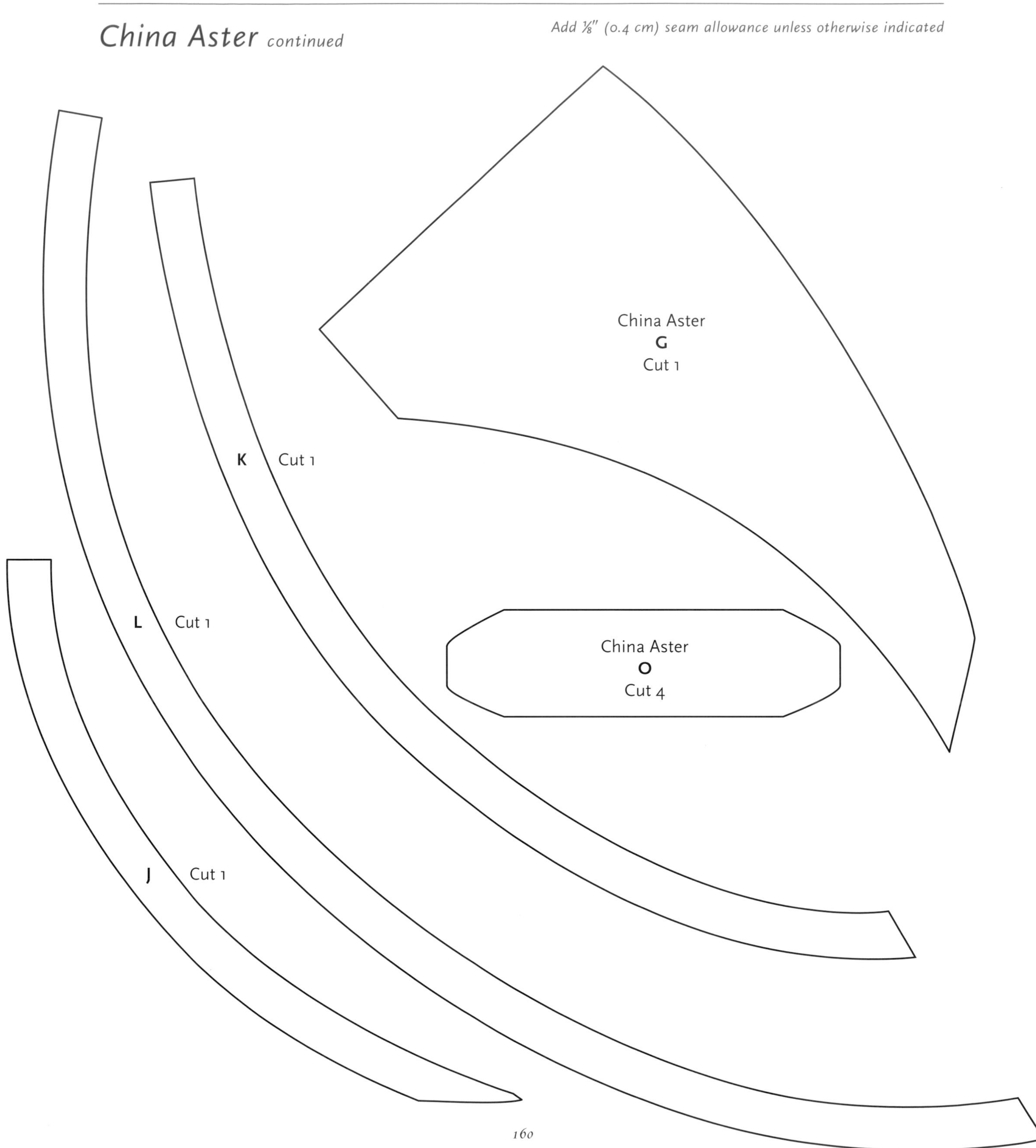

Add ⅛" (0.4 cm) seam allowance unless otherwise indicated

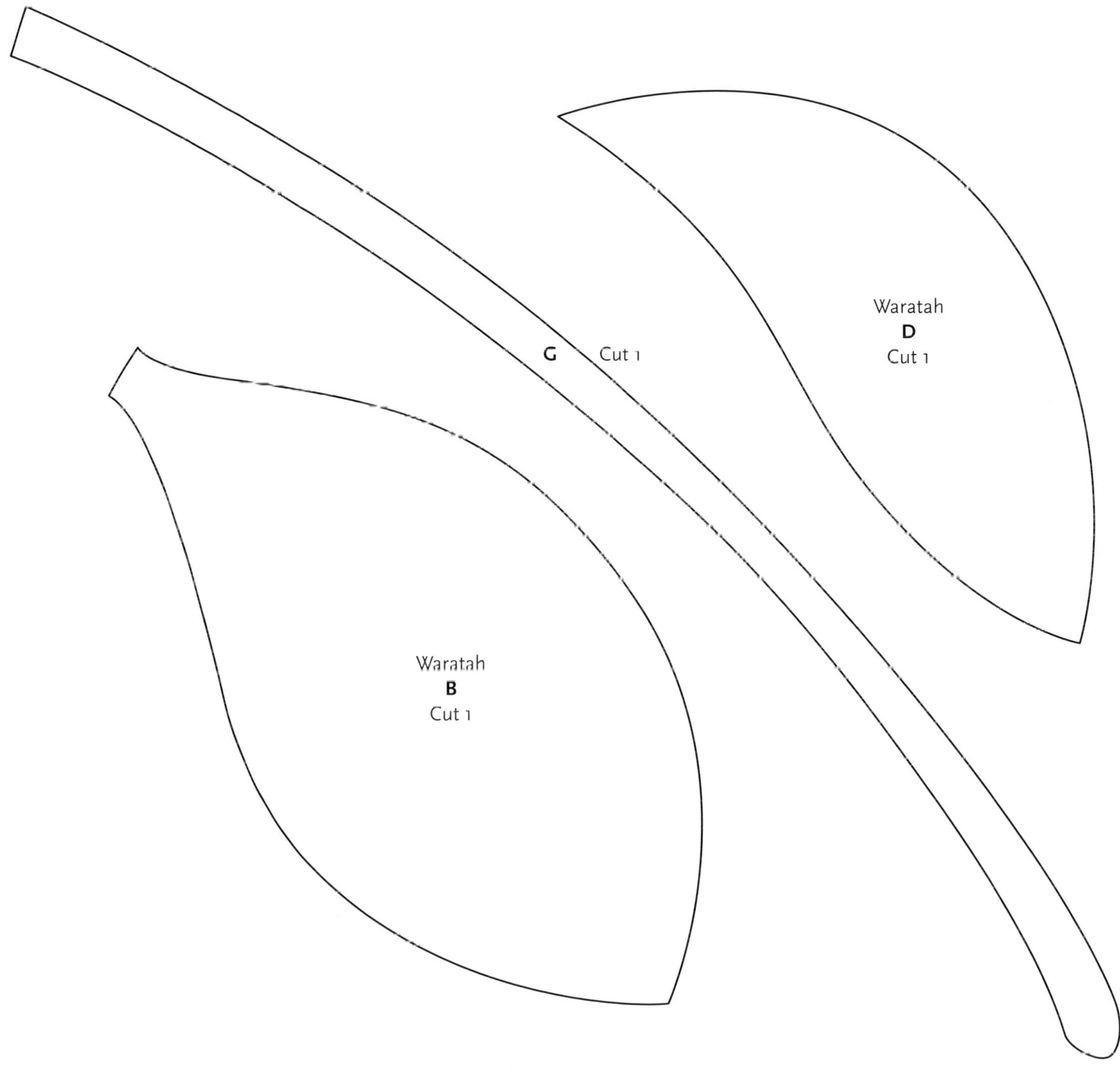

Add ⅛" (0.4 cm) seam allowance unless otherwise indicated

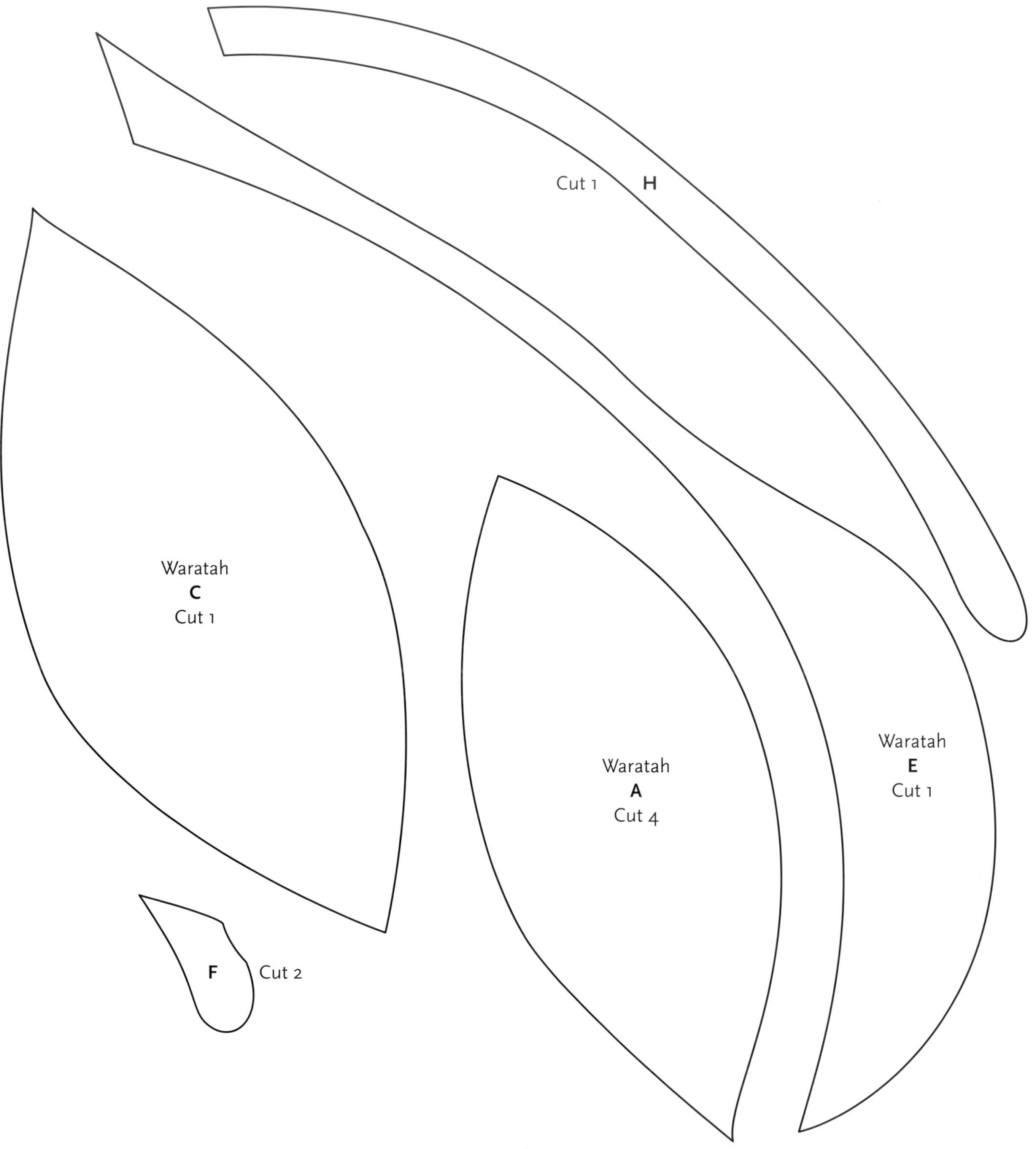

Waratah *continued*/ *Autumn Glory*

Add ⅛" (0.4 cm) seam allowance unless otherwise indicated

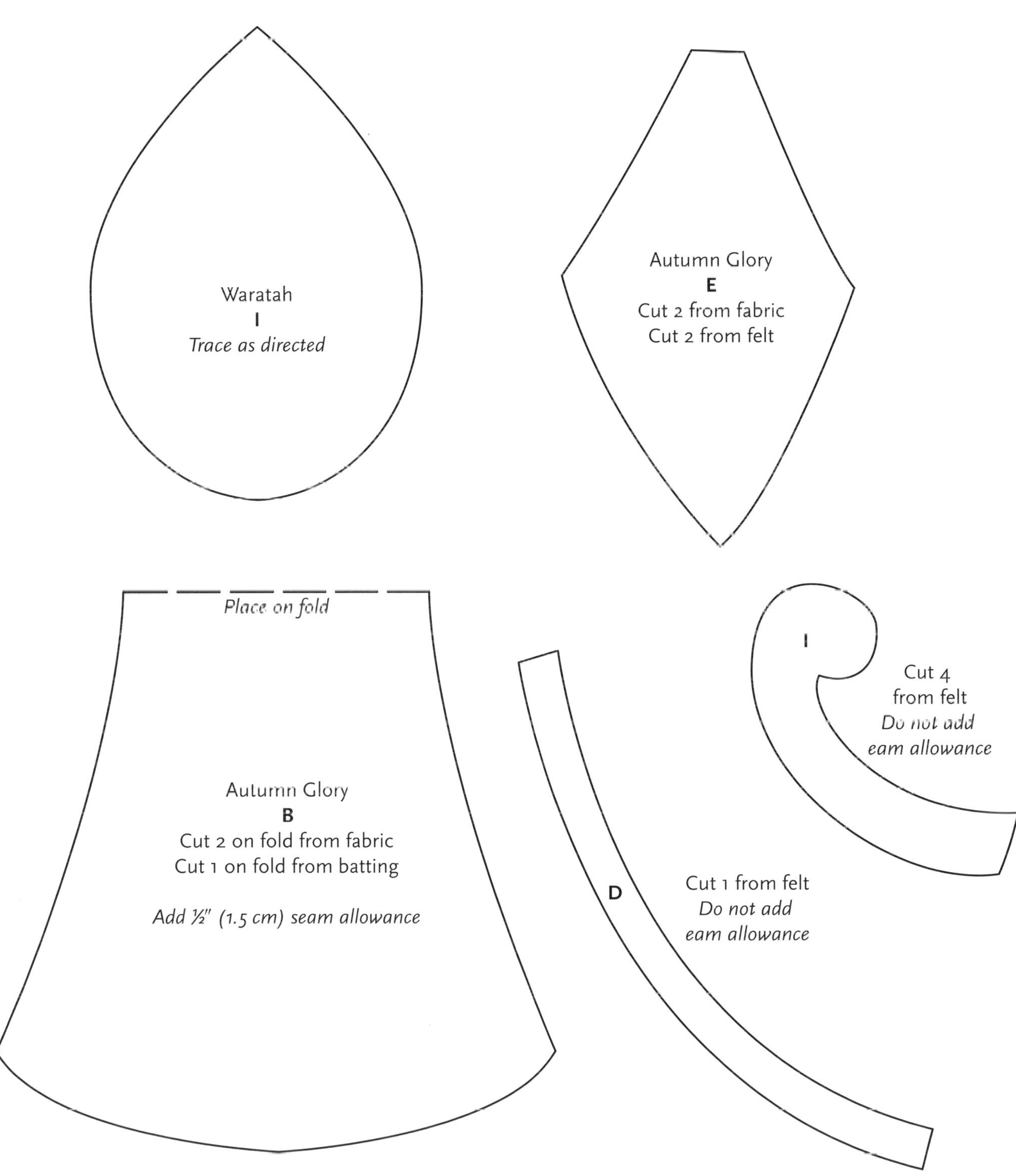

Autumn Glory

continued

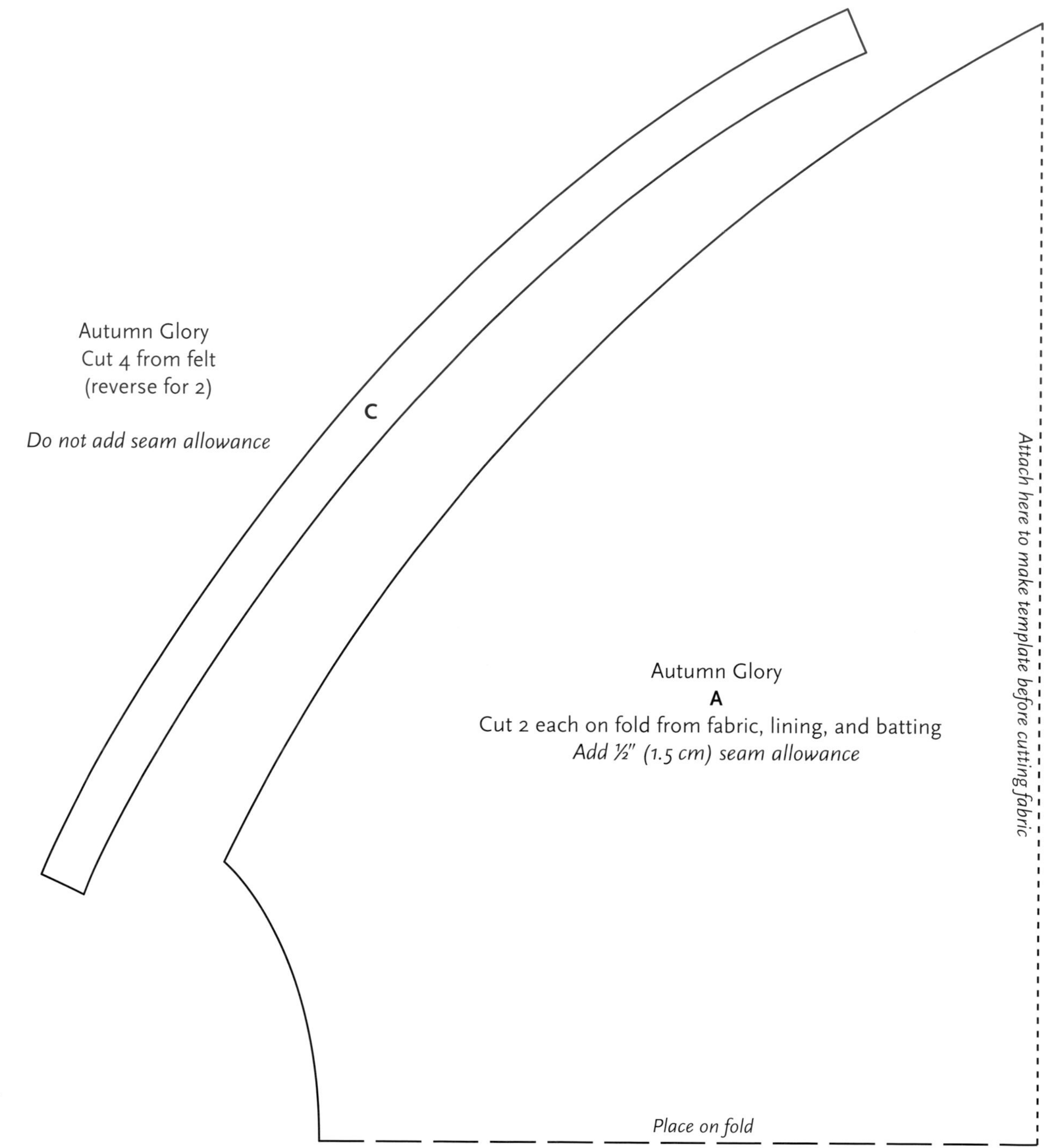

Autumn Glory

continued

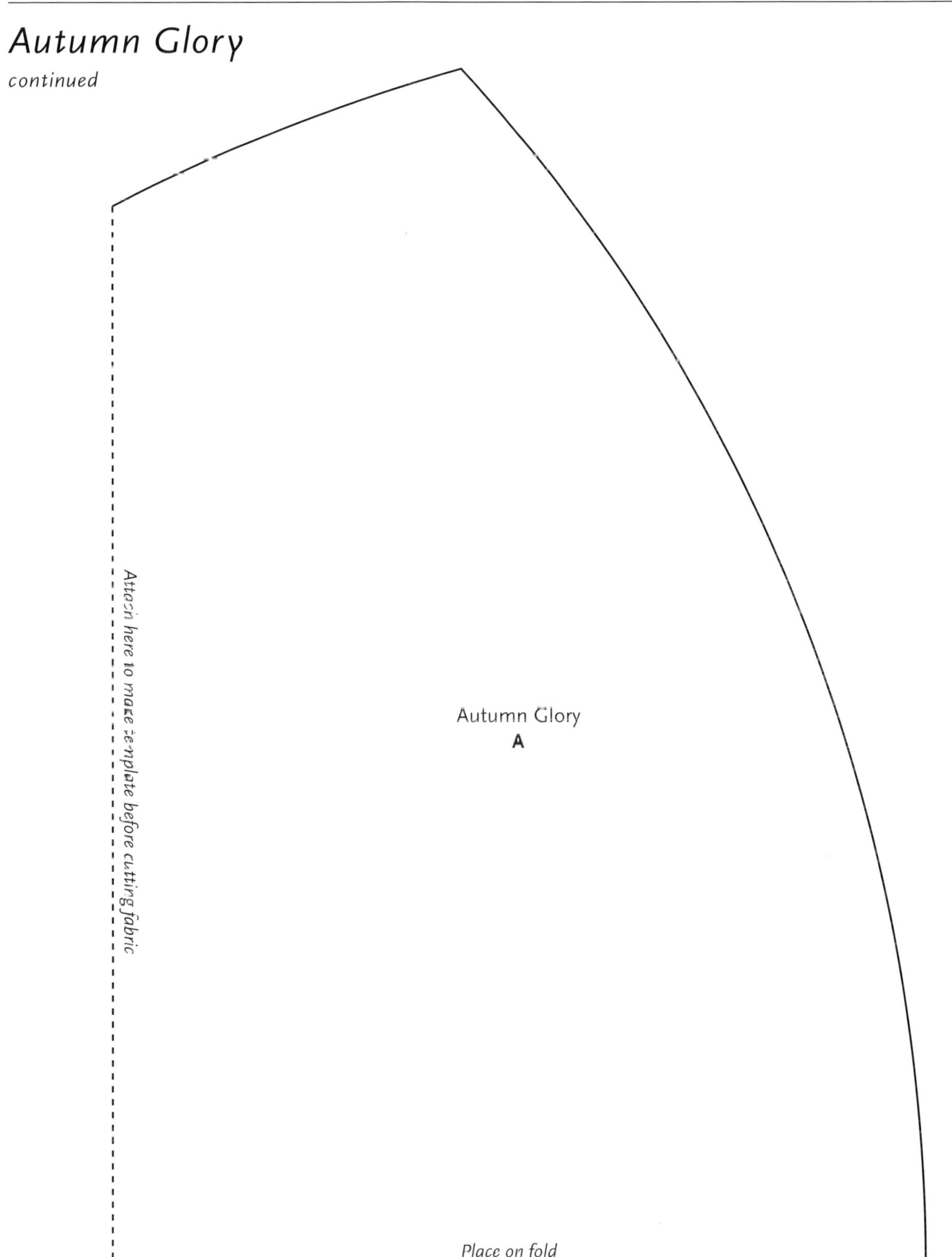

Add ⅛" (0.4 cm) seam allowance unless otherwise indicated

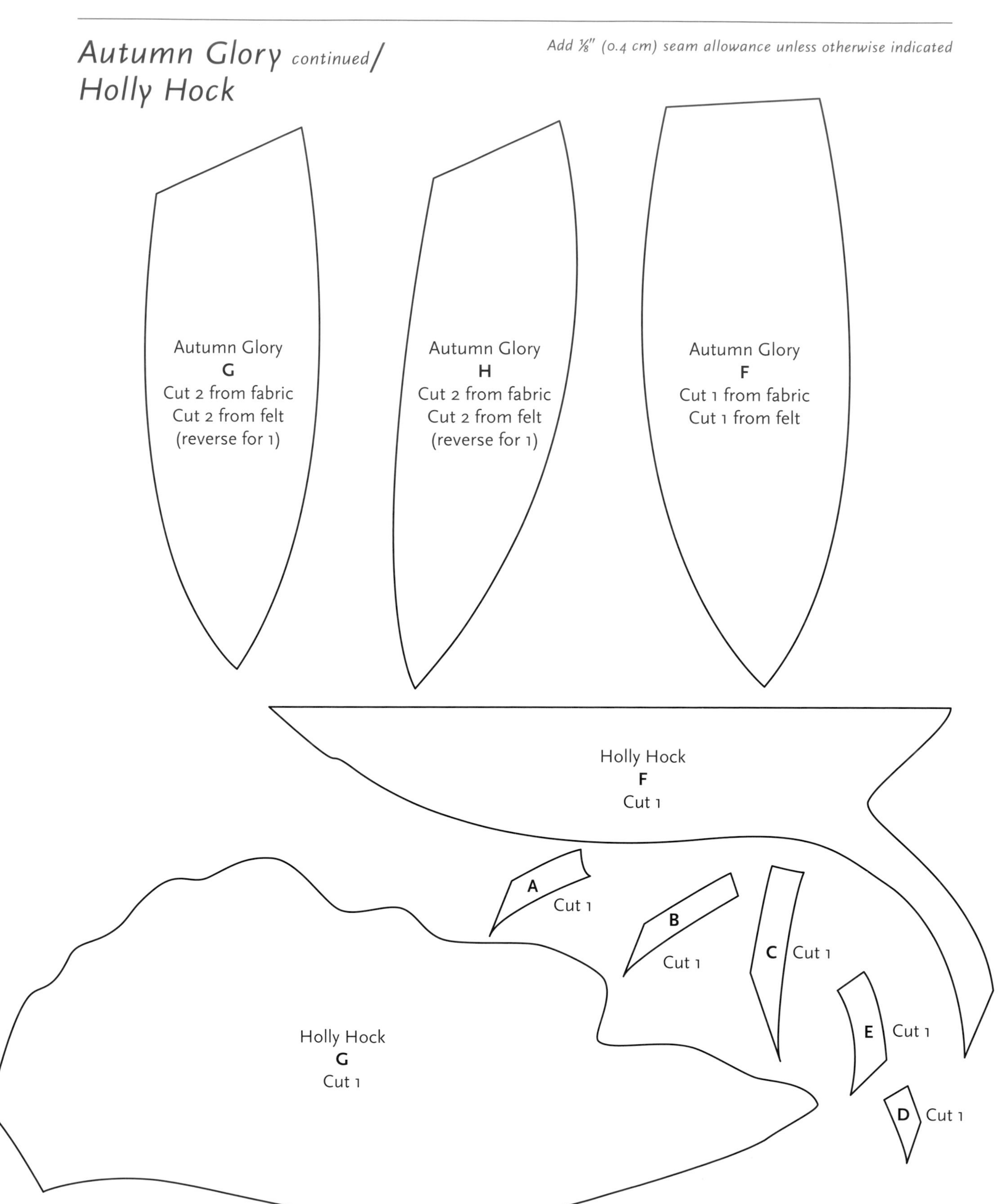

Holly Hock
continued

Add ⅛" (0.4 cm) seam allowance unless otherwise indicated

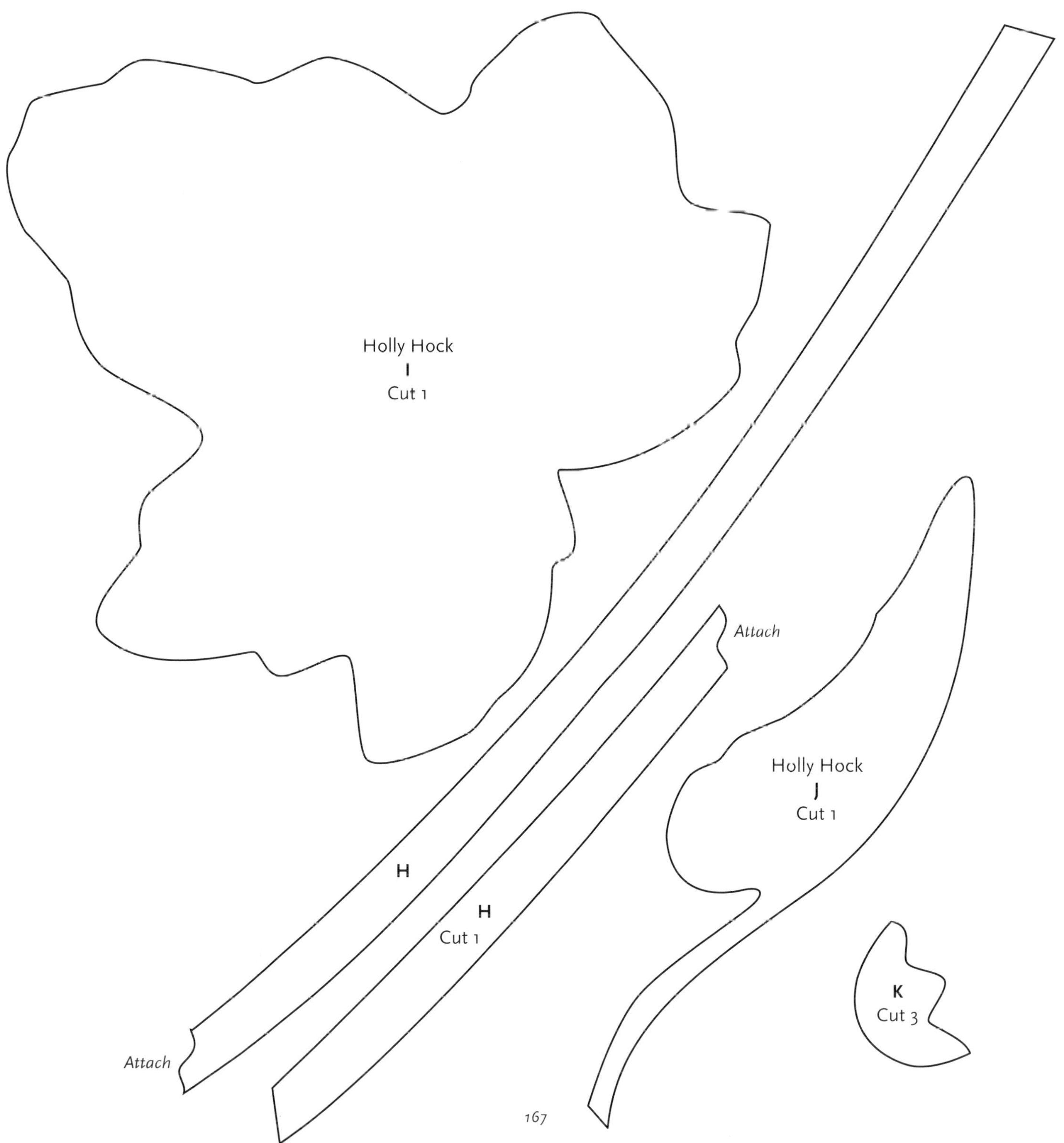

Kalanchoe/Qualup Bell

Add ⅛" (0.4 cm) seam allowance unless otherwise indicated

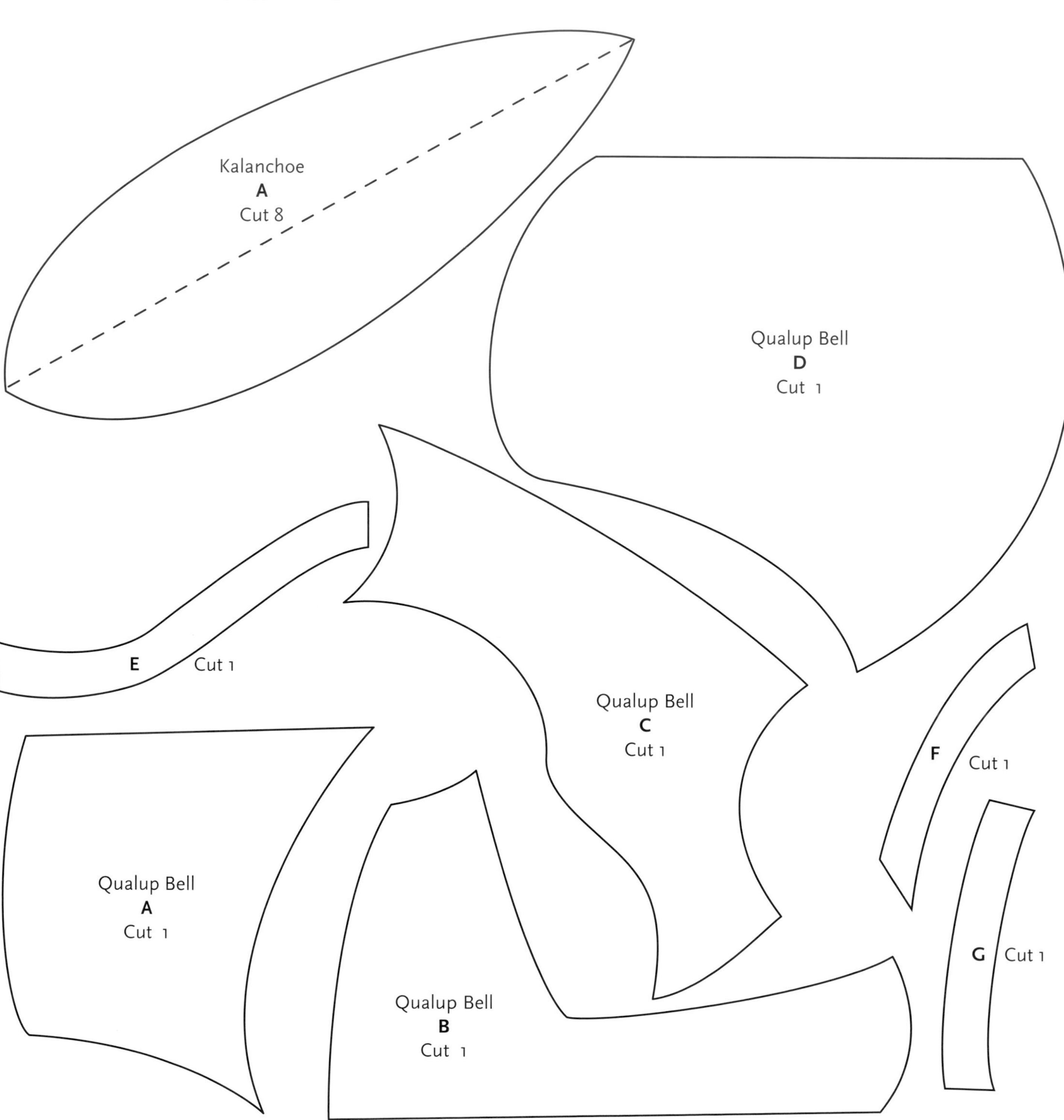

Qualup Bell *continued*

Add ⅛" (0.4 cm) seam allowance unless otherwise indicated

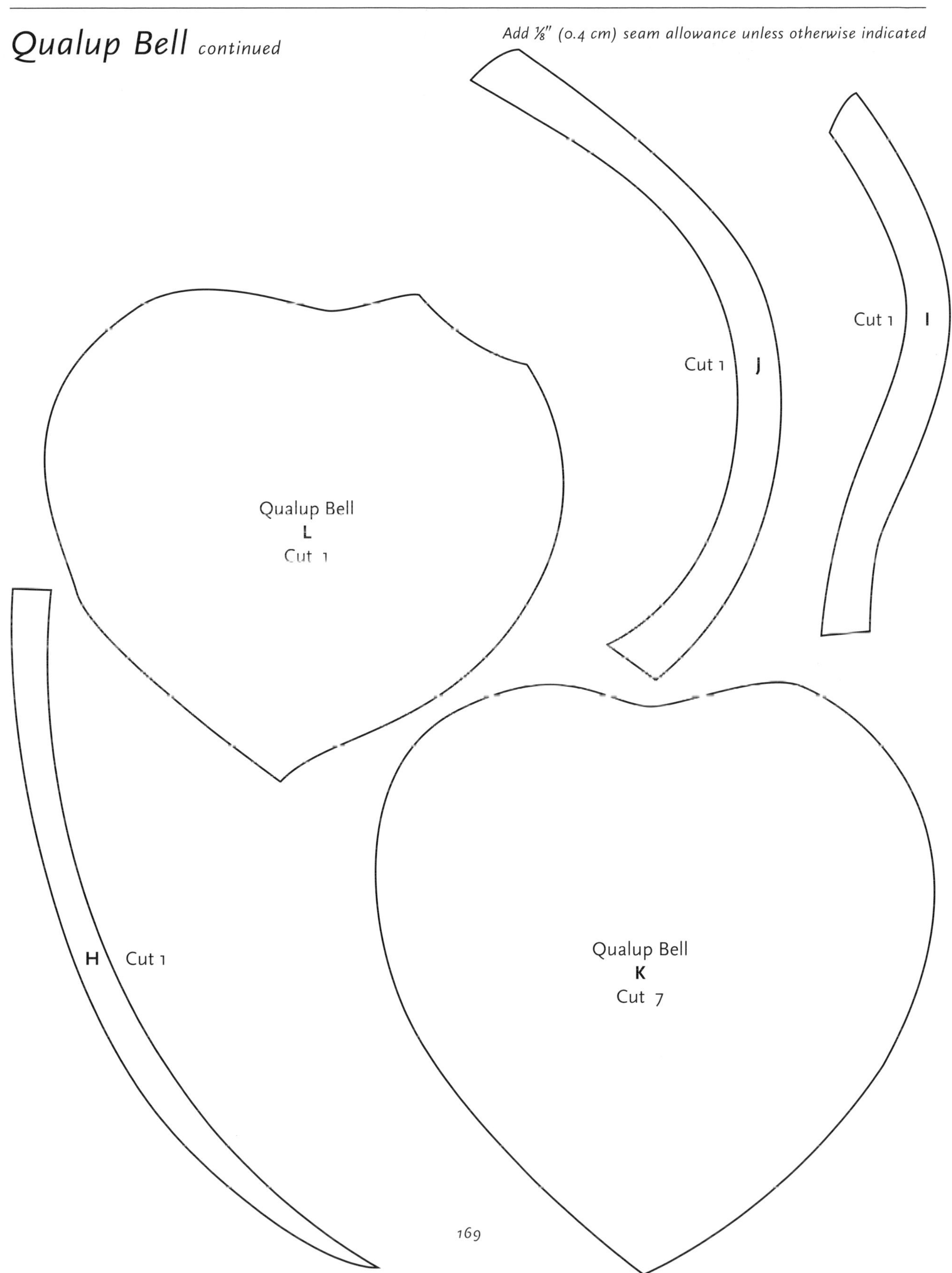

A Valentine's Gift

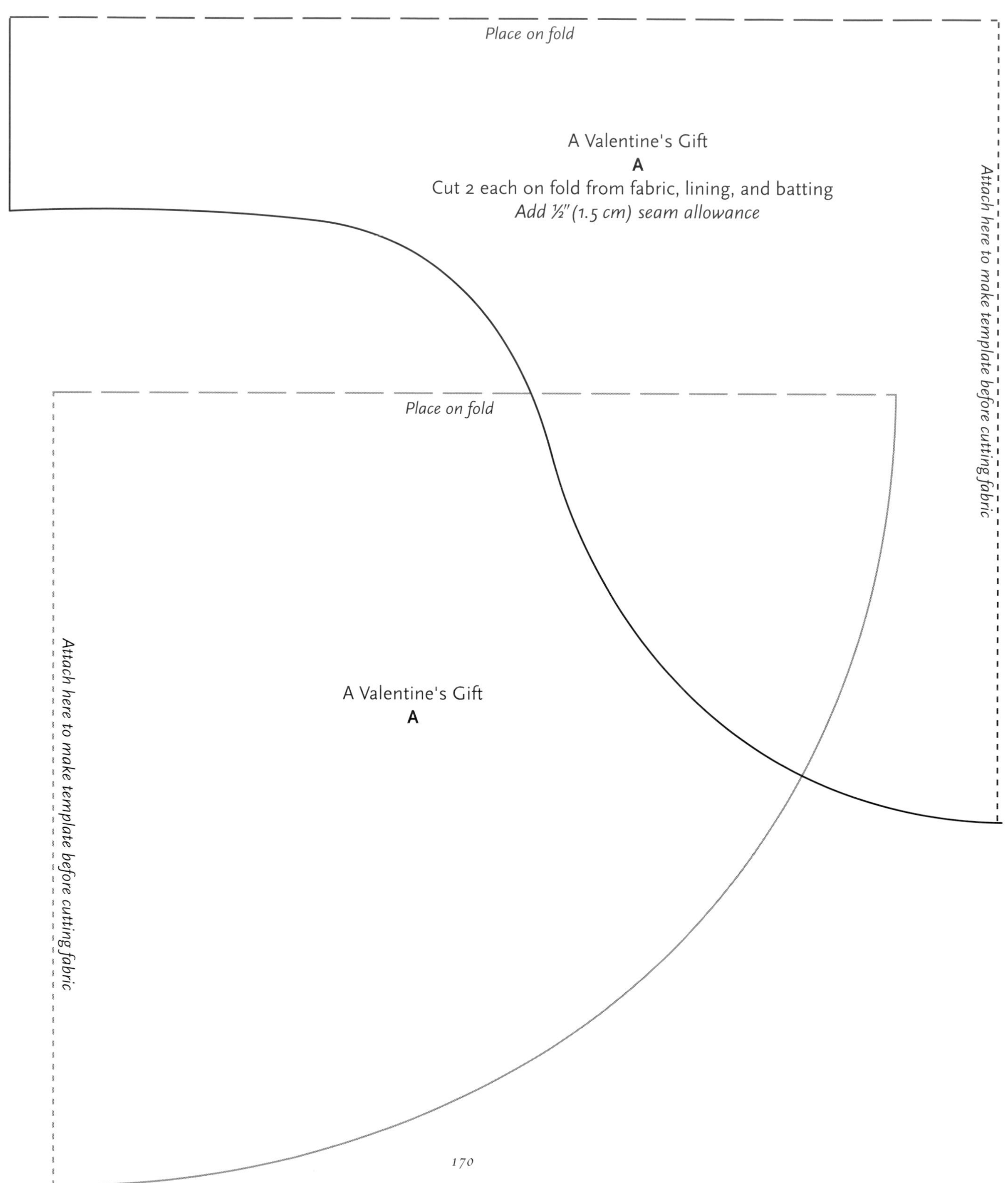